CITIES OF STRANGERS

Cities of Strangers illuminates life in European towns and cities as it was for the settled and for the 'strangers' or newcomers who joined them between 1000 and 1500. Some city-states enjoyed considerable autonomy that allowed them to legislate on how newcomers might settle and become citizens in support of a common good. Such communities invited bankers, merchants, physicians, notaries, and judges to settle and help produce good urban living. Dynastic rulers also shaped immigration, often inviting groups from afar to settle and help their cities flourish. All cities accommodated a great deal of difference – of language, religion, occupation – in shared spaces, regulated by law. But when, from around 1350, plague began regularly to occur within European cities, this benign cycle began to break down. High mortality rates led eventually to demographic crises, and, as a result, less tolerant and more authoritarian attitudes emerged, resulting in the violent expulsion even of long-settled groups. Tracing the development of urban institutions and using a wide range of sources from across Europe, Miri Rubin recreates a complex picture of urban life for settled and migrant communities over the course of five centuries and offers an innovative vantage-point on Europe's past with insights for its present.

Miri Rubin is Professor of Medieval and Early Modern History at Queen Mary, University of London, where she specialises in European history between the eleventh and sixteenth centuries. She is the author of, most recently, *Mother of God: A History of the Virgin Mary* (2009), *The Hollow Crown: A History of Britain in the Late Middle Ages* (2005), and *The Middle Ages: A Very Short Introduction* (2014). She has made numerous media appearances, including the radio programmes *In Our Time* and *Making History* for BBC Radio 4.

THE WILES LECTURES

The Wiles Lectures, given at The Queen's University of Belfast, is a regular, occasional series of lectures on an historical theme, sponsored by the University and published (usually in extended and modified form) by Cambridge University Press. The lecture series was established in the 1950s with the encouragement of the historian Herbert Butterfield, whose 1954 inaugural lecture series was published as *Man on His Past* (1955). Later lecture series have produced many notable Cambridge titles, such as Alfred Cobban's *The Social Interpretation of the French Revolution* (1964), J. H. Elliott's *The Old World and the New, 1492–1650* (1970), E. J. Hobsbawm's *Nations and Nationalism since 1780* (1990), and Adrian Hastings' *The Construction of Nationhood* (1997).

A full list of titles in the series can be found at:
www.cambridge.org/wileslectures

CITIES OF STRANGERS

Making Lives in Medieval Europe

Miri Rubin

Queen Mary University of London

CAMBRIDGE
UNIVERSITY PRESS

CAMBRIDGE
UNIVERSITY PRESS

University Printing House, Cambridge CB2 8BS, United Kingdom

One Liberty Plaza, 20th Floor, New York, NY 10006, USA

477 Williamstown Road, Port Melbourne, VIC 3207, Australia

314–321, 3rd Floor, Plot 3, Splendor Forum, Jasola District Centre,
New Delhi – 110025, India

79 Anson Road, #06–04/06, Singapore 079906

Cambridge University Press is part of the University of Cambridge.

It furthers the University's mission by disseminating knowledge in the pursuit of
education, learning, and research at the highest international levels of excellence.

www.cambridge.org
Information on this title: www.cambridge.org/9781108481236
DOI: 10.1017/9781108666510

© Miri Rubin 2020

First published 2020

Printed in the United Kingdom by TJ International Ltd. Padstow, Cornwall

A catalogue record for this publication is available from the British Library.

Library of Congress Cataloging-in-Publication Data
Names: Rubin, Miri, 1956– author.
Title: Cities of strangers : making lives in Medieval Europe / Miri Rubin.
Description: Cambridge ; New York, NY : Cambridge University Press, 2020. |
Series: The Wiles lectures | Includes bibliographical references and index.
Identifiers: LCCN 2019038908 (print) | LCCN 2019038909 (ebook) |
ISBN 9781108481236 (hardback) | ISBN 9781108740531 (paperback) |
ISBN 9781108666510 (epub)
Subjects: LCSH: Cities and towns, Medieval–Europe. | City and town life–Europe–
History–To 1500. | Strangers–Europe–History–To 1500. | Immigrants–Europe–
History–To 1500. | Europe–Emigration and immigration–History–To 1500.
Classification: LCC HT115 .R83 2020 (print) | LCC HT115 (ebook) |
DDC 307.76094/0902–dc23
LC record available at https://lccn.loc.gov/2019038908
LC ebook record available at https://lccn.loc.gov/2019038909

ISBN 978-1-108-48123-6 Hardback
ISBN 978-1-108-74053-1 Paperback

Contents

List of Figures   *page* vii

List of Maps   ix

Acknowledgements   xi

1 Cities and Their Strangers 1

   Words and Their Meanings   1

   Europe's Cities   2

   Urban Culture: Cohesion and Diversity   8

   Patterns of Urban Governance   13

   Citizenship   16

   Thinking the 'Medieval' City   18

   The Making of This Book   19

2 Strangers into Neighbours 25

   Public Policies and the Movement of People   26

   Between Dynasts and Townspeople   28

   Beyond Conquest – Further Factors That Made Cities Diverse   30

   Urban Statutes and Newcomers   33

   The Short-Stay Stranger   35

   Newcomers Who Stay   37

   Desirable Foreigners   43

   Strangers into Neighbours, into Strangers Again?   45

3 Jews: Familiar Strangers 50

   Traces of Jews Where There Are None   50

   Lords and Jews   51

   Mixing in Neighbourhoods   56

CONTENTS

Changing Urban Sensibilities   59

Reform and the Enhancement of Strangerhood   62

Siena – A City and Its Jews   64

Purifying Cities   66

Cities of Exclusion   69

4 Women: Sometimes Strangers in Their Cities. 71

There, and Not There   71

Women's Work in Urban Spaces   75

Women and Urban Courts   80

Women's Religious Places   82

Women about the City   84

Women at Risk   87

Conclusion 91

Notes   99

Bibliography   145

Index   185

Figures

1.1 Provisioning the City of Paris, *Vie de Saint Denis*, 1317, Bibliothèque
Nationale de France, ms. 2091, fol. 125r . . . . *page* 15

2.1 The Ceremony of Entry into Citizenship of the City of Agen,
Costuma d'Agen, c. 1280, Bibliothèque municipale d'Agen,
ms 42, fol. 56v. 39

3.1 The Size and Shape of the Jewish Badge, Entry in the Register of
the General Council of Siena, 1425, Archivio di Stato di Siena,
Consilio generale 123. 65

3.2 The Ideal City, Urbino, Fra Carnevale, *La città ideale*,
c. 1480–4, Walters Art Museum, Baltimore. 70

4.1 Simone Martini, Altarpiece of Sant'Agostino Novella, 1324,
Pinacoteca Nazionale, Siena 74

Maps

0.1 Europe and the Mediterranean Region, c. 1200 . . . . *page* xiv

0.2 Italy in the Eleventh Century, cities mentioned xv

Acknowledgements

I accepted the invitation to deliver the 2017 Wiles Lectures at Queen's University Belfast, knowing that this was a series like no other. The descendants of Thomas S. Wiles, who founded the Lectures in 1953, created an occasion to 'encourage the extension of historical thinking into the realm of general ideas'. At the height of the Cold War, members of this transatlantic family, represented by Mrs Austen Boyd of Cottee-nagh, Craigavad, sought to share historical ideas with a wide and diverse audience. Our historical conversations have since been enriched not only by the Lectures – splendid events effectively organised by gener-ations of historians and administrators at Queen's – but also by the books in the Wiles Lectures series, published by Cambridge University Press. It was an honour to deliver the Wiles Lectures and a pleasure to turn them into this little book.

Mrs Boyd believed that history-making depended on deep discussion, so she provided for the presence of several experts at the Lectures and in the discussions that followed each of them. The critical friends I chose for this task all possess profound understanding of medieval urban life: Marc Boone, with his mastery of the history of Flanders; Emma Dillon, who explores the sounds of medieval cities; Serena Ferente, who studies both political thought and political lives; Thérèse de Hemptinne, who researches the lives of women in Flemish cities; Katherine Jansen, who has an unrivalled understanding of religious life in Tuscan cities; Gabor Klaniczay, who traces the cultural links that bound medieval Europe's regions; and Daniel Smail, with his profound knowledge of urban life in southern France. It was particularly pleasant and helpful that Bruce Campbell attended the Lectures and contributed valuable insights.

Other historians joined me in Belfast: Virginia Davis, Bronach Kane, Ella Kilgallon, Lauren Mulholland, Jon Parry, and Simon Sandall. Everything that happened during that memorable week was made possible by Peter Gray, the most gracious of hosts and a subtle historian, who is Chair of the Wiles Lectures Trustees. In all his efforts on my behalf Peter was ably assisted by Susan Templeton.

As I prepared these lectures from materials and studies arising from several historical fields, I turned to experts for advice. Extended conversations with Mario Ascheri and Magnus Ryan helped me understand the legal culture of Italian cities; discussing migration and citizenship with Milan Pajic was a constant pleasure as we worked in the Cambridge University Library side by side; Joe Canning offered advice on legal *consilia* for Italian cities; and John Arnold shared a then unpublished article on rituals of shaming in cities of the Midi. Most of the research for this book was conducted in the Cambridge University Library, and it is a pleasure to offer thanks to its obliging and able staff, particularly those in the Reading Rooms and Acquisitions. Archival trips were made more productive and enjoyable thanks to local friends. I am grateful in particular to historian François Arbelet, who introduced me to the archive of Gourdon; to Max Aussel, who shared his unrivalled expertise in Occitan, and stories about his childhood too; to Delphine Soubiroux-Magrez, who welcomed me to the Hôtel de Ville de Gourdon; and to George and Giles Murray, and Naomi and Nigel Yandell, who opened their family homes.

Some friends read the lectures with great care: Vivian Bickford-Smith, Jim Bolton, Ira Katznelson, Patrick Lantschner, Chris Moffat, Shulamith Shahar, and Paul Strohm. I was also privileged to have two of the lectures (the core of the current Chapters 3 and 4) scrutinised by the medievalists who gathered at the Dartmouth Medieval Colloquium 2017, an event organised by Cecilia Gaposchkin and Walter Simons. I am grateful to all the participants who animated discussion there, and particularly to Sean Gilsdorf, who caused me to think about the effects of precarity on the social fabric of communities. Sean Field, who also attended that event, offered his comments on the lectures, even though he was engrossed at the time in completing a book of his own. I benefited from attending the colloquium 'The Medieval City: A Question of Trust' at King's College, Cambridge in April 2018, and for this I thank the organisers, David

Napolitano and Milan Pajic. My visits to the project Visions of Community at the University of Vienna were enriching occasions thanks to the comparative frameworks that its leaders so deftly employ.

Marc Boone, Scott Bruce, Duncan Hardy, Yitzhak Hen, Richard Keyser, Fabian Kümmeler, Beat Kümin, Ora Limor, David Napolitano, Cecil Reid, and Katalin Szende answered questions and suggested readings with swiftness and generosity. The final draft of this book was read by expert and generous friends, who helped me improve it: Matthew Champion, Ronnie Ellenblum, and Katalin Szende. Another friend, Mary-Rose Cheadle, brought her intelligence and acute reader's eye to the final draft. The anonymous readers for Cambridge University Press were smart and constructive in their comments. Together with Liz Friend-Smith they have helped me turn four lectures into a short book.

Gareth Stedman Jones and Joseph Stedman Jones read this book with profound historical sensibility, as did Abigail Thaw with her characteristically warm curiosity. As in everything I do, on this journey too I have been fortunate in the support they and other members of my family offer daily. Alongside many dear friends, they have lived with me the challenges and possibilities of being a stranger, by always making me feel very much at home.

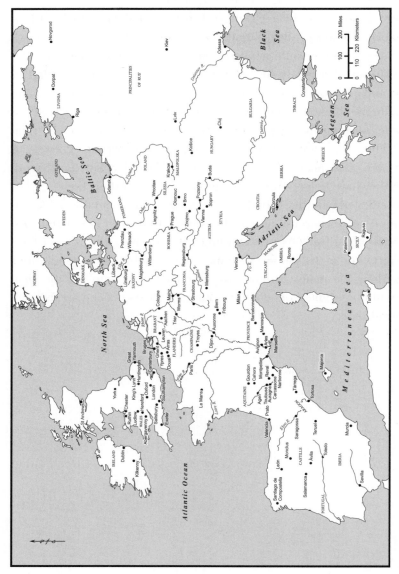

0.1. Europe and the Mediterranean Region, c. 1200

0.2. Italy in the Eleventh Century, cities mentioned

CHAPTER 1

Cities and Their Strangers

Stranger in a Strange Land
What's a man supposed to do?
Just a Stranger in a Strange Land
(Waiting and watching and wondering)
When will the light come shining through.

Rik Emmett,
Stranger in a Strange Land (1984)

WORDS AND THEIR MEANINGS

THE TERM 'STRANGER' – *FORINSECUS, FORENSIS* – WAS USED IN MEDIEVAL TEXTS to describe a whole array of groups and individuals. It was most usually used to describe newcomers from villages or small towns in proximity to a city, in the first stages of their relation to the town or city, before they became settled, *incolae*. These were usually people of modest means – variously trained and skilled – whose absorption into urban life often went undocumented. 'Strangers' also described newcomers from further afield, people with distinctive dialects and occupations, associated with other cities or realms, whose presence was often reinforced by chains of migration, like German merchants in twelfth-century London, or Tuscan bankers in thirteenth-century Provence. A pathway to citizenship was open to such newcomers if they wished to associate their lives with the city. To these two groups we may add individuals and groups in towns and cities who were not foreigners, yet to whom a quality of 'strangerhood' was attached, what Simona Cerutti has called 'extranéité'.[1] Indeed, a cognate word was sometimes used, as in the statutes

1

of Marseilles: 'a foreigner, that is a strange person' ('forensis, id est persona extranea').[2] They were never described as strangers by their contemporaries, but they were touched by difference even after decades of settlement, like Jews in most parts of Europe, Muslims in Iberia and Sicily, or Greeks in Venice.

Towns also experienced a constant stream of passers-through – traders in their markets, pilgrims, students, ambassadors, mercenaries, artisans, and servants – each type with its own effect on urban life, each with its own marks of difference. In going about their duties, civic officials sought to assess the disposition of each type – a peasant from the contado, a foreign student, a Jew – and their opinions were affected by custom and law, as well as by religious instruction. Living in towns and cities meant living with strangers.

EUROPE'S CITIES

The urban centres of the later Roman world – *civitates* – were hubs for administration, where imperial law held sway, manufacture and commerce flourished, a rich public life was on display, and entertainment was offered in stadia and hippodromes.[3] Such cities were most densely located all around the Mediterranean, and they reached as far as London, Cologne, and Trier in the north. Early in the fourth century, the practice of Christianity was permitted throughout the Empire, and by the next century this had become the official religion. So cities became centres for church administration too, where bishops presided from their urban cathedrals over Christian life within their dioceses. Bishops assumed authority and responsibilities beyond the solely religious domain: they were keepers of the peace, supervisors of their city's water and food supplies, managers of charitable distributions, and founders of schools. In the fifth and sixth centuries, the western part of the Empire was transformed into a set of kingdoms – such as those of the Ostrogoths, Visigoths, Franks, and Vandals – and in them city life persisted, though the overall volume of trade declined. From the seventh century, the Mediterranean was re-ordered following the Muslim conquests and the establishment of the Umayyad Caliphate in large parts of the old Roman world, in North Africa, Iberia, Sicily, and Italy.

In the space we may usefully call Europe, cities were resilient centres to which refugees often fled for safety. Some European cities were seats for ambitious new dynasties, like the Ravenna of the Ostrogoths or Aachen of the Carolingians. When in the later eighth and ninth centuries, Northern people – Vikings – forcefully settled in the regions of northwest Europe, they linked existing inland cities and ports with the sinews of trade, promoting such centres as Dublin and York. Cities old and new required food, services, and manufactured goods; they generated demand and stimulated commercial activity.

New types of urban settlement developed in response to the notable growth of population around 1000. So existing cities grew, and thousands of new towns were created. According to its greatest historian, the Belgian Henri Pirenne (1862–1935), this new type was the *medieval* city.[4] New urban centres were often situated on the site of former Roman forts, on bends in rivers, or adjacent to monasteries, at places where the exchange of agricultural produce and some manufactured goods – pottery or armour – could take place in safety.[5] Drawing from the immediate countryside, but also attracting merchants from further afield, such new settlements were largely composed of newcomers, strangers assembled with a shared cause.

Such urban life was varied in its quality and reach, and those who lived it sought to make it viable. So inhabitants strove to win customs and freedoms through negotiation with whoever held local authority: a monastery, a bishop, a count, or a king. By 1000, a complex coming together of demographic, technological, and political processes prompted the developments that, over the next three centuries, saw the threefold rise in Europe's population, together with growth in areas of settlement, in the amount of food produced, and in the scope and pace of trade.[6] The number of Europeans living some form of Christian life was also on the rise, and it came to include people in large parts of Scandinavia, in the kingdoms of Poland and Hungary, and in those lands of Iberia, Italy, and Sicily soon to be taken from Muslim rulers.[7]

The economic stimulus was felt earliest in the south and northwest of Europe, and it was experienced by millions of peasants in their daily lives.[8] Some would choose to be involved in urban life through manufacture, service, or commerce; and as they came together they created urban communities for profit and safety.

3

This was nothing short of an urban transformation of Europe. In the Low Countries, a quarter of the population lived in urban settlements, while in Italian regions perhaps 30 per cent did.[9] In towns and cities trade and manufacture set the tone of life, where a variety of religious and educational institutions offered their services, while walls provided safety. Such walls marked the space within which townspeople interacted in administration, where governance was conducted in promotion of commerce and craft, safety and sociability, and stable family lives. All these activities were also moulded by criteria for inclusion and exclusion.

As the extent of manufacture and exchange grew, urban groups came together with the aim of gaining rights for their communities. These efforts were often led by men who already enjoyed some connections with landed families or with the local bishop. Sometimes lords initiated the formation of urban communities as centres for the marketing of agricultural produce yielded by their own lands. Lords – be they secular men or religious institutions – habitually ceded some jurisdiction to a community of town dwellers and in turn benefited from the annual payment of a fee from a market for agricultural goods and from a share in the income from justice or customs on trade.[10]

Sworn associations soon emerged in these growing urban centres.[11] There was a rush of such activities from the later eleventh century: in Le Mans, in 1070, we are told by the bishop's chronicler that 'thus was made a conspiracy, which they called a communion' – communion being a word rich with religious meaning.[12] Such leading organised groups were sometimes empowered by royal charters to create their own officials, as in Arras in 1111, York in 1154, Dublin in 1171, or Oxford in 1199. In Italy, similarly, Pisa negotiated in 1099 with Emperor Henry IV its privileges and rights to elect officials, as did Genoa, which acted through a *compagna* of townsmen. From Italy this communal movement seems to have spread to southern France, as it reached Marseilles in 1128, Arles in 1131, Avignon in 1136, Montpellier in 1141, and Narbonne in 1148. These processes of enfranchisement were associated with the election of officials sworn to uphold the town's interests, and to execute the will of its governing group; in southern France and Italy these officials were often called consuls.

4

Membership in the city was associated with settlement, and the owner-ship of a plot of land, a 'burgage' plot. As the new settlement was defined and soon surrounded by walls, plots of equal size were measured out within it, to form the basis for the emergent community.[13] Representa-tives of the lord may live in castles or grander habitations, alongside local bishops or other religious institutions, but townspeople first dwelt on fairly equal plots, just as centuries earlier Plato had imagined his perfect urban polity city, made up of 5,040 citizens occupying 5,040 plots, 'owning a share of the land and set to defend their allocation'.[14] When Duke Barnim of Pomerania founded the city of Prenzlau in 1234, he laid out 300 'mansos' – 200 on one side of the river Ucker and 100 on the other.[15] From this basis there developed a variety of status and of wealth, and this became visible in the subdivision, or accumulation, of urban land. The rich emerged alongside the poor, and new forms of association and civic action developed: the craft guilds with their mutual support of workers in a given trade; political assemblies and participatory governance in local councils;[16] and hospitals for the urban sick and poor, as well as schools as centres for critical thinking and useful professional training.[17] Urban architecture developed to match, with squares and city halls.[18] In all of these initiatives were enshrined precepts and prejudices, some of which were long to persist, like the exclusion of women, and civic rights depend-ent on the possession of property and religious orthodoxy.

Urban life spread across Europe, but not always in the same way or at the same pace. The legal heritage, location, climate, agrarian regimes, and natural endowments of settlements varied across the continent, as did the political capacity of rulers to direct economic processes and migration. While new towns were created in England and France (which included Flanders) from the late eleventh century, they only emerged in Bohemia and Poland later, in the twelfth century. By 1300 there were large cities aplenty in northwest Europe: Cologne with 80,000 inhabit-ants, Bruges with 50,000, Ghent with 80,000, and, greatest of all, Paris with 200,000. In central and northern Italy there were many large cities too: Venice unique with 120,000, Genoa and Milan both with 100,000, and Florence with 90,000; England had London, with 80,000; but no such large cities existed in Iberia, the Nordic sphere, or Central Europe.[19]

Contemporaries noticed the differing rates of urban growth. When the Franciscan scholar Bartholomew 'the English' (1203–72) surveyed cities in Europe and beyond, he mentioned none in Iceland, Finland, the Baltic, Denmark, Norway, Sweden, or Hungary. In Bohemia, he only mentioned Prague.[20] Cities also differed in character: there were capitals, ports, ducal residences, cities with cathedrals, and a few with universities; some cities were important pilgrimage centres, others were noted for the manufacture of particular goods, such as silk in Paris and brocade in Venice. Smaller urban centres were kept buoyant as administrative hubs or regional markets.

The diversity of urban populations was hardwired into the lives of whole regions. The county of Champagne became familiar with Lombards, the financiers and merchants most likely to offer credit at its fairs, those hubs of commerce in late twelfth- and thirteenth-century Europe.[21] The cities and towns that made up the Hanse were similarly diverse.[22] The Hanse sphere was an association of merchants around the North and Baltic Seas and along the rivers that fed into them. It encouraged ease of movement, legal protection, and fiscal advantages to its members, from England to Livonia, as far north as Gotland and as far south as Cologne.[23] Merchants could move from one Hanse city to another, becoming for a while familiar neighbours, if not citizens, thanks to the possession of a shared language – Low German – and trust in the fair and lucrative trade to which they all contributed. Ties through marriage and business partnerships further thickened the Hanse network, and the sociability of confraternities helped socialise its young and rising merchants.[24]

Some strangers therefore benefited from arrangements that rendered their difference an accepted feature of city life. Cosmopolitanism is a word often used to describe cultures acquainted with ease of movement.[25] It can be used to describe those who travelled the Mediterranean through the network of hospitality maintained in its ports, and which Olivia Remie Constable has studied so well. This network of *funduqs*, with its roots in late antiquity, offered to foreign traders lodging and support designed to 'meet the needs of travellers' and provided safety for merchants who were far away from home.[26] By the early thirteenth century, these were emulated in Venice for the accommodation of its northern visitors, with the Fondaco dei Tedeschi; and other trading cities followed suit.[27] Foreign merchants were allowed to settle for long periods without seeking citizenship: Germans in the Steelyard of London, men of Lübeck in St Olav's Court in Novgorod, or Tuscans in Bologna's Compagnia dei Toschi.[28] The city of Lucca approved the statutes of its merchants in Bruges in 1377, as it did for other Lucchese communities in Avignon, Genoa, London, and Paris. This society in Bruges dealt with matters ranging from arrangements for the burial of members in the church of St Augustine in Bruges, where they had their chapel, to banking contacts with London.[29]

These were men who remained as foreigners for long periods of time, who wielded influence and enjoyed wealth, and who were occasionally buffeted by the political fortunes of their hometowns.[30] Sharon Farmer has recently suggested that the Lombard financiers in Paris, men who lived with other male kin, and away from their families, were disruptive, even violent, in their treatment of the women they employed, or of those who approached them for loans.[31] Such men were both settled and different, embedded yet keen to maintain their native connections. They lived as foreigners, and their connections elsewhere underpinned their prosperity.

The world of high scholarship, of study–work sociability in cities with schools and universities, was highly cosmopolitan, too. Men who shared the experience of Latin pedagogy, and the career prospects it made possible, could move across Europe with ease. This world expanded greatly with the creation of fifty new universities in Europe over the course of the fifteenth century. Men associated with religious orders were a regular presence in cities.[32] Such organisations were European in scope, and hence members travelled in the course of administration and study for periods of varying length. The orders of friars were quint-essentially urban institutions, and the military orders also possessed urban bases, where travelling or visiting members were hosted.[33]

People settled in some strangerhood, with meaningful attachment to another place, and to others who shared that affinity, in what is now frequently thought of as a diaspora.[34] The idea of diaspora is a powerful one, and it is linked to identity and memory maintained by groups, expressed in their rituals; it is a state of being. Diaspora is powerful in capturing how lives are constituted in the aftermath of trauma – exile, famine, enslavement – new lives, powerfully linked to old. Diaspora is a deeply subjective experience, even when its members are well settled in their new homes. We should bear it in mind as we think of exiles and banishments, and encounter the aftermaths of expulsions, of conquest and reconquest.

URBAN CULTURE: COHESION AND DIVERSITY

All that was new and flourishing in towns and cities depended on a diversity of talents and endowments: on lawyers and notaries, merchants and bankers, physicians and teachers, on artisans in dozens of crafts; on priests, actors, and street vendors. At their inception, towns were composed of strangers who came together to create an effective community. Towns were soon shaped by the ideas and interests of merchants, lawyers, and bankers, as well as by the preaching of friars.[35] The history we are about to encounter in the period of economic growth witnessed an imaginative willingness to attract and receive into towns and cities those who could provide services and skills: Genoese ship-makers in twelfth-century Seville; Italian and Jewish financiers in thirteenth-century Hungary and Poland; or Flemish weavers in fourteenth-century England. The resulting urban mix varied according to region, and it changed over time. It always preoccupied those who governed, those charged with maintaining economic growth, safety, and fiscal viability for their urban communities.

Alongside the clerical and diplomatic Latin culture of religious institutions and royal courts, there were European zones characterised by a *lingua franca* – a shared vernacular language – which facilitated commerce and the spread of civic culture. The arc of linguistic comprehensibility, which stretched from Catalonia to Piedmont, allowed business contacts to develop with ease, as they did, for example, for Tuscan bankers in Provence.[36] Marco Polo (1254–1324) chose this Romance *lingua franca* when writing about his travels in *The Description of the World* (*Le divisament dou monde*), a work rendered into Tuscan by Rustichello da Pisa (fl. late thirteenth century) as *The Million* (*Il milione*).[37] At the same time, as we have seen, in northern Europe a sphere of trade and a civic culture evolved for ease of movement and interaction in the area between the Baltic and East Anglia, and its common language was Low German.[38] Low German in its many dialects also served the cities of central Europe – Buda/Ofen, Krakow, Liegnitz/Legnica – where German traders settled as privileged newcomers. They were allowed to operate in their mother tongue under protective privileges offered by the kings of Hungary and Poland.

In these urban spheres, the heritage of classical legal and political theory combined with local custom to inspire the aspirations of leaders and to inform discussions about the urban common good, the *bonum comune*.[39] Urban writers – and these were often holders of important offices, such as Galbert of Bruges (d. 1134), Brunetto Latini (1220–94), Dante Alighieri (1265–1321), and Geoffrey Chaucer (1343–1400) – reflected on how cities should be governed, and how their inhabitants might live as moral communities. Yet the meaning of the common good was always ideologically charged and contested, since so many claimed to be its promoters and defenders: kings, prince-bishops, dukes and counts, city councils, craft guildsmen, and friar-preachers, each type with its own understanding of what made cities thrive.[40]

Those who theorised about urban life believed that townspeople shared more than mere closeness in space: they saw in the coming together of townspeople a rational, and hence moral, act. They all knew the definition offered by Isidore of Seville (d. 636):

A city, *civitas*, is a multitude of people united by a bond of fellowship. It is named from the citizens, *cives*, that is, the inhabitants of the place (because it decides upon and holds the lives of many people). *Urbs* is the town itself, the *civitas* is not rocks, but the inhabitants.[41]

The Florentine notary, scholar, and politician Brunetto Latini reworked the classical tradition in his encyclopaedic *Le Livre dou Tresor* of the 1260s:

From that time they began to build houses and strengthen cities and fortresses and enclose them with walls and ditches. 3. From that time on they began to establish customs, and laws, and rights, which were common to all the citydwellers. For that reason Cicero says that the city is an assembly of people for living in one place and under one law.[42]

In the following century, the jurist Bartolus of Sassoferrato (1313–57) made it clear that a mere collection of houses did not make a city; that a moral dimension was essential to true urban flourishing.[43] The fourteenth-century jurist Nikolaus Wurm (d.1383), who worked in Lieg-nitz/Legnica, set out his digest on urban laws for his and other Silesian towns in Low German. Educated at the university of Bologna, he expounded in the form of a dialogue:

> *Menius*: Why should one call something a city, and what should one call a city?
>
> *Gayus*: It is called a city because the people therein should live peacefully in a union and keep and strengthen the laws.[44]

The search for urban stability and prosperity led to the development of distinctive genres of writing about urban affairs. The city of Arras, from its inception as a self-governing community in 1111, valued the composition and performance of poetry and drama. Its *Jeu de St Nicholas*, composed by town clerk Jean Bodel, even featured a pious local magistrate as a protagonist. Such vernacular eloquence was a sign of what Carol Symes has called the city's 'prosperous diversity', and Bodel was member of the confraternity of poet-performers, *jongelurs*.[45] Notaries and judges, jurists and preachers, all tried to define the essence of good urban living. Judge Albertanus of the city of Brescia composed in 1245 – ostensibly as a guidebook for his son – his *Book of the Art of Speaking and Keeping Silent* (*Liber de doctrina dicendi et tacendi*), a summary of classical and later maxims on comportment and prudent speech in the civic sphere.[46] To be a citizen was to speak, advise, and discuss in a manner that newcomers had to learn and emulate. Alber-tanus, and Brunetto Latini a few decades later, emphasised that com-mand of bodily comportment, and especially of speech, through the rhetorical training of citizens, was central to the city's well-being. Wise use of language was not just a matter of style: it helped to avoid strife and to promote civic peace. For this reason a moral tract, like the Dominican William Perault's (c. 1190–1271) *Summa of Vices* (*Summa vitiorum*) of 1236, was so widely disseminated and translated throughout Europe, with extended sections on 'sins of the tongue', malicious speech, and its consequences.[47]

Reason was meant to govern human relations within each city's distinctive environment. Reason was implicit in the rules for the election of officials, and explicit in the making of statutes and civic rituals. It was meant to promote liberty, a concept that had animated makers of urban communes since the twelfth century.[48] In their urban statutes, communes expressed their priorities: the regulation of trade, justice, and the reception of strangers. These also regulated the treatment of animals, trees, and water, both within the city and in its surroundings.[49] Towns paid attention to waste management, the paving of roads, control of livestock, and regulation of access to light.[50] The quality of housing, and spaces for work and recreation, all affected town dwellers' sense of place and identity. This in turn influenced attitudes to those who might come to share these resources with them.

Even before its rich written sources were systematically produced and kept, by the mid thirteenth century Siena was able to design and manage important communal projects. This is well demonstrated by its *bottini* – the subterranean system of water supply – so carefully planned and managed by urban officials.[51] Access to water for industrial use – in fulling, dyeing, and tanning – was regulated through the framework of guilds (*arti*), associations open only to citizens.[52] So civic status intersected with the amenities offered in cities, with the quality of life, and with the sense of flourishing and belonging.

Managing the city meant making it a good and safe place to live and flourish. As jurists and public servants considered how a city was to be ruled, artists imagined its appearance. In 1338–9, at the invitation of The Nine (*I nove*) – the council of nine men that governed Siena between 1285 and 1355 – Ambrogio Lorenzetti (1290–1348) painted allegories of city life in times of peace and war, in the room from which The Nine governed.[53] These wall-paintings came to be known as the allegories of Good and Bad Government. The well-governed city was imagined as being at peace with itself and its surroundings. Its people were at work, as roofers, shoemakers, teachers, and weavers; others were at study, and some were at play. And all this was made possible thanks to government based on the combined virtues of its magistrates and the force of law, delivered without fear or corruption.[54] Such a city enjoyed a flow of food through its gates under the rule of Security – *Securitas* – portrayed as a female figure. She hovered over the verdant fields just outside Siena, with her comforting words:

> Without fear, let every free man walk safely
> and let everyone cultivate and sow
> as long as this commune
> remains under the signoria of this lady
> For she has taken all power from the guilty.[55]

When citizens and their officials felt secure in this manner, they were willing to accommodate the extension of paths to citizenship to suitable newcomers. They were even willing to live with various forms of difference – of religion, language, or lifestyle – in their midst.

Newcomers contributed diversity to urban life, even as they gradually became more familiar with – and to – their new community. Lasting, and even overwhelming, forms of diversity resulted when newcomers arrived in the wake of domination and conquest, those words used by Rees Davies in the title of his 1988 Wiles Lectures.[56] In regions like Wales and Ireland, Livonia and Iberia, indigenous people formed substantial rural majorities, and sizeable groups within towns ruled by incomers from afar. After the Norman conquest of Sicily, King Roger II (1095–1154) attracted Tuscan and Lombard settlers, to enhance the Latin and Christian character of cities inhabited by Greek Christians and Muslims.[57] In the city of Lviv, after its incorporation into the Polish kingdom in 1356, Germans, Poles, Armenians, Jews, and Greeks all lived under German urban law, and the indigenous population became but one group among many.[58]

Diverse urban polities developed throughout central Europe, where dynasts invited foreigners – *hospites*, guests – to settle and encourage economic development in cities and towns. Governance in these urban centres was performed by Low German-speaking merchants and artisans, immigrants from contiguous regions of the Empire – Saxony, Thuringia, Prussia – under royal protection. Kings offered attractive privileges which made these newcomers into ruling castes of cities like Buda or Prague. The Teutonic Order did the same in its Baltic sphere, developing urban centres such as Reval/Tallinn, Riga and Dorpat/Tartu. In all of these cities German urban customs influenced the legal framework for civic life, those of Magdeburg and Lübeck being favoured models for emulation.[59] Indigenous people like the Livs of Riga were excluded by guilds, and so they worked as hired hands, servants, or porters. In Buda, Hungarians could join 'German' guilds; some were mixed, like the Butchers,[60] or of purely Hungarian membership, like the Tailors. With Jewish communities, and some *latini* – French, Iberian – too, the cities of central Europe experienced a diversity of languages, lifestyles, and religions.

PATTERNS OF URBAN GOVERNANCE

Siena was one of several cities in Italy to gain a great deal of autonomy in the twelfth and thirteenth centuries, within the political framework of the Holy Roman Empire. Cities in other regions achieved similar communal government, but the degree of autonomy operated differently where dynastic rule was keener to impose its interests and will. Paris, for example, became a capital city in the twelfth century, directed from the Ile-de-la-Cité by a *prévôt* (*praepositus*) on behalf of the king of France.[61] When the need for credit was felt in the growing city, bankers from Asti in the Piedmont were invited by King Louis VIII in 1225 to offer financial services.[62] Krakow, the residence of the dukes of Małopolska (Little Poland) and a cathedral city, received from King Bolesław V in 1257 a charter of autonomy. Yet it was managed by German merchants who had been invited and settled there by royal edict alongside Tuscan bankers and Jewish merchants.[63] So in Paris and Krakow the decisions about the settlement and treatment of strangers were taken by kings, while in thirteenth-century Siena or Milan the city council formulated policies, framed them in statutes, and enforced them, however imperfectly. European cities confronted strangers – ranging from migrant peasants to 'invited' foreign merchants – with differing degrees of autonomy, and hence with varying degrees of local consultation and acceptance.

This political framing of the treatment of newcomers mattered, because urban life depended above all on trust.[64] Townspeople had to be able to trust new neighbours, to be sure that their presence had been scrutinised by credible officials after an entry that met the criteria laid down by local statutes. Newcomers, in turn, had to be able to trust the city, to rest assured that they would be treated decently – or at least predictably – in keeping with the tenor of local statutes. And all towns-people had to be able to trust that food would be available in the shops every day, that malefactors would be punished, and that the market would be fair.[65] Local merchants and artisans had to be trusted, as had those officials who supervised the quality of bread and beer, fish and meat.

Provisioning great cities was the work of hundreds of producers across vast regions, whose own environments were shaped by the demand generated by urban centres.[66] Feeding a city like London affected cropping, planting, and husbandry decisions made on manors and farms throughout the southeast of England, and west as far as the Cotswolds.[67] The resulting contact of rural producers and manorial officials with urban markets offered the first encounter with town life, and a familiarity that could in turn prompt rural dwellers to consider migration.[68]

All cities needed such migration. Economic growth required a sustained flow of labour, due to an urban demography with high rates of mortality and many households of single people. Skills learnt on farms and manors could be easily transferred to urban centres, where unskilled hands were also needed. At the same time, there was demand for rare expertise: for lawyers and stonemasons, physicians and moneylenders. And while cities had to be able to attract incomers, immigrants could make choices too, so a city's reputation mattered a great deal. *Sefer Hasidim* – a collection of precepts and *exempla* to guide a rigorous Jewish life, by Rabbi Judah the Pious of Regensburg (1150–1217) – reported as common knowledge that Jews eventually adopted the ethics and habits of those communities within which they settled:

> When [Jews] look around for a place in which to live, they should take stock of the residents of that town—how chaste are the Christians there? Know that if Jews live in that town, their children and grandchildren will also behave just as the Christians do. For in every town . . . Jews act just like Christians.[69]

Those who could choose a new home would seek to learn about its laws and ethos, its *fama*.

1.1. Provisioning the City of Paris, *Vie de Saint Denis*, 1317, Bibliothèque Nationale de France, ms. 2091, fol. 125r

Towns regulated the entry and stay of visitors by erecting gates and chains, and appointing guards.[70] Gates opened to useful entrants and stood fast against those who might bring harm; walls and gates were often represented on city seals, a symbol of urban authority.[71] Jurists thought of walls, ramparts, and fortifications as a material expression of the city's essence, borrowing concepts from Roman law, where walls were considered as common goods, to be enjoyed and maintained by all citizens.[72] City walls represented 'the power of the *universitas* that the ramparts individualized and reinforced, fixing its geographic contours',[73] although in reality much activity often took place in ports situated outside such walls.[74] The city opened cautiously to those who brought food, as the miniature in Figure 1.1 depicting Paris in the early fourteenth century shows. *The Life of St Denis*, presented to King Philip V in 1317 by the monks of that monastery, shows bridge-gates from the river, with shiploads of barrels bearing provisions.[75]

Walls were reassuring in many ways, and the maintenance they required was a major item of expenditure for any city. The patricians of Ypres expressed their trust in walls for safety at a time of political upheaval, some time between 1320 and 1332: 'And it is well known that gates are needed by the city ... and if the gates are opened, the good people of the city would be in danger of being murdered at night, and robbed of their goods.'[76] Those entering were usually expected to leave their arms at the gates, apart from some professionals who were exempted, like office-holders and bodyguards.[77] People who passed through the wall into a city that was not their home were allowed to stay in inns, where they were scrutinised by innkeepers acting as gate-keepers too. Officials were allowed to stop people and ask them for their name, and expect an answer, and to enter houses to enquire into the identity of any strangers lodging there.

Such strangers were usually described in terms derived from Latin *foris* (out, outer): *forinsecus* or *forensis* in Latin, *forestiere* in Italian, *forain* in French.[78] The English word *stranger* was derived from Latin *extraneus*; the word *alien*, from Latin *alienigenus*, was used for those born outside the composite kingdom of England, Scotland, Ireland and Wales. Those who had arrived and stayed, working in a city without citizenship, were often called *inhabitants*, *habitatores* or *incolae*.[79] But cities also imagined a pathway from occasional to settled presence, and on to citizenship.

CITIZENSHIP

Citizenship accorded the highest form of integration, with its offer of political and economic rights, and it was enjoyed only by a minority of any city's Christian men.[80] Citizenship was usually available to sons of citizens and was acquired at birth by those born in the city. Yet it was a distinctive personal status, not to be assumed as belonging to a family. So Siena's 1309 Constitution made clear that one man's accession to citizenship did not mean that his brothers in the contado were citizens too.[81] Citizenship could also be earned *ex gratia* or *ex privilegio*, by special concession.[82] Bartolus de Sassoferrato, himself an adopted citizen of Todi, spoke for many jurists when he defended the equality of citizenship, whatever its origin. The city was its citizens, and the city could fully make citizens, since it recognised no higher authority in the matter.[83] The jurist Baldus de Ubaldis (1327–1400) opined nonetheless that 'natural' citizenship and that achieved by law were to be distinguished, even if they were in practice exercised similarly by their holders.[84] Indeed, that was sometimes the case: in 1358 a list of citizens of Avignon described their oath of loyalty to the pope as that of citizens belonging to, or originating in, the city (*civium originarium*).[85] From the later thirteenth century, theological and legal discussions also incorporated considerations of a moral nature – like intention – in reflection on the qualities of a good, trustworthy citizen.[86]

Systems of citizenship varied greatly. Becoming a citizen usually followed a period of residence during which a person had paid taxes, worked, built a house, and established a family.[87] And because citizens had duties – fiscal, political, and military – both kings and urban communities often sought to encourage inhabitants to become citizens. In the course of the fourteenth century, both England and France developed a process of naturalisation, or 'denization', as it was called in England, where it was managed by royal officials.[88] It was in the interest of sovereigns to ensure the status of those inhabitants of their cities whom they considered to be particularly useful. The case of France is especially interesting. In the fourteenth century, there was a lively debate that ultimately detached the association in Roman law between city of origin and citizenship, and reoriented it towards a relationship with the crown and kingdom.[89] By separating citizenship from paternal endowment, the children of foreigners could become 'naturalised' and defined by their place of birth.[90] Granting citizenship of the kingdom became a regalian privilege, and its reach followed royal sovereignty.

Most newcomers arrived as migrants from villages and smaller towns.[91] The lives of such newcomers were soon fitted into networks of labour as they became part of the working population, those of both lesser wealth and political influence. On occasion, even the more modest townspeople might gain citizenship. In 1266 the city of Parma created more than 400 new citizens of its restive *popolares*, previously unenfranchised. In 1282 fifty-two were created, paying 'according to what they had promised and what had been ordained by the commune'.[92] Among artisans it was guild membership that made further political participation possible.

THINKING THE 'MEDIEVAL' CITY

How might we approach this multitude of urban experiences? When historians and theorists have thought about medieval cities, they have tended to consider them in the period of growth and institution-building. The medieval city served as a model for the reflections of Max Weber (1864–1920) on the origins of modernity. He saw the 'Occidental' city as an important starting point, a harbinger of rational, modern social organisation, which fostered individuality tempered by civic responsibility. Weber imagined the medieval European city as free from the yoke of dynastic intrusion, which he believed dominated the 'Oriental' city.[93] Here he was quite wrong for, as we have already seen, most medieval cities existed under royal jurisdictions – in England, France, Castile, Aragon, Poland, Hungary, Sicily, Portugal, and the Nordic sphere (*Norgesweldet*). Weber's contemporary, the Belgian historian Henri Pirenne, saw the cities of the Low Countries emerging – as the archives of so many urban communities showed – out of a world of lordship based on the tenure of agrarian land and jurisdiction over servile village populations. Pirenne saw towns as the creation of merchants seeking profit, protection, and freedom from seigneurial imposition. Here was an inspired vision that still powerfully affects our thinking about towns and cities in Europe. What interested Pirenne far less were the ways that freedom was tentative and exclusive in those cities, as any reflection on their diversity soon shows.[94]

We also think of medieval cities through the imagination of medieval historian Jacques Le Goff (1924–2014), who admired the freedom of thought enjoyed by townspeople. Le Goff encouraged historians to study the city as a creative space, where new attitudes to time and the afterlife developed.[95] Critical and inventive thinking underpinned much urban life; scholars at the schools of Paris from the late twelfth century, a time of urban flourishing, discussed questions that were quintessentially urban, even mercantile: What is the just price? Should cities have brothels? Can alms be given from ill-gotten earnings?[96]

The questions raised by our historical subjects in the written and visual traces that they have left behind are often very close to those we still seek to answer. We approach these traces with appropriate humility, but also with the plenitude of our intellectual traditions. We sometimes do so by using concepts unfamiliar to their own usage. I follow ancient historian Nicole Loraux here in naming such a practice 'controlled anachronism' (*anachronisme contrôlé*).[97] In what follows, we shall consider concepts and behaviours regarding strangers as these arise from past deliberations, but we shall also disrupt those categories by pointing out their inconsistencies, and their silences. For example, while Jews were rarely described as *forinseci* or *alieni* in period documents, it is useful to think of them alongside – and in comparison with – other groups marked by difference, as we shall do in Chapter 3. Similarly, medieval sources do not describe women as strangers in their hometowns, but we shall explore in Chapter 4 a range of disabilities in women's civic participation that rendered their lives comparable to those of newcoming strangers. Working historically requires sensitivity towards the terms of past lives and conversations, but historians can also know much that people in the past never knew – or never asked – about themselves.[98]

THE MAKING OF THIS BOOK

The opportunity to enrich our public discussions with historical insight is perhaps more precious than ever before. I began research for this book in summer 2015, as the chancellor of the Federal Republic of Germany allowed the afflicted and dispossessed of Syria's civil war – about 1 million newcomers – to settle. No historian could fail to be moved, and moved to reflect. I wondered how these newcomers would make their homes, how these strangers would become neighbours. Like so many immigrants over the generations, parents would no doubt make sacrifices so their children could live better – different – lives. I wondered, too, how settled Europeans would support these efforts, or hinder them.

Historians are inclined to turn to the past with questions arising from their present. As they do so they must take care. The dramas of human flight, as well as migration in search of a better life, are always with us.

The movement of people always challenges the suppleness of institutions, their ability to respond to newcomers, to the opportunities and the challenges these create. Encountering strangers is also an emotional experience, as feelings veer between sympathy and fear of the unfamiliar; between the desire to benefit from another's labour or talent, and resentment at a newcomer's perceived effect on habits and common practices.

The routes travelled by newcomers are determined by a vast array of economic, demographic, and legal conditions, and these are all historically specific; they also involve complex individual feelings and calculations. When a city or a state allows a newcomer to join it, there are a myriad ways in which the settled and those arriving soon interact: as business partners, fellow workers, neighbours, or parishioners, in processes that make the new increasingly mundane, the strange more and more familiar. All of this unfolds over time and depends on the building of trust. As we shall see, communities and individuals are most trusting, or willing to take risks, when they are at ease with themselves.[99]

This short book aims to introduce the reader to some of the ways that urban communities dealt with strangers, whether migrants from a neighbouring village, merchants bearing goods from afar, or invited experts. We shall consider how civic leaders and law-makers discussed the risks and the benefits, the moral imperatives and the social consequences, of allowing newcomers into the spaces that townspeople called home.[100] As we struggle everywhere to figure out how to facilitate and manage the movement of people, the answers to these questions are particularly pertinent. By exploring the varying efforts made in towns and cities in the past to encourage useful newcomers and keep out dangerous ones, we shall encounter different attitudes across regions and change over time following the great surge in urban life after c. 1000. We may also learn some modesty as we compare our own efforts with theirs.

Cities of Strangers is not another history of cities, nor a history of migration. It is rather a set of interlocking essays based on the Wiles Lectures of 2017 that consider how we may think about the reception of strangers in medieval towns and cities. Most attempts so far have taken the form of local studies, and these have been invaluable for the making of this book. I aim to offer some *comparison*, and so to show the variety between European regions; I shall also introduce some helpful *concepts*; and always attend to *change* in attitudes and policies.

This book offers some approaches that have not been tried so far, and works through a wide range of sources and scholarship with the hope of animating future research. The scholarship I have been able to consult is far more plentiful for those areas that were early and highly urbanised, like the cities of northwest Europe and of north–central Italy, where traditions of scholarship on urban life are also long and intricate.[101] Whole regions, like Poland and Hungary, have suffered from acute losses of documentation, so that only the later medieval segment of their urban story is amenable to detailed study.[102]

My thinking about strangers in cities has been inspired by a wide range of encounters, with reflection on migration and settlement. Migration – the making and the breaking of solidarities that it may cause – can be located at the heart of national histories, which is where Gérard Noiriel placed it in 1988 in *Le Creuset français: Histoire de l'immigration, XIXe–XXe siècles.*[103] This image of the melting pot, used so frequently to describe the making of the United States, poses a useful image against which to test the experience of medieval towns and cities.

The most powerful studies of the movement of people have dwelt not solely on the betterment of lives, but have also considered the sense of loss and the lingering experience of unsettled identities. Oscar Handlin's classic study of the experience of migration to the US in the nineteenth century, *Uprooted* (1951), captured the ambivalence of the attempts to establish male honour in the new homeland, a world so different from the tough, yet intimate, villages of Sicily, Sweden, or Ireland left behind. He opened *Uprooted* with something of a motto: 'Once I thought to write a history of the immigrants in America. Then I discovered the immigrants *were* American history.'[104] More recent studies of citizenship have deftly probed the malleability of the categories of inclusion and exclusion, as these were tested against the reality of slavery and its legacy, and the indigenous 'extraneity' of Native Americans.[105] I too have found that studying the treatment of strangers is an education in many related spheres of European life: ethics and economics, urban space and kinship, ideas and practices.

Handlin's approached is echoed in E. Annie Proulx's 1996 novel *Accordion Crimes*. This is the story of an accordion made in later nineteenth-century Sicily, of its movement with its immigrant owners across the United States, where it was pawned, stolen, and gifted by men from Sicily, Germany, Mexico – immigrants all. This reminds us that however much the stranger hopes for acceptance, he or she also retains important attachments to objects and practices – to food, language, habits of the body – that are from another place, like the music played on the accordion.

I hope to offer some points of entry into the history of the neighbouring lives of strangers and those already settled, though much of my work here is based on documents that record the norms of civic behaviour.[106] It was in such legal and administrative domains that much thinking about strangers was expressed. And strangers took the law seriously too, for it ensured their safety and defined their prospects. Nowhere was this more evident than in the lives of non-Christian strangers.

Such operation of the law through the work of magistrates intersected with the attitudes of neighbours and the exhortations of preachers, and with factions everywhere within urban communities. All of these combined to make living in cities volatile and creative, and that was as true for those who felt at home as it was for those who were yet to become trusted neighbours. Reflecting on the treatment of newcomers and strangers, I have found it useful to think of urban centres as assemblages, a term first coined in French as *agencement*.[107] This means approaching a city (like all aspects of the social)[108] as an entity made up of many parts – human, material, animal – combined to form a dynamic whole, with attendant forms of behaviour and emotions: fear, pride, envy, anger, and anxiety.[109] Historians have over recent years tried to understand cities through patterns of civic identity, based on ritual and often on what has been called 'civic religion'.[110] We may do so too, but only in a weak sense. For even when townspeople habitually met at great processions that portrayed order and magnificence, lives returned on the morrow to the challenges of daily living with varying forms of difference and diversity.

Cities emerge as processes, unfinished, never fixed, always in flux.[111] They were carefully planned and measured spaces, in which habits and routines unfolded in time – with bells, curfews, market days, and festivals, with outdoor sermons and processions, and calendars, both civic and religious.[112] The urban space was also dramatically divided: separated into parts, marked by neighbourhoods, gates, and barriers;[113] cathedral jurisdictions carved out precincts, with their own building styles and sociability.[114] The city was of parts – parties – in other fundamental ways, too. Patrick Lantschner has described the cities of north–central Italy and the southern Low Countries as 'polycentric', their endemic political unrest arising from deeply held party, clan, and family allegiances.[115] Cities were faction, gangs, and competition; no city was ever truly 'at rest'. Every city was an assembled process, ever responding to a host of challenges, with the endowment – material and conceptual – that was its history and legacy. Diversity in the city was both a challenge and a tool.

Through comparison and juxtaposition we shall discern differences and identify patterns in attitudes to strangers in cities. This book does not offer colourful biographies of people who fashioned shape-shifting lives in cities, men like the three 'aliens' recently studied so well by Sanjay Subrahmanyam.[116] Rather, it offers a comparative illustration of how in different parts of Europe newcomers – more or less challenging in their unfamiliarity – were treated in laws and social practices that allocated to them tasks and spaces, and that laid down pathways for increased familiarity and integration into urban life. A whole variety of strangers will be considered, from the recent immigrant assimilated into the urban workforce within a generation, to long-standing communities of one-time immigrants whose strangeness formed part of their identity, even their usefulness to the city. We shall meet them at the city gate, and consider the laws and procedures that enabled their journeys from strangers to neighbours.

We shall find that while cities devised ways to receive and integrate newcomers in the periods of growth and opportunity, their officials were equally adept at revising these provisions once times and prospects had changed. In large parts of Europe, urban elites perceived their condition to be precarious and worsening in the later fourteenth century. Economic downturn was evident in parts of western Europe already in the early 1300s, during and following the terrible famine years of 1315–22, when it seemed never to stop raining in northern Europe. Cities experienced then the desperation of hungry people, locals as well as refugees from the countryside, and a dizzying volatility of prices that caused spirals of debt.[117] And soon Europe's cities were truly devastated, literally laid to waste, by the Black Death of 1347–1352, which hit urban centres particularly hard and continued to do so over the following decades, and on into the fifteenth century.[118]

This economic downturn created in cities a range of political alignments often associated with the desire of workers to assert themselves, since labour was now scarce and skills much in demand.[119] The new order disrupted communities where mercantile elites were hard-pressed, and workers often insistent and effectively organised. Several Italian cities were soon absorbed into dynastic lordships, where princely administrations now decided the fate of newcomers. Central Europe, which suffered far less from the ravages of recurrent plagues, became an attractive destination for those who were now less welcome in cities, especially Jews from regions further west. In Italian and imperial cities we witness urban elites no longer able to deliver the common good through effective fiscal administration handing over the public space to charismatic preachers, who communicated programmes of root-and-branch reform of business ethics, of the gendered order, and of the marriage bed. Through strategies of exclusion, magistrates and preachers alike sought to define the 'us' and 'them', to develop techniques of record-keeping and discipline to match. This was the age of exclusion and expulsion.

When the world history bestseller, the *Nuremberg Chronicles*, was published in 1493, it included some 2,000 images of cities. Cities were where history was made, by those settled and by newcomers alike.[120]

CHAPTER 2

Strangers into Neighbours

You may not like them much
(Who does?) but we owe them

basilicas, divas,
dictionaries, pastoral verse,

the courtesies of the city;
without these judicial mouths

(which belong for the most part
to very great scoundrels)

how squalid existence would be,
tethered for life to some hut village,

afraid of the local snake
or the local ford demon. . .

From W. H. Auden,
Horae canonicae,
Sext (between 1945 and 1954)[1]

MEDIEVAL URBAN CENTRES BECAME LARGER AND MORE numerous after c. 1000. Ranging from market towns of hundreds or a few thousands of inhabitants[2], to cathedral cities of thousands, and to metropoles of tens of thousands and more, they attracted immigrants, and invited individuals and groups to settle. In areas of recent conquest, such as Iberia, Ireland, Sicily, or Livonia, cities saw the settlement of newcomers among indigenous populations as political power changed

25

hands. Townspeople with different capacities interacted in workshops, marketplaces, and in public spaces. There were urban manufacturers and consumers, entertainers and audiences, preachers and parish communities, office-holders and those they disciplined. Town life was organised through membership in multiple groups: the family, the occupational guild – *arte, Zunft, métier* – and, for the purpose of worship, the parish. Like-minded people often created associations for enhanced religious[3] experience, confraternities of prayer formed by the living for their dead.

PUBLIC POLICIES AND THE MOVEMENT OF PEOPLE

Contemporaries noted that towns differed in their power to determine their own affairs. Brunetto Latini (1220–94) wrote in his *Le livre dou Tresor* that cities fell into two types:

> one, which exists in France and in other countries, who are subject to the lordship of kings and of other perpetual princes who sell the office of magistrate and give it to those who seek it (they are little concerned with their goodness or the advantage to the citydwellers).

And the other type is in Italy:

> for the citizens and the citydwellers and the communities of cities elect as magistrates and lords those they consider to be better and more profitable to the common good of the city and all its subjects.[4]

This idealising view nonetheless captures a distinguishing factor in the treatment of some indigenous as well as newly arrived groups in European cities: in some regions policy was governed by royal statute, whereas in others it was made by local assemblies, sometimes subject to imperial approval.

The making of policies about the settlement of newcomers was a matter for all rulers. Henry III's son, King Edward I, expelled the Jews from England in 1290, and this caused him to realign the provision of credit and financial services. The Crown developed intricate relations with foreign merchants and bankers who already had commercial interests in English wool.[5] In 1293 the Provençal merchants in London had to acknowledge under oath that they understood they were not 'of the freedom' of the city, that is, were not its citizens. In 1298 a group of foreign merchants took an oath and declared they were not unaware of the customary restriction on their stay, to no more than forty days.[6] By 1303 their rights and duties were codified in Edward I's *Carta mercatoria*, which encompassed merchants of 'Germany, France, Spain, Portugal, Provence, Catalonia, our Duchy of Aquitaine, Toulouse, Cahors, Flanders, Brabant and all other foreign lands and places'.[7] Royal policy governed entry from abroad, so when political unrest in Flemish cities between 1323 and 1328 resulted in the large-scale banishment of weavers from their hometowns, King Edward II encouraged such exiled textile workers to settle in England.[8] Citizenship had become the business of the state, as we have seen in France. By 1350 royal officials in England had developed the possibility of denization, a process that also produced a new source of income.[9] The English crown extended the reach of letters of denization, so that by 1390 those born in Ireland were also required to be naturalised if they wanted to enjoy the status of the English.[10]

The lands of the kings of Castile and Aragon were growing apace in the twelfth century, following the conquest of territories from Muslim rulers, hence policies for those areas with large Jewish and Muslim populations had to be devised. Kings provided cities with law codes – *fueros* – with wide-ranging provisions for life in what had long been – and continued to be – frontier regions. Adding to the ethnic and religious mix of their lands, kings also invited foreign workers by royal edict. In this manner, Genoese settled in Seville first as shipbuilders in the twelfth century, and from 1251 officially as merchants and financiers too. They were allowed to have a church in their neighbourhood and to judge their own non-criminal cases. In 1261 Alfonso X granted them a mosque to turn into a palace for their use.[11] Castilian merchants in turn seem to have arrived in the Low Countries only later, by the fourteenth century.[12] Royal intervention in Castile and Aragon, just as in England and France, provided the framework for the settlement of professional strangers, and to this reality local communities had to adapt.

In some regions kings and territorial rulers vigorously encouraged groups of foreign settlers to move to their cities, as drivers of economic growth and thus of royal income.[13] In a series of privileges between the

1250s and 1271, the Swedish ruler Birger Jarl exempted from taxes first
the merchants of Lübeck, then those of Hamburg, and lastly those of
Riga.[14] Polish royal privileges offered attractive terms to migrants from
Low German-speaking lands, and to small numbers of incomers from
Italian cities, from the Midi and Iberia.[15] The terms were laid down in
royal legislation, which each king confirmed upon his accession. After
the Mongol invasion of 1241, Bela IV (1206–70), king of Hungary, sought
to rebuild the settlements on the Danube, including the royal residence
at Buda.[16] A German mercantile elite dominated the city council of ten
Germans and two Hungarians. The important role of city judge was held
by one of full German descent, that is 'from all sides' of his parentage
('deutscher art sey von allem geschlächt').[17] Buda grew into a bilingual
city – with Low German and Hungarian – and its commercial and social
activities were organised along ethnic lines. Buda's statutes became the
model for other towns in the kingdom, like Sopron/Ödenburg, Košice/
Kaschau, Cluj/Klausenberg, and Pozsony/Pressburg.[18] These arrangements endured until the mid fifteenth century and were always closely
scrutinised by royal officials.

   Such involvement of dynastic rulers in the local settlement of foreigners continued to extend further east. When the erstwhile Kievan territory
of Ruthenia became a duchy of the Kingdom of Poland in 1356, its towns
were already extremely diverse.[19] Lviv/Lemberg, for example, had a
staple for 'mercibus de Thartaria', 'Tartar' goods handled by Armenians,
Jews, Muslims, and indigenous Ruthenians. With the region's amalgam-
ation into Poland, German migrants from Polish towns began to run the
city. Lviv soon became officially Catholic – having been Russian Ortho-
dox – and it too lived by German urban law. Armenians and Jews had
privileges for protection and freedom of worship, as they did in other
parts of the kingdom: 'in their customary habits that is, advocates,
bishops, priests and churches'.[20]

BETWEEN DYNASTS AND TOWNSPEOPLE

Between rulers and urban communities there existed on occasion
other layers of authority, and these determined how royal statutes were
interpreted and enforced locally. In areas of recent conquest and little

peace – Ireland, Wales, Prussia – the power of such lords was especially strong. An active lord, like William Marshall (1190–1231) in Kilkenny, rebuilt fortifications and promoted trade in his towns. His seneschal of Leinster, Geoffrey Fitz Robert, granted Kilkenny a charter in 1207–11, with privileges and exemptions from tolls. Here was the basis for mercantile growth, led by Kilkenny's merchants, who were allowed to form a guild, as other towns in England and the Low Countries had done for some decades.[21]

In the aftermath of Edward I's conquest between 1277 and 1283, the Crown created well-fortified boroughs in Wales, just as it had done in Ireland, and it provided laws to govern life in them. Wales was divided into lordships held by English magnates who shouldered the burden of defence, and benefited from the income generated by trade and the provision of justice. These men enjoyed relative freedom of action and used it to invigorate the economy of their regions through urban growth. Lord Grey of Ruthin held lands in the northeast of Wales. At the heart of his lordship he nurtured the town of Ruthin, where a wide range of crafts and manufacture flourished: baking, meat preparation, tanning, and brewing.

Ruthin's court rolls for the early fourteenth century have been studied by Matthew Stevens, and these reveal a great deal about life in the town. People with identifiably Welsh names were on the whole about one-third poorer than their English neighbours, but they were represented at all levels of town life, bar Lord Grey's highest administration.[22] There were partnerships, and hence relationships between English and Welsh. There was no strict spatial separation between them, though people habitually lived close to those of similar origin. So in Ruthin, of thirty-six Welsh burgesses active in 1324, twenty held modest properties on Welsh Street, usually fractions of a burgage plot; while of Ruthin's thirty-five English burgesses, only four held property on Welsh Street, and those who did held full burgages (often more than one), dwellings most probably let to Welsh residents.[23] This intermingling was not what royal legislation had had in mind for its Welsh boroughs, but it was a state of affairs allowed by the officials of the local territorial lord, and it resulted in mixed urban living, if not quite assimilation.

BEYOND CONQUEST – FURTHER FACTORS THAT
MADE CITIES DIVERSE

As we have seen, urban centres were diverse by their nature, yet political change, such as conquest and colonial settlement, could contribute to that diversity. Less violent changes in regime also affected the composition of cities. The arrival of the papal court in Avignon in 1309 caused the population to rise from around 5,000 to 60,000 in the 1370s. The papal court employed hundreds of people, including merchants, bankers, tailors, butchers, and labourers, recruited from all the regions surrounding it, with perhaps half the newcomers being from Italian cities.[24] And when the papacy returned to Rome in the fifteenth century, the population there grew, attracting men and women as pilgrims and artisans, and also causing women to become sex workers. A notable Slavic minority developed, probably of refugees from the Balkans, and its women developed religious and charitable institutions to alleviate their need in the vast city.[25]

Cities became particularly diverse when they were incorporated into maritime empires such as the so-called 'Commonwealth Veneziano'.[26] From the early thirteenth century, the city ruled large parts of the eastern Mediterranean – where colonial rule was created with the hegemony of Latin Christianity and Venetian administration. This also meant interaction with Greeks, Jews, and Armenians, who entered into joint-business ventures with Venetian citizens and for some time immigrated to labour in workshops of the mainland – the *terraferma*.[27] Dalmatian immigration intensified from 1420, following Venetian domination, and so an island such as the Dalmatian Curzola/Korčula developed an international port and became home to diverse groups from the *Stato del Mar*, the Venetian Empire.[28] The inhabitants of these Venetian lands joined immigrants from other Italian and German cities. There they lived and created networks of support, with distinctive religious confraternities and churches. Colonial extension made the metropolis ever more diverse, even if most immigrants could not accede to full Venetian citizenship.[29]

The sphere created by the Hanseatic network of alliances was integrated into a League after the Treaty of Stralsund of 1370, and within it was experienced yet another type of diversity: the presence of familiar strangers from the associated towns. The Hanse was a daily reality for communities around the North and Baltic Seas. This meant that a merchant of Riga could stay indefinitely in Gdansk/Danzig, while a Genoese merchant could only stay for a limited period. In Flanders, Hanse merchants were so active that some men of Lübeck applied in the 1270s to Margaret, Countess of Flanders, for permission to found a town of their own, on the Zwin outside Bruges – 'novam villam de Dam'.[30]

Yet there was a distinction still between the Hanseatic *incola* – inhabitant – and a citizen of a Hanse city. An interesting example was John Kempe, son of the famous mystic, Margery Kempe (1373–1438) of Lynn. John married a local woman from Gdansk/Danzig, and settled and traded there. When his mother was widowed and he sought to visit her in 1431, he had to obtain permission and produce surety for the debts in which he was involved before a permit to leave was issued.[31]

Mention of a pilgrim like Margery Kempe brings to mind the urban diversity that resulted from the presence of such visitors who lived in cities for fixed terms. Cities like Rome, Canterbury, Siena, Wilsnack, or Santiago de Compostella attracted a constant flow of such visitors. These stimulated local economies with their demand for accommodation, food, and financial, sometimes medical, and always pastoral, care. In Siena, the hospital of Santa Maria della Scala accepted deposits and arranged credit for pilgrims at the final destination, even securing their wealth if they died on pilgrimage, for post-mortem restitution to their heirs.[32] Similarly, Treviso regularly saw the passage of pilgrims – alongside merchants – from central Europe on their way to Rome and the Holy Land. Here too provision was made by the creation of the hospital of Santa Maria del Piave for their care.[33] Series of the seven Works of Mercy, often painted on church walls or sculpted on portals, interpreted the duty to 'lodge the stranger' in terms of giving shelter to a pilgrim, as did the scene on the Redeemer portal of Parma cathedral of 1196.[34] But lodging the stranger was nowhere interpreted as the work of welcoming a newcomer.

University towns hosted hundreds of students who stayed in a city for a period of years. Students were usually young men who posed a risk to public order. But they were also consumers, whose needs were anticipated by royal patrons. The kings of England granted the universities the right to hold their own courts and to import food from their estates.[35] Those of France offered privileges and protections, and in Paris controlled the price of food, as they did the price of the straw from which modest beds were made. The needs of foreign students inspired new forms of scrutiny and provision, like the rent control evaluation of 1231, or the charitable foundation of the Collège de la Sorbonne of 1257.[36] Students in turn, just like foreign merchants, were organised into 'nations' – *nationes* – social groups based on language and regional identity: French, Norman, Picard, and English.[37]

Towns also attempted to supervise mariners on shore leave. The *Oak Book* of Southampton, from around 1300, cited for use the law code of northwest Europe, the Roll of Oléron:

> Mariners hire themselves to their master, and there are some of them who go on shore without leave, and get drunk, and make quarrels, and some of them are hurt; the master is not bound to have them healed, or to provide them with anything; on the contrary, he may put them ashore, and hire another in his place ... But if the master sends them on any service ... and he wounds himself or is hurt, he shall be cured and healed at the cost of the ship.[38]

Similarly, Mantua's statutes of between 1303 and 1313 regulated any movement in the city's ports after the sounding of the third bell, rung in the evening, until the day bell was sounded on the morrow.[39]

So cities offered temporary homes to a variety of groups that took part in their markets, benefited from their hospitality, were drawn to their relics and holy images, and enjoyed their charitable provision. In those regions where royal and imperial privileges guided the settlement of foreigners, urban communities had to accept strangers. Their presence might be beneficial to economic growth, but it might also inspire fear of competition, resentment over privileged exemptions, or anxiety when such strangers were young men away from home. In the case of non-Christian newcomers, other emotions arising from current religious ideas affected attitudes, too.

Those urban communities with greater degrees of autonomy were able to deliberate and legislate their own attitudes into the statutes that governed them. Such statutes reflect what civic officials considered to be the risks and the benefits of accepting newcomers, from nearby or from further afield. As the historian of Roman law Mario Ascheri has put it, referring to Italian cities: 'the statutes ... are naturally the first sources one should confront when treating the regime to which the stranger was submitted in our cities'.[40] We shall study several of these Italian statutes and seek out similar trends, where these emerge in other regions.

URBAN STATUTES AND NEWCOMERS

Frederic William Maitland once noted that the first act of an enfranchised town in England, a borough, was to give

> itself a constitution, to develop a conciliar organ, one council or two councils, to define the modes in which burgherhood should be acquired ... and generally to be as oligarchic or democratic as it thought fit.[41]

And so did many towns and cities across Europe, cities that lived in relative freedom from any sovereign's involvement in their affairs. The communes of north and central Italy from the twelfth century were early and prolific makers of statutes. The laws they created for self-governance were based on existing privileges and local customs accumulated over centuries, to which were added regulations on trade, election to office, and the treatment of foreigners or strangers – *forestieri*.[42] Venice, Pisa, Pistoia, and Genoa all blended the legacies of Lombard and Carolingian law,[43] with new stipulations regarding taxation, the maintenance of roads, water supply, and control of the market. As the study and teaching of law were systematised in the twelfth century – earliest in Padua and Bologna – it inspired the collation and publication of statutes, which were frequently updated and soon also attracted legal commentaries.[44]

It is useful to think of urban statutes as products of deliberation and design by office-holding citizens charged with the city's safety and interested in its prosperity. Cities called on experts in Roman law to draw up their statutes and – when necessary – to interpret them.[45] These were often members of landed aristocratic families and of wealthy merchant ones. Legal experts developed the *ius proprium*, the right to legislate over local affairs, within the frame of the *ius commune* – the Roman Law – that held strong in all parts of the Holy Roman Empire south of the Alps.[46] The zone of active statute-making stretched from central Italy into southern France.[47] So great was the utility of making and enforcing statutes that several rural communities in these and other regions also produced them with the aim of managing common land and controlling the environment.[48] Over time, statute-makers increasingly turned to experts for technical knowledge on fiscal, environmental, and industrial regulation through statutes.[49] This expertise was appreciated throughout Europe. When the city of Lübeck received its freedom charter from Emperor Frederick II in 1226, it began a search for a legal expert in both Roman and canon law hailing from Lombardy.[50]

Books of statutes were kept in town halls and were sometimes copied for the personal use of civic officials.[51] In Ferrara in 1173 the statutes were carved in marble as an inscription on the cathedral's south façade.[52] Statutes were adopted locally and constantly improved and updated.[53]

Yet changes could be contentious. A chronicler of Piacenza recorded that when in 1250 a new statute regarding the election of the rectors of the people was read out, it caused great commotion.[54] Dante considered symptomatic of Italy's poor political condition changes to customs regarding citizenship and public office, areas regulated by statutes:

> How often, in the time you can remember,
> Have you changed law and coinage, offices
> And customs, and revised your citizens?
> (*Purgatorio*, Canto 6, 145–7)[55]

Statutes soon served other groups within the city, like guilds and confraternities. The statutes that governed notarial work in Bergamo, compiled between 1264 and 1281, laid down the responsibilities of notaries, who provided essential legal services to both officials and citizens.[56]

The need for public engagement with communal law soon required that it be provided not only in jurists' Latin, but also in the common language. When the commune of Siena decided in 1309 to have its statutes rewritten in the vernacular – *in volgari* – for which service it paid a notary and an illuminator tidy sums, it claimed to have done so:

So that poor people and other persons who do not know (Latin) grammar, and others who wish to, will be able to see and make a copy of them.[57]

The notary who copied the statutes of the commune of Porlezza on Lake Lugano in 1336 attested that he had them read publicly:

> The statutes written above have been read and published by me, Parisio Beto, notary of Porlezza, at the order and command of lord Giacomazzo Ferraro of Vigevano, podestà of the said community of Porlezza, in the commune's square.[58]

A whole array of archival provisions, recordings of transactions, tax lists, and the related seals developed to underpin and regulate urban life. In many German cities by the thirteenth century a city book (*Stadtbuch*) was kept, and in it were recorded transactions between citizens.[59]

Cities observed each other and adopted good practices that seemed to work for their neighbours on many matters, including the making of statutes.[60] The communes of the Macerata in east–central Italy often followed the statutes of Ancona, the region's ancient port.[61] The statutes of Ragusa/Dubrovnik of 1227 borrowed a great deal from the laws of Venice – its most important commercial partner – even though it formed part of the kingdom of Hungary.[62] Where cities did not legislate for themselves, as in Poland and Bohemia, kings often allowed for German urban law codes to prevail, the *ius teutonicum*.[63] In Hungary the influence of German law is evident, although kings there were reluctant to have foreign law applied in their realm.[64]

THE SHORT-STAY STRANGER

Cities made provision for strangers in their midst, traders and visitors who stayed for fixed periods. And thus Camerino in the Macerata required that those coming to sell salt did so on Saturdays and Wednesdays at the allocated stand (*starium*) provided in St Mary's Square, and always using the local measures.[65] Towns and cities were eager to control what in England acquired a distinctive name – forestalling. This meant selling outside the market, and so undercutting local traders – even licensed foreign ones – who paid dues for the right to trade. The royal statutes of 1192 granted to Dublin decreed that no foreign merchant 'buy, within the city, corn, hides, or wool, from a foreigner, but only from citizens', that is, in the market.[66] Bologna's statutes of 1288 similarly punished 'foreign merchants who buy and sell merchandise, exchanging wares with another foreign merchant outside the piazza'.[67] And lest the presence of such 'foreign' traders embroil locals in court cases, whose punishments included banishment, the commune of San Gimignano sought to limit the damage to its citizens from any such case in its statutes of 1255: local courts were 'not to banish or cause to be banished any person of our castle or town for any money or debt to any foreign person'.[68] The statutes of Forlì from 1359 reminded the local judge of his duty to enforce the well-supported rights of citizens or residents of the city's contado against foreigner debtors (*forenses*).[69]

Urban communities attempted to order into categories a complex web of lives, relations, and aspirations.[70] Most statutes recognised that those who only stayed a while, with no great stake in the local community, posed the greatest risk to the city's well-being. And so the statutes of Pistoia of 1284 did not allow *forenses* to reside there during periods of political unrest (*rumor*).[71] Statutes regulated taverns and inns where such strangers lodged.[72] Local householders were often forbidden to offer strangers bed and board. The statutes of Valsolda, north of Como (decreed in 1246 and reformed in the 1370s), made this clear:

> And it has been deliberated and decided that no person of the said valley should accept or receive, nor give lodging to any foreigner, unless someone of the said valley has given a good account, and security of at least 25 lire of our currency.[73]

Innkeepers scrutinised visitors to their establishments, hence they were often licensed, as well-known locals.[74]

Forenses laboured under several restrictions. In Mühlhausen in Thuringia, a settled non-citizen was obliged to buy local wine at double the going price (*bis tantum dabit quantum civis*).[75] Many cities forbade the sale of property to non-citizens. Pistoia's statutes of 1296 were explicit that no business in real estate should be done with foreigners:

that no person of the city of Pistoia or the district sell, commit, pawn, hire or in any ways alienate lands or possessions or any immobile goods to any person or place that is not of the city of Pistoia or its district.[76]

In Buda's statutes, created by 1403, it was laid down that 'no burgess of Buda city should sell his goods to a foreigner'.[77] Foreigners were excluded from sharing in natural resources available to settled citizens. So in the Tuscan town of Cecina, in 1409, a fine was paid for each of the *bestie forestiere* put out to pasture in the settlement's wood:

> And the small animals of the said foreigners, those which are being pastured in the wood of the said Commune, for every head their lord or guardian will pay 12d, and for each big beast, 2 soldi.[78]

Similarly, the statutes of Montebuono (a town in northeast Lazio, near Rieti), collated in 1437, made it clear that 'no foreigner who is not a resident of the land of Montebuono should dare to pasture his animals both large and small within the confines of the territory'.[79] If he did, he would be fined.

NEWCOMERS WHO STAY

Yet cities also encouraged some newcomers to stay. Everywhere there was movement into urban centres from communities nearby. Where we can evaluate the scope of such entry, and this is rare, newcomers appear to have made up a large portion of the population: around 1165 in Léon they were 20–30 per cent of the inhabitants.[80] During the thirteenth century, notaries developed practices for recording citizens by given and by family names, so that the various types of townspeople could be logged correctly.[81] This is when we encounter the first lists of 'new citizens' – *vecinos nuovos* – from Murcia.[82] Officials were allowed to stop people and ask them for their name, and expect an answer, to enter houses and enquire as to any strangers residing there. But when a person had regular business in the town and wanted to make his home there – and the statutes always treated such a person as a man – he could embark on a process aimed at setting up a new, productive urban household, and building a home. When women married a citizen of another city, and moved to set up household there, they were absorbed into that new household, although jurists insisted that they also retained the citizenship – however qualified – of the community of their birth.[83]

Incoming men and women were the lifeblood of urban communities in a period of growth, as was vividly described by the consuls of Toulouse in 1226:

> Many men and women with lords and others without lords ... some with their goods and others without them ... greatly improved the city of Toulouse and its suburbs and the community which grew and daily received more.[84]

This flow was particularly important in the region of Toulouse after decades of warfare and strife, so becoming a citizen was made simple. A free man had to say: 'I wish to enter Toulouse and become a citizen of Toulouse' ('Ego volo intrare Tholosam et facere me civem Tholose').[85] The statutes of the city of Agen in southern France, made by 1298 but reflecting customs that had probably prevailed since 1248, show a man asking for entry into citizenship ('estre ciutadas o borzes'). (See Figure 2.1.)[86]

He had to

> with his hand on the Holy Gospels, forswear heretics and vaudois and all manner and all errors of heresy

and swear to the lord and council that

> he will appear before the lord and his council at their judgment to answer all complaints against him; and that within a year and a month he will buy in Agen a house or land or a vineyard ... and for that year and a month he must be excused from military service and the watch.[87]

During that time he was to free himself from any remaining duties to a lord outside Agen.

Rural migrants had to be released from duties to a lord outside the city. Perugia's statutes of 1279 provided that:

> Anyone from our vicinity or district who stays in the city or burgh of Perugia with his family for ten years continuously, and does not owe servile homage, and against whom there are no complaints during these ten years, will be free and unrestricted with all his goods.[88]

2.1. The Ceremony of Entry into Citizenship of the City of Agen, *Costuma d'Agen*, c. 1280, Bibliothèque municipale d'Agen, ms 42, fol. 56v

Here was the path to belonging: continuous residence, property ownership, hearth and family, a good reputation, and service to no other lord or city. While the famous saying 'City air makes one free' (*Stadt luft macht frei*) was a creation of the nineteenth century, it is true that towns and cities encouraged newcomers to become free agents as they began their urban life, allowing for a period of transition.[89] And once they were citizens, they had to stay in the city – *senza fraude*, no cheating! – except for the periods of harvest and the gathering of grapes.[90]

The entry into citizenship was a process marked by stages of scrutiny. The statutes of the city of Forlì from 1359 describe the process of entry into citizenship in some detail: a person who wished to join had to be faithful and devoted to the Roman church; he was then examined by the podestà and the city's *antiani*, who deliberated, and finally voted

> with white and black beans, by those *podestà* and *antiani* so that the person of the captain or *podestà*, or his deputy count as 12 votes.[91]

Venice was particularly restrictive in offering its citizenship. In 1305 it adjusted its law to require fifteen years' residence before a merchant or artisan could set up a shop, and twenty-five years before a more substantial import and export business might be established.[92] Where participation in civic life depended upon membership in guilds, joining one was a road to citizenship. In early fourteenth-century Venice, the glass-makers, 'cristallai', expected an oath and a payment:

> And if any foreigner comes to Venice and wants to work in this art, he will be obliged to swear to the art, and pay 5 soldi, of which one-third goes to the chamber of Justice, and two-thirds to the craft guild.[93]

A local entrant paid 3 soldi. So the *arte* acted as a gate-keeper by scrutinising entrants to the guild, and thus to the public life of Venice. Higher up the social scale, guilds were used for the scrutiny of foreign merchants in Florence. The *Mercanzia*, the union of the main crafts (merchants in foreign cloth, finance, wool, and silk, and physicians, apothecaries, and mercers) from 1309/10 arbitrated between Florentine merchants, but also between foreign ones and Florentines.[94]

New settlers were often exempt from taxes for periods that varied in length.[95] In Recanati they were free of local taxes for up to fifteen years, and upon arrival received some marshy land to dry and make fruitful.[96] But non-citizens also laboured under restrictions, with asymmetrical fines when violence erupted between a citizen and a foreigner. The statutes of the commune of Cairo Montenotte, near Genoa, of 1214 stated that in all matters foreigners (*extranei*) will pay double in fines.[97] But there was also some leniency in fines for transgressions committed by newcomers, perhaps because they were considered to be less well informed about local customs. The Ragusa/Dubrovnik statutes of 1272 prohibited everyone – foreigner and citizen, *extraneus sive civis* – from carrying arms; the fine stood at 2–5 hyperpers and the loss of the weapons concerned; but a foreigner (*non tamen habitans ibi*) was only fined at 1 hyperper.[98]

Becoming less of a stranger and more of a trusted neighbour was everywhere seen as a process. Crucial to all its stages was the earning of trust. Trust and reputation were fragile, and some occupations and life experiences rendered people unlikely to ever achieve a good name. Surety had to be provided for those passing through a town or city, probably by relatives, business partners, or established immigrants from the town or village of origin. Reputation followed people even abroad. Men who had been banished from their hometowns as punishment for a crime were rejected by other towns, too.[99] Cities bound in leagues and associations were obliged to reject for settlement those who had been banished by a sister-city.[100]

The frontier towns of Castile, so eager to attract settlers, were more lenient towards newcomers: simply renting a dwelling made a man – or a woman – a *morador*, one who was there to stay.[101] Paying taxes was an important step on the road to acceptance. Some cities took initiatives aimed at ensuring sufficient migration. In 1315, Treviso introduced an addition to its statutes – *additioni nuove* – including a recommendation that countrymen (*contaddini*) who had two sons and sufficient property send one of them to the town to train in a craft or profession.[102]

Cities were imagined as a collection of households led by their male heads: at work, paying taxes, sensible in their treatment of their dependant servants and apprentices, and, in some parts of Mediterranean Europe – Iberia, Sicily, and from the later fourteenth century Italian cities – of their slaves. Hence, statutes dealt with aspects of family life: they regulated dowries, attended to the rights of widows, and protected the rights of orphans.[103] Since the remarriage of local widows to foreigners could result in the removal of wealth from the city, this was closely observed. The statutes of Sassoferrato, a town in the Marche, clearly stated:

> If any woman is married or given as a wife to any foreigner or one who does not pay dues to the said commune, and gives by contract or gift of her goods to him, this will not be valid at all, and the goods will remain forever obliged to yield the owed dues to the said commune.[104]

Statutes sought to regulate relations between parents and offspring, and so to discourage feuds.[105] And since inheritance arrangements could so often create conflict, statute-makers aimed to control the solemnity of making wills.[106] Porlezza's statutes of 1338 provided that seven witnesses attend the testator, of whom three were men who had known the testator and who could confirm the good standing of the other four witnesses; the event was also to be attended by two notaries.[107]

Trust and good standing could be enhanced through the powerful bonds of marriage. This was true for all newcomers within their religious communities, and it could fortify unions involving converts. There was also patronage that could operate within particular professions and crafts, and that allowed sons of immigrants to become better integrated in the city. Demographic realities determined how open the ranks of locals were to newcomers. Andrée Courtemanche's study of the Dodi family, which moved from Barcelonnette to Manosque in the mid fifteenth century, shows a variety of pathways into considerable integration. First there was the marriage of the widowed daughter of the labourer, Guillaume, to a notary; the couple were in turn adopted – taken as *filios adhoptivos* – by another, childless, couple. When the next daughter married, this was witnessed by prominent citizens, among them councillors. Within twenty years, the younger generation of men were considered to be local *manosquins* with a strong local family network.[108]

Building a home was concomitant with settling down, unlike for those who repeatedly spent short periods as guests in public hostelries. The Advocate and Council of the Swiss town of Fribourg stipulated in 1289 that someone who did want to settle down 'must buy himself a house in our city, and must make it his personal home there with his family and his wife. And if he does not, that house he bought will remain with the city, and he will no longer be a burgess.'[109] In Siena the entry to citizenship of Gerino di ser Tano of Casole, an immigrant from the contado, took place in stages between October 1311 and October 1312. It included his commitment to build a house, and then proof that he had indeed built one in S. Pietro in Castelvecchio, and that this would serve as surety against any future debts he may owe the commune. The city's builder-assessor soon reported that he had checked the house and confirmed its value.[110]

The statutes of the cities of the region of the Marche are particularly detailed in their provisions for the reception of newcomers. Its towns and cities sought to attract those workers who transformed the raw materials of the countryside into goods for sale in towns: butchers, tanners, shoe-makers. Ports like Fermo, Recanati, and Ancona had long been home to immigrants. In 1085, the town of Fonte Avellana had a 'street of the Bulgars, who are called Slavs' ('Vicus Bulgarum qui vocatur Sclavi-norum'), and soon the inland towns did too.[111] Notable Lombard groups of 'magistri di pietra' – specialist stonemasons – lived in these towns, often groups of brothers, who migrated and settled, still maintaining their group identity, as the creation of their confraternity in Recanati shows.[112]

In Camerino, a town of the Marche, a newcomer had to work for a month and prove his usefulness to the local community before he could build a house. Statutes regulated the size of such starter homes, as well the materials to be used in their construction.[113] In Monte Milone, the starter home was to be built on an area of 12.25 (3.5 x 3.5) square meters with a single room on one floor. If built in stone – with plaster and cement – it could go up to 2.8 meters high. Local materials, such as shingle from the river, or stone spoil from ruins, were also made available for use. Those building in wood could cover their habitation with a paste of chaff mixed with sorghum stalks.[114] The distance between houses was regulated too, to provide ample lighting and spaces for the removal of refuse; the distance between houses was to be about 1 meter.[115]

Holding office was the ultimate mark of acceptance into a new urban community. In Chioggia, according to the statutes of 1272, one could only serve on the councils or hold the office of chancellor after twenty years' residence;[116] in Cecina, after ten years, and if paying at least 8 soldi a year in tax, an inhabitant could 'hold the offices of the commune'.[117] In Florence, the statutes of the early fourteenth century allowed civic office to be held only by those who had been born within the city or its contado and who belonged to a family that had been settled there for at least three generations. In Bologna, new citizens were forbidden from holding the office of *anziano* or *gonfaloniere*, that is, city magistrate or neighbourhood representative.[118]

DESIRABLE FOREIGNERS

Once able to act for themselves, communes sought to use statutes and rituals in the anticipation and resolution of strife. In every city there were factions and competition, not least between the families that controlled high office and economic activity. The fault-line that defined Italian politics was loyalty to the pope or to the emperor, parties known respectively as the Guelph and the Ghibelline. But even these categories were open to further division, like the Black and White factional strife, which caused Dante's exile from Florence. The Florentine chronicler Dino Compagni lamented around 1310 that his beautiful city, endowed with well-bred citizens, lovely women, useful crafts, and a good climate, had been undone by its citizens' strife.[119] Or, as Dante put it, it had become a divided city, *città partita*.[120] Although cities aimed to control access to arms, their militias often fomented division and intimidation: in Bologna, members of the city militia assembled publicly in ranks of nobles or knights.[121]

Consequently, by the later twelfth and thirteenth centuries, communes turned to outsiders – usually men with legal or military experience – to govern their fractious communities. These were the podestà, foreigners appointed to enforce local laws for a fixed period of time.[122] In such cases, the lack of local attachments is valued as a quality that ensured the impartiality no citizen could possess. Cities turned to foreigners for other services too, namely those that required expertise and discretion: in its statutes of 1296, Spoleto required its chamber notary (its treasurer) to be a *forensis* – a foreigner.[123] Alongside the ideal of an active local citizenry existed the desperate need to call in impartial men to enforce justice and ensure peace within cities.

Trust was fragile in these complex cities, and so some – like Siena and Piacenza – developed long-standing relationships with religious houses whose monks acted as overseers of the annual financial audit of civic officers.[124] Pistoia's statutes of 1284 required that the judge and notary in charge of communal property should be foreigners.[125] This choice is significant, because most cities were reluctant to allow even those men in minor religious orders to become civic officials, or indeed citizens. Verona's statute of 1327 excluded any cleric from holding office.[126] If citizenship created a bond between citizens who made laws for their mutual benefit, then the clergy, whose lives were regulated by canon law, could not easily qualify as citizens.[127]

Other groups were invited by cities, such as those with useful expertise in law, medicine, or finance.[128] Ascoli Piceno in the Marche negotiated in 1297 the foundation of its first bank with a consortium of twenty-two individuals: sixteen Tuscans, two Aretines, and four Jews of Rome (*Iudei de Urbe*). These were to provide loans at a set interest rate and act as sole lenders to the commune.[129] The city made them 'exempt of all of the said Commune and city's other assessments, both in real and personal property'; it promised to protect the bank from competition from 'foreigners', who might lend when a particular need arose.[130] About the same time, the city of Berne received loans from three settled Lombards, each described as 'a citizen of Asti living in Fribourg of Üechtland'.[131] A few years later, two of the men made another loan to the city without interest, and so were exempted from taxes owed, since they were now described as 'citizens and merchants of Asti and our co-citizens (*comburgenses*)'. The last is an intriguing term, which was sometimes used to describe women's status in towns:[132] a fellow citizen, yet not one able to exercise full civic rights, in particular to assume public office.

While the traditions of preaching and pastoral care drew a highly negative image of the lender at interest,[133] thirteenth-century scholars also developed new ways of justifying such lending. As Joel Kaye has shown, concepts from Roman law facilitated thinking of interest as compensation for the loss of opportunity that lending caused the lender.[134] Yet such approaches contrasted with the content of sermons, which reminded audiences of the turpitude of lending at interest. The level and content of such preaching would become shrill in the fifteenth century.[135]

By welcoming strangers, cities were doing what we have seen sovereigns do all over Europe. Bankers and financiers, large-scale traders in luxury goods, and those with technical expertise were all allowed to settle and contribute to the common good. After the entry of Friuli into the Milanese sphere in 1273, a lively Lombard community developed in that city. Perched at a crossroads leading across the Alps, Friuli also welcomed German immigrants, in particular expert workers and traders in iron. It developed a *fondaco* – a lodging complex – to accommodate northern merchants, among them Jews from the Holy Roman Empire.[136]

STRANGERS INTO NEIGHBOURS, INTO STRANGERS AGAIN?

The statutes we have studied here reflect the concerns of community leaders as they thought of the effect of letting newcomers into their cities. They made settlement easy for those who worked, built a home, and behaved well. Such newcomers could also aspire to citizenship, after years or decades. But we have also seen that cities contained groups from further afield, with distinguishing skills, languages, networks, or religion, to which they adhered. The identities of the Astensi in Paris, Lombards in Manosque, Flemings in London, Jews in Ascoli, or Armenians in Lviv were made of clusters of ideas and practices, chosen and cherished. These familiar strangers could remain just so – both belonging and different – for generations. Christians could aspire to become fully assimilated, and acquire citizenship, but where the sources allow us to judge – as in England and in Venice – many preferred not to seek that citizenship, but to live safely as a distinct element in the complex array of the city.[137] The Flemish weavers in London or the Tuscan bankers in Avignon mostly felt safe enough to live as an embedded yet distinct entity in those cities. Yet both also suffered serious losses that followed from political struggle attached to blatant hatred of – even long-settled – foreigners. In 1376 the Tuscan bankers were expelled from Avignon 'like dogs' during the war between the papacy and Florence. In 1381, the men of Kent who marched on London to bring their grievances to the king as part of the 'Peasants' Revolt' sought out a parish where many Flemings had settled, and cut off the heads of many. One chronicler even claimed that the shibboleth was whether they could say 'breede and chese', like native Londoners, rather than 'case en brode'.[138]

The urban sense of purpose in this period of growth enabled a certain latitude in the incorporation of newcomers both from nearby and from afar. Those who made rules for living imagined newcomers mobilised towards the common good at various levels of society, but always in settled families, hard at work, and contributing to the city's efforts. Yet the reality was far more complex, and cities were homes to many single men and women. Many settled members might choose still to retain certain marks of difference, to mentor newly arrived relatives, to continue trading with their community of origin, to speak a foreign language or dialect, and to worship with others like them in dedicated chapels or synagogues. They were all performing complex identities that cities were – for decades – large and inclusive enough to contain.[139]

Everything we have seen so far regarding the incorporation of newcomers took place within the enabling environment of economic growth and commercial expansion. But when these circumstances changed, each city struggled with the new realities in its own way. A transformation of the civic mood is evident, and it was the result of long-term changes in European life, brutally obvious everywhere after the Black Death, and during its long and dramatic aftermath into the fifteenth century. Bruce Campbell has called this period of European history the Great Transition. Cities lost up to half of their populations, and the volume of trade fell – and continued to fall.[140] And that was not all. For decades cities were visited and revisited by outbursts of epidemic disease that had become endemic, and so the shape of cities changed, with large sections covered by vacant buildings that yielded no contribution to the urban tax base.[141] In such cities the sense of the common good shifted and, with it, the attitudes to newcomers and strangers did, too.

Social relations in cities became even more unsettled, and the results varied in scale and in import for different social groups. A set of contradictions faced urban elites of merchants and guild members: on the one hand, they required workers who were tax-payers, and to these workers they had to pay higher wages; on the other, decline in well-being bred attitudes of suspicion and exclusion between groups, with those marked by difference the first to feel the effects. With dramatic depopulation – a city like Siena shrunk to about 40 per cent of its pre-plague population – officials sought to attract immigrants to their crafts and as contributors to its fiscal burden of defence. Yet at the same time those very officials were directed by the council to exclude Jews from public life.

In these very decades, several Italian cities moved from communal forms of government to control by dynastic lordships that took over the business of administration, including decisions on citizenship.[142] A good example is the case of Milan, where in 1389 Duke Gian Galeazzo Visconti began using the system in order to reward political allies in the city. His administration saw the grant of citizenship as an aspect of lordship, just as it had formerly been in the city's gift. The underlying orientation, however, was no longer the civic common good, to create a reliable and cooperative body of citizens who helped support the city. Rather, interests of seigneurial patronage prevailed, and hence the equality of those born and those made citizens was eroded too.[143] Similarly, when the county of Flanders came to be ruled from 1384 by the dukes of Burgundy, following a dynastic marriage, the considerations of townsmen in a city like Bruges became ever more distant from the seat of administration and from the policy about citizenship.[144]

The politics of citizenship reflected the sharp divergence of interests between urban groups. Some towns made entry simple, like Auxonne in Burgundy in 1367, where a man presented himself to a notary in the presence of three witnesses to draw up the document of enfranchisement. The obligation on him was to pay all taxes due from a citizen. Here notaries were empowered to make citizens![145] Lords could intervene in cities' aims to attract immigrants: Count Verde, hoping to repopulate the Piedmontese town of Rivarolo in 1376, offered a year's exemption from tolls and five years' exemption from all taxes.[146]

Yet the bars to citizenship were sometimes raised too, where privileged urban groups attempted to protect their advantage. In Flemish towns which were more economically buoyant this process coincided with what Marc Boone has called 'institutionalisation poussée', 'forced institutionalisation'.[147] With enhanced protection from Duke Philip the Good, the fifty-three crafts of Ghent now also conducted greater internal scrutiny of their membership, thus bolstering the city's activities of inclusion and exclusion. This period also enhanced the disciplining and punishment of those deemed sexually deviant, homosexual men.[148]

Guilds often closed ranks, excluding newcomers, and restricted membership to the sons of members, as in London and Venice.[149] Where ethnicity was a marker of difference, it could become a new criterion for exclusion. In Lüneburg, where people of Slavic origins habitually joined craft guilds, a new regulation of 1409 excluded them, and since craft membership led to citizenship, this was a meaningful blow;[150] Danes, Swedes, and Norwegians there were also excluded from guilds.[151] In Iberian cities, the ethnic mix included Jews and Muslims, yet King Alfonso V of Aragon (r. 1416–58) confirmed statutes for the guild of goldsmiths in Valencia that forbade the teaching of the craft to non-Christians.[152]

We witness a shift in mood, in what was said and done in the public domains of towns and cities. The willingness of some rulers and urban communities to tolerate, and even support, diversity in work and lifestyle was tested and in many parts lost. City life was becoming more regimented and disciplined, and this is reflected in civic language and practice. When Avignon was issued with new statutes in 1441, its new council of forty-eight included members from each of its three 'nations': native, ultramontane (Italian), and cismontane (French).[153] City oath-books now contained myriad categories of citizen, each with a distinctive oath, and oath-taking occasions became more frequent.[154]

Some challenging religious ideas – not so much new, but preached more vigorously than ever before – were gaining prominence. These interpreted the common good as a new moral disposition directed at every Christian: to reject the prevailing norms of profitable commerce based on the exchange of credit at interest, to cease social activities that seemed frivolous and wasteful, such as family parties, to desist from games of chance, and to promote in the place of all of these a lively Marian devotion.[155] Renewed attention to religious probity, often led by friars who wielded inquisitorial powers too, was exploited by competitors in the city: an accusation of heresy could tarnish the reputation even of a well-established citizen.[156] Long-established groups, like the beguines, became victims of preaching campaigns against begging. Following the preaching of the Dominican Johannes Mulberg, they were expelled from Basel in 1405, whereupon he turned his critique on to usurious clergy.[157]

The fifteenth century saw in many places a combination of royal policies aimed at taxing foreigners, and social attitudes aimed at distinction and exclusion. The long decades of intermittent warfare between England and France created a fertile environment for anti-'alien' policy and feeling. First in 1439–40 in London and then in the following decade reaching further north, the fiscal registration of 'aliens' was undertaken by royal officials.[158] What began with the French and the Flemings soon stretched north to include the Scots and Irish.[159] Soon a distinction was being made between wives and other women, and judgements about offspring and servants. At the same time, Jews were being expelled from dozens of cities in the Empire, often moving to smaller towns and large villages, and in large numbers to central European towns and cities.

CHAPTER 3

Jews: Familiar Strangers

In my heart I told him that my father too
Had such a store of threads and buttons.
In my heart I explained to him about all the dozens of years
And causes and accidents, that I am here now
And my father's store was burned there and he is buried here.

Yehuda Amichai, *Jerusalem 1967* (1967)[1]

TRACES OF JEWS WHERE THERE ARE NONE

I N 1507 THE HUMANIST SCHOLAR ANDREAS MEINHARDI (1470s–1525/6) composed an imaginary dialogue. In it he cast himself as the character Meinhard, who tries to convince a student – Reinhard – to come and study at the new university of Wittenberg. Meinhard extolled the city's fine air, its proximity to the countryside, its learned professors, and the fine doctors who kept its inhabitants healthy. As they walked the streets of Wittenberg, Meinhard pointed out interesting local sites, and when they reached a running stream, his companion asked:

REINHARD What is the name of the quarter through which the Citus rushes?

MEINHARD It is the Jewish Quarter, named from the Jews who once inhabited it.

REINHARD But who have now been expelled?

MEINHARD Completely.[2]

Such a conversation could have taken place around that time in dozens of cities of the Holy Roman Empire, Iberia, England, and France, and in some Italian cities, each with its ghostly remains of Jewish neigh-bourhoods.[3] And Jews were not alone. For the technique of expulsion was frequently used in the fifteenth century as a cure for perceived ills: economic, demographic, and moral.

So far we have witnessed cities creating spaces and procedures for the absorption of newcomers through a variety of processes. We have noted the resulting diversity of city life. Now let us explore the challenges of living as a group marked by difference – Jews. The word *stranger* is awkward here, as these were long-standing inhabitants. Their situation was in some ways like that of Tuscans in Avignon or Venice, Flemings in London, or Danes in Lübeck. Jews too were a deeply embedded urban group, yet one also marked by religious difference.

It is interesting to think of Jews as one among several groups of strangers in any city, rather than as radically different. Jews had inhabited many cities in southern Europe since the Roman era, and by 1000 were also settled in cities further north, usually in communities of some dozens of families. They arrived and stayed under the protection of sovereigns or regional lords, and became locals – in some cases even citizens of sorts – adopting local dialects, habits of comportment and dress, and taste in consumption.

This early settlement of Jews reflected the growth and expansive extension of urban life, and attitudes towards them in later centuries are equally a touchstone of the new urban ethics of exclusion. In large parts of Europe Jews gradually lost the places they had long inhabited in urban neighbourhoods.

LORDS AND JEWS

Old Jewish communities were present in Rome, and in the cities and regions of southern France, Iberia, and Sicily. In these Mediterranean areas, Jews held land, and lived as farmers, artisans, and vine-growers.[4] A new pattern of Jewish settlement developed as Europe's economy grew, and so by the year 1000 Jews had migrated to major cities further north, such as Mainz (by 950), Magdeburg (by 965), Meresburg (by 973), and Worms and Regensburg (by 980). By the time of the 1096 Rhineland 'crusade' massacres, these had become flourishing communities, often under the protection of prince-bishops.[5] The Iberian traveller Benjamin of Tudela (1130–73) described a trip in 1165 from Saragossa through southern France and on to Italy and beyond, recording each city with its Jewish community, many with famous schools supported by prosperous members.[6]

As dynastic kingdoms became more ambitious and capable in their administrations from the later eleventh and twelfth centuries, they developed explicit policies regarding groups of foreigners in royal service. A good example is the settlement of Jews from Normandy in England following the Norman Conquest of 1066 by the duke of Normandy who became King William I. The aim of settlement was to provide the Crown with reliable financial services. Initially, these services included the exchange of coins, which reached England from King William's continental domains, and the minting and reminting of royal coinage; English Jews soon became providers of credit to monasteries and to the Crown, and to landlords and urban dwellers too.[7] Small communities of Jews soon became a feature of all county towns, from Huntingdon to Hereford, where they worked closely with the royal official in charge, the sheriff. Jewish lives were highly regulated by royal statutes, and their business dealings – as serfs/servants of the royal treasury – were scrutinised by royal officials through the Exchequer of the Jews, founded by the 1190s.[8] Throughout the thirteenth century, royal legislation became increasingly intrusive as it restricted business by and with Jews. So they moved to smaller towns, such as Ludlow and Abergavenny, in search of business opportunities.[9]

The ideology of Christian kingship allowed rulers to treat non-Christians as servants of their treasury.[10] A theology much marked by the thought of Augustine of Hippo (354–430) linked Jewish service to the toleration of their presence in Christian polities. Within the concept of Jewish servitude this presence was combined with the Roman legal concept of service to the imperial *fiscus*, its treasury.[11] By the twelfth century, Jewish servitude had become an idea familiar in the Holy Roman Empire, and current in England and Sicily. It was used in the royal statutes, the *fueros*, that ordered urban life in Castile and Aragon, in the vast areas recently conquered by Christian rulers. Such *fueros* contained ample sections on relations between Jews, Muslims, and

Christians.[12] The vastly influential *Fuero de Teruel* issued in 1177 stated 'that the Jews are servants of the Lord King and always count as part of the royal purse'.[13] Throughout Europe, authority over Jews became a touchstone of royal and imperial sovereignty, over and above royal vassals, and ecclesiastical authorities.[14]

The policies towards Jews – and towards other groups marked by moral difference within mainstream clerical culture – were more than just expedient choices: they went to the heart of a conception of royalty, increasingly touched by imperial grandeur and religious ambition. William Chester Jordan has described the reign of Louis IX of France (1226–70) as 'redemptive' governance: prostitutes were offered alternative life chances, moneylenders were corrected, and a public disputation attended by the king's mother was meant to show that the Talmud by which Jews lived was full of error.[15] Kings could make unexpected grand gestures in religion, like that of Louis IX, who converted a few hundred Muslims while on crusade and then arranged for them to settle among the communities of northern France, where they were to live as Christians.[16] In 1284 King Pere II of Aragon arranged for his officials to transport *jenets*, professional soldiers from North Africa, to become a force of distinctive excellence. He paid them for their service, granted them gifts of rich clothing, and protected them, a small number of men within a Christian kingdom.[17] As Hussein Fancy argues, such gestures – hiring Jews or tiring of them, making Muslims a cherished and trusted group of royal fighters – went to the heart of ideas of sovereignty, which rulers sought to realise within the expansive and enabling mood of twelfth- and thirteenth-century Europe. And this affected the lives of Europe's Jews, as it did the experience of living in cities.

While kings and emperors saw authority over Jews as their special privilege, territorial lords within their kingdoms also issued privileges and settled Jews. Territorial lords conducted their own policies. They protected Jews settled in their cities, as did Count Thibaut of Champagne in 1230 in his charter for Troyes, where he reserved the privilege to offer justice in cases involving clerks and knights – men loyal to him – and his Jews (*mes geis*).[18] Within the Holy Roman Empire, similar initiatives flowed from territorial rulers. Duke Frederick II of Austria (1211–46) granted rights in 1244 that regulated the settlement of Jews in his cities.[19]

As servants of rulers at all levels, Jews held positions of trust and offered services that underpinned the vigorous money economy: as minters, traders, and tax-collectors; in 1182 Emperor Frederick I had granted them the privilege to trade in gold, silver, and other metals.[20] When Margaret of Constantinople, countess of Flanders, expected the arrival into her domain of Jews hard-pressed by the policies of Henry III, she wrote to authoritative scholars – among them Thomas Aquinas (d. 1274) – for advice as to whether a Christian ruler might receive them.[21]

The medieval economy was thirsty for credit, but Europeans were taught to feel ambivalent about lending at profit.[22] In reality, every local merchant was a creditor of sorts, embedded in networks of debt. Manufacturers and artisans required regular and plenteous credit, as did cities in support of public works, such as the building of walls, bridges, and city halls. Dynastic rulers and cities alike invited those best suited to offer sophisticated financial services to settle in their parts: King Bela IV of Hungary (1206–70) encouraged the immigration of Christians and Jews from Austria and Bohemia – and this was renewed by his successors.[23]

Dynasts often granted privileges to Jews alongside others, who were similarly seen as useful to the kingdom: Italian bankers or German merchants. Such privileges were embedded in charters granted to cities. In 1291 King Andrew III of Hungary (1265–1301) provided a set of privileges for Pozsony/Pressburg, addressing first the settlement of any newcomer, and then that of Jews:

> And if any person from whatever town wishes to come to settle in the city of Pozsony, the lord of that town or possession will not presume to impede this, but will allow him to hold his goods freely. A just and customary land tax should be paid. Also the Jews settled in that city have the same freedom that citizens do, saving the right of the archbishop of Esztergom and the provost who resides in Pozsony.[24]

In 1358 Emperor Charles IV (1316–78) treated his relations to Jews and 'Cahorsin' – a word often used to describe Lombards – as a regalian right, inherent to his kingship: 'All Cahorsin usurers and Jews are our servants and those of the Imperial treasury.'[25] Such bankers and merchants came from regions with highly monetised economies, and formed

professional networks across Europe and sometimes beyond. Their operations were facilitated by the trust that arose from kinship networks,
enhanced by religious or regional identities, just as they were to be for
the Quaker bankers of the eighteenth century.

At the very same time, intellectuals – often in cities and soon within
universities – developed new genres for discussion of Jews and Judaism.
These were disputations both imagined and real, where the biblical Jew
and the Jew next door merged into a figure that confounded Christians,
and yet always lost in these contests.[26] By the thirteenth century, polemics with Jews were staged by kings who involved leading theologians, as
in Paris in 1240, and in Barcelona in 1263; debates were also imagined
as taking place between merchants, as in the Majorca Disputation of
1286.[27] New anti-Jewish narratives were born out of the rich religious
culture of cities: child murder in twelfth-century Norwich, host desecration in thirteenth-century Paris, and in 1348 the accusations of well-
poisoning in dozens of German cities. These were social dramas that
unfolded only rarely, but when they did, there was violence in city
streets and loss of life. Such violence sometimes spread throughout a
region, as in the Rintfleisch massacres in Franconia of 1298–1300,
prompted and justified by the rumour of host desecration.[28] These
conspiratorial narratives, which cast the Jew as intent on harming
Christians, often in a ritualised manner, were available at times of
trauma, such as during the Black Death, when ravaged populations
turned against Jews in the German and French cities they had inhabited
for so long.[29]

Jewish liturgy had included since late antiquity a prayer for the well-
being of the sovereign, *Tefilah li-Shlom Malchut*. Rabbis explained that it
was necessary to 'pray for the wellbeing of the king, for without the fear
of it, man would swallow up his fellow man'.[30] The prayer acknowledged
the Jews' dependence on rulers – rulers who were often capricious, and
always voracious – for their settlement throughout Europe, for the
opportunities to work and prosper, for relative safety. Like other groups
marked by difference, Jews were always aware of their identity, and were
reminded of it particularly strongly at certain times of the Christian
liturgical year, such as Lent and Easter. Some Jews no doubt felt the
burden of such strangeness to be too heavy, and converted to

Christianity. Following conversion they often moved to a town where they were unknown.[31]

Like other groups with useful skills to offer, Jews sought out opportunities for migration and settlement. The Jews of Rome branched out into the Marche, Tuscany, and Umbria in the thirteenth century, joining forces with other Jews, or other foreign bankers, as we saw them do in Ascoli in 1297.[32] They also responded to political change. Under the heavy taxation, harassment, and pressure to convert experienced in Henry III's England, some Jews moved to that king's lands in Gascony in the 1260s, where such policies did not hold. When the region of Quercy came under the lordship of the king of England in a treaty of 1263, Izaac, a Jew of Bordeaux, approached Pons, lord of the bourg of Gourdon, with a request to settle there. The resulting charter accorded 'customs and rules' (*costumas et etablismens*) to a group of Jews – men and women – for settlement in Gourdon.[33] They were allowed to trade like any other Gourdonnais, both in the town and in the surrounding territory.[34] The Jews were to provide credit, so several clauses dealt with the keeping and sale of pawned objects, listing those items usually prohibited for pawning: chalices, vestments, skins from illegal slaughter, bloodstained clothes, and ploughshares. Finally, if the Jews did not enjoy their experience in Gourdon, Lord Pons promised to have them accompanied safely out of the bourg on their departure.[35]

MIXING IN NEIGHBOURHOODS

One of the principles of Jewish settlement was that Jews should never exercise authority over Christians.[36] This principle was not always respected in practice: Jews employed Christian servants, they held senior positions in royal administrations – in Iberia, in Hungary – and entered into business partnerships. But it did mean that Jews were not welcome within the administrative and judicial – the civic – spheres of urban life. Those who were sufficiently affluent and highly skilled accordingly played a part in urban life, but not as elected officials, with only exceptional cases of service in the militia and membership of city councils.[37] Jurists interpreted the late Roman legislation that barred Jews from office for contemporary use. Bartolus of Sassoferrato (1313–57) discussed whether Jews should receive university degrees. At stake was the issue of *dignitas*: was it fitting for a Jew to be endowed with authority? He resolved that they could hold honours granted by their own communities – as rabbis, judges – but not that of a civic judge or a university professor.[38]

Medieval legislators and chroniclers struggled to find a suitable term to describe the position of Jews in their cities, one of utter embeddedness and yet of not-quite-full enfranchisement. Jews were occasionally described as *concives*, 'fellow citizens', a term also applied to foreign merchants, just short of 'citizens'.[39] Alfred Haverkamp has described the deep integration of Jews within the legal and civic culture of German cities; in some forty German towns, Jews appear to have been such citizens, a category also extended to women, as we shall see in Chapter 4.[40] When cities extended citizenship rights of this kind to Jews, *concivilitas* was a useful term to describe it.[41] There was an attempt to find civic titles to describe the administrative integration of Jews. An official was sometimes appointed a *iudex Iudaeorum*, who helped supervise Jewish financial business.[42] In the Austrian duchy of Styria, he was called *Zechmeister*, a 'guild' master of sorts.[43] Civic language was used creatively to describe the peculiarities of Jewish life in the city.

If Jews were to do business with Christians, they had to be able to secure documents, so some Jews styled their own seals.[44] Rabbinical opinions were divided on whether a Jew ought to take an oath on relics or on a Christian bible. In cities of the Empire, Jews took an oath on the Hebrew bible. The beautifully illustrated *Stadtbuch* of Bavarian Landshut of 1361 included a version of the Jewish oath accompanied by a drawing of a prosperous Jew, 'Feifelein'.[45] But as competition with Christian bankers grew throughout the thirteenth century, this form of assurance became more necessary, and so Jews accepted awkward – and sometimes embarrassing – forms of oath-taking.[46]

However imperfect the civic status of Jews, they were visible and integrated into urban life. Officials and notaries in Italian cities noted the residence status of Jews. Hence Oswaldo Cavallar and Julius Kirshner have concluded that what mattered most for Jews was to be able to 'enlist the statutes as the basis for seeking redress of grievances against fellow citizens, noncitzens, and public officials'.[47]

The labyrinth of urban tenure meant that no neighbourhood in a medieval city was truly homogenous. Daniel Smail has reconstructed an itinerary from the notarial records of Marseilles from 1357: walking through town involved passing from 'the house of Carle de Montoliu near the Jewry, to the house of a Jewish dyer, past the drains of the old Jewish wells, thence to the gate where the Jew, Durant de Bedarides, lives, and finally to the alley that leads to the church of St Martin where – [the very great banker] Bondavin's garden is'.[48]

In Iberian cities patterns of settlement were an even more complex mix, with Christians, Jews, and Muslims side by side. A survey of settlement in the town of Ávila conducted in 1306 is rich in telling details of neighbourhood proximity. In the quarter of S. Tomé, the carpenter Master Lopez lived close to the doctor Master Juan, Abdalla the painter, and Abrahem.[49] On a street in another neighbourhood, the house of a Christian woman, Acenar Ximeno, abutted that of the Jew Yuçaf Davila; indeed, she reported that 'The water drips off the roof of the house of Yuçef Davila, and it should not.'[50] Her husband is named as sharing a courtyard, a *corral*, with the Jew Yaco and the widow of Santius Munoz. Such patterns of neighbourhood led to the intricate forms of violence and litigation that David Nirenberg has studied so well in the cities of the Crown of Aragon.[51]

Rarely was there separation, and usually there was close neighbourhood, combined with a mutual awareness of who was who. Non-Christians lived their difference in proximity to Christians, yet all were aware of the boundaries that governed comportment in the public sphere. Individuals knew what was appropriate – and inappropriate – in gestures or eating habits; they understood what privacy meant in sharing close quarters, where it was easy to cast an intrusive gaze through a window, or to inflict unwelcome sounds on others.[52] Precious objects – heirlooms, jewellery – were left by Christian borrowers to secure loans, and so inhabited Jewish houses.[53] All this blended into a tentative but intimate familiarity. It was an arrangement both fragile and enduring.[54]

Such proximity resulted not only in neighbourliness, but also in the possibilities of transgressive intimacy. A vast literature developed in Iberia, ranging from rabbinic legal opinions to elegant verse in all local vernaculars, reflecting sexual fascination between Jews, Muslims, and Christians.[55] A Christian poet expressed the male gaze and feeling:

> Beautiful, gentle Jewess, when I met you the day before yesterday, I experienced a glory which cannot be described ... My lady, I trust your discretion and hope you will return what you have taken from me ... Not to become a Jew I defy all pains, because I must not convert, but only to serve and praise you.[56]

There was consequently great anxiety about sexual contacts between Christians and Muslim or Jewish partners. Muslim women were particularly vulnerable, since the consequences of a tarnished reputation were probably greater for them.[57] In the more mundane records of local courts, Jewish men appear habitually as the sexual partners of Christian women. Guillelma, a married woman of Manosque, was accused of adultery in 1310; Davidonus was named 'and many other men (*et pluribus hominibus*)'.[58] It is hard to judge the truth in this matter: a woman having sex, or just a woman consorting with Jews for business, but such transgression weighed on the minds of contemporaries.

Jews – and, in Christian Iberia and parts of Sicily, Muslims too – were inhabitants of these working urban communities: it was their only home. They paid dues, attended some civic rituals, settled in streets dedicated to a trade – as all occupational groups did – and occupied homes built of the same fabric and style, and, as everywhere, the rich more sumptuously than the poor. When they chose to commission expensive books or build a synagogue, they turned to local craftsmen, and guided them to use well-established and fashionable patterns of art and architecture; they even wrote poetry in the local metre.[59] They did so despite the fact that around them were texts and performances supported by important institutions (cathedrals and churches) that portrayed them as evil, dangerous, and responsible for the violent historical act that underpinned the Christian story – the Crucifixion.

CHANGING URBAN SENSIBILITIES

The long fourteenth century saw a series of changes that threatened the fragile arrangements in towns and cities. Crises inspired sentiments – and encouraged theories – of blame attached to strangers and other dangerous groups. A sophisticated community like that of Carcassone appealed to the king of France around 1320 with a list of complaints for which it sought redress. In those hard times 'Jewish voracity' plagued the poor. In the next paragraph, the drafters described the libidinal desires of lepers who wished to seize the properties of the healthy and infect them with their own disease, 'with poisons and pestiferous potions and magic'.[60]

In that very year violence was inspired by the marching band of young men known as the Shepherds Crusade, a social movement of discontent that marched through the kingdom of France equally poised against royal castles and rich priests. Its aggression was directed against authority, so Jews, as protected servants of the Crown, were often targeted alongside royal officials. When the 'shepherds' reached Aragon, they gathered around a royal castle and massacred the Jews of the village of Montclus.[61]

The state of public distress and violent outrage was even more pronounced in the course and long aftermath of the Black Death, which affected parts of Europe between 1347 and 1351. In the short term, rulers attempted to retain the status quo, to stabilise prices and wages, which had risen owing to the disruption of agricultural routines and communications. The stark new demographic order threatened the carefully crafted urban hierarchies in the spheres of work, family, and politics. Polities and local governments reacted with contradictory policies and impulses: legislating to fix prices while paying higher wages; controlling access to work in cities while lavishly granting privileges aimed at attracting migrants to urban centres.[62] And within this thicket of policies and initiatives Jews had to make their lives.

In hundreds of settlements across Europe, in cities and small towns, Jewish communities were destroyed, by death or expulsion.[63] The Jews of Tàrrega described the situation to the officials of the Crown of Aragon:

> Incited by a diabolical spirit, with armed hand and deliberate intent, they came maliciously to the *call* of the Jewish community [*aljama*] and with unwarranted recklessness they violently broke down the gates of this *call* with axes and other types of weapons, and they even destroyed the *call* itself, entering it all together and shouting loudly with raised voices, 'Kill the traitors.'[64]

Pope Clement VI (pope 1342–52) tried to maintain the terms by which Jews lived among Christians. In several letters of 1348 he desperately reminded the clergy, those in a position to affect public opinion, that 'Our saviour chose to be born of the Jewish stock when he put on mortal flesh for the salvation of the human race.' In a later bull of that year, he tried common sense, reminding people that 'the same plague, by the hidden judgment of God, has afflicted Jews themselves and many other races who have never lived alongside them'.[65] At the same time urban communities seriously considered the possibility that Jews had caused the mortality. In January 1349, the councillors of Cologne wrote to those of Strasburg to report the widespread claims that the Jews had caused the plague by poisoning sources of water, and to announce their intention to remove the Jews from their city.[66]

Activities that had attracted stranger-communities – commerce and finance – were now denigrated in the public sphere, their practitioners, often Jews and Lombards, humiliated and disbarred. Civic leaders invested great effort not only in making their communities clean – with new-found attention to urban hygiene[67] – but also in purifying them. A radical discourse of difference developed, and it resulted in heightened judgement, distinction, and separation within urban communities.[68] While many groups were affected by this change of mood, one failed the test of purity and probity most spectacularly – and these were Europe's Jews.

Being a Jew did not go unnoticed, even when and where Jews flourished. Marks of Jewishness could be irksome, even when not dangerous. Consider the distinction revealed by a list of property owners in the Hungarian city of Sopron compiled in 1392: among 110 recorded within the town walls, there were 10 Jews who between them owned 11 plots of land. While every Sopron landowner was also eligible to hold a cabbage patch on the outskirts of the city, the Jews alone were not: 'Only the Jews' houses have no cabbage patch.'[69] Through similar distinctions, through their languages and habits, other groups were recognisable as both local and different. The terms of their difference were variously assigned to them and espoused by them. Being different by language or religion was a way of life by choice and by necessity. The terms on which Jews related to the body politic were historically changeable. The later medieval decades were such a period of change.

REFORM AND THE ENHANCEMENT OF STRANGERHOOD

Embedded in the city as merchants, artisans, and specialists in financial services, the Jews of Italian cities were an ever-present source of finance in times of war. The traditional critique of lending at interest could be invoked when a big loan was required. When Perugia was at war with Gubbio in 1351, it exacted a loan from its Jewish bankers, to be repaid without interest – just the 'pure capital'.[70] Later in the century, a distinctive reforming language was developed by intellectuals, who proclaimed a new Christian moral order. Popes had supported the arrangements that tolerated Jews within Christian communities, but they were increasingly obliged to confront the revision of traditional positions on the business practices of Jews and their place in Christian communities. Pope Martin V (pope 1417–31), who was enmeshed in intensive reform activity at the Council of Constance between 1414 and 1418, licensed extravagant preaching itineraries across Europe for such charismatic preachers as Vincent Ferrer (1350–1419) and Bernardino of Siena (1380–1444). Yet in 1418 he also renewed the privileges accorded to the Jews of the Empire, at the request of Sigismund, King of the Germans (1368–1437), and these also protected Christians who rented houses to Jews.[71] In 1419 a new *Sicut Judeis* bull reinforced the need to apply 'distinguishing markings' on Jews, a requirement that had been in place since the early thirteenth century, though little applied in practice.[72] The pressure on Jews, and on those who protected them, was now acute.

Such initiatives, in ecclesiastical legislation and preaching performances, posed challenges to cities and polities forced to re-evaluate their attitudes to strangers, especially to those involved in moneylending, large and small. Rowan Dorin's discussion of the changes in interpretation of the canon *Usurarum voraginem*, promulgated at the Council of Lyons 1274, is highly instructive. This canon had aimed to discourage support for Christian – mostly Italian – moneylenders by excommunicating those who rented houses to them. In the early fifteenth century, this canon was re-interpreted as applying to Jewish moneylenders too, against prevailing custom.[73] Indeed, Lombards and Jews were treated similarly in this age of expulsions.[74]

Other long-standing arrangements were also being radically questioned. In Mainz, where Jews had lived under the protection of bishops since the tenth century, in 1438–44 the Dominican Siffridus Piscator (d. 1473) wrote a tract on the question 'May a bishop tolerate Jews?', a clear challenge to the current archbishop, and to all his predecessors.[75] Piscator's answer was no. Jews were financing the Antichrist with their moneylending; those who rented houses to them should be excommunicated, for Jews were a real danger to their Christian neighbours.[76] Here new ideas of religious reform, carried by a friar of the Observant movement, was inserted into a local dispute between city council and bishop overturning the tradition of allowing Jews to offer loans at interest.

In those parts of Europe where Jews still lived – they had already been expelled from England (1290), France (1306, and again in 1394) and Brabant (1370)[77] – kingdoms and communities had to decide how to treat them in the face of the changing quality of life and tone of public discourse. Central European polities still welcomed refugees from the west.[78] Several northern and central Italian cities in the 1410s and 1420s handed their public spaces over to the charismatic preacher Bernardino of Siena, son of the Sienese Albizzeschi family.[79] Brescia, Verona, and Massa Maritima all legislated under his influence; in Perugia his preaching was enacted as articles of the local law code, as against blasphemy, games of chance, and usury.[80] Public displays of virtue and devotional emotion saw the burning of bangles, earrings, and gaming cubes in a surge of civic devotion associated with the comforting figure of the Virgin Mary.[81] In Modena in 1423, Bernardino's preaching

> lasted for three or four hours, and he had people burn about 116 game boards, a bag of cards, dice, and gambling tools which were also burned in the piazza of Modena on December fifth, because the friar was considered a saint. On the tenth of that month he caused the burning of 2000 pamphlets of every kind, and more than a sack of women's hair and trinkets . . . On the 13th of the month, the said friar Bernardino gave the big Name of Jesus of gold against a blue background in a wooden frame for [pious] use for the Virgin by the Confraternity of the Annunciate.[82]

The expert on Franciscan economic thought, Giacomo Todeschini, has described Bernardino: 'his work and his action ... now assume all the strength of a political and government project oriented toward clearly distinguishing between the Christian economy and the economy of those who were not Christian'.[83]

Deliberation on the common good now emphasised the danger of moral difference, and encouraged uniformity in appearance and comportment within urban communities enlisted into and excited by this purifying vision.

SIENA – A CITY AND ITS JEWS

In Siena a Jewish community of forty families was attested by Benjamin of Tudela in 1165; by 1229 it was considered a *universitas Iudeorum*.[84] Yet an ambivalence governed the city's attitude towards its Jews. Siena's population had fallen from 42,000 c. 1300 to about 14,000 in the later fourteenth century. In May 1384, Siena's General Council determined that since the Jews disparage the faith of Christ and of the most glorious Virgin Mary:

> some wise men, lovers of the faith of Christ and of the honour of the glorious and most blessed Virgin Mary, and of the good present state and honour of the people of the commune of Siena, have provided that no Jew be able to stay or reside in any house or palace which abuts on the Campo of the city of Siena nor in any house or palace which abuts on the road or street which goes from the *punta San Marco* to the *Croce al Travaglio* [the current Via di Città].[85]

In 1425 Siena legislated for the wearing of a Jewish badge, yellow and highly visible:

> Each and every Jew, both men and women, of whatever age they be, those who are, will be, and will come in the future ... A big and ample O of the roundness indicated below, and of crocus-coloured – that is, yellow – cloth.[86]

This 'O' was to be worn on the outer garment. And lest people wear too small an 'O', the notary drew a neat circle to show the appropriate size: 11cm across (see Figure 3.1).[87] It was a particularly humiliating sign,

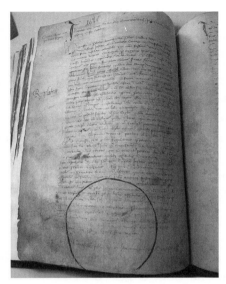

3.1. The Size and Shape of the Jewish Badge, Entry in the Register of the General Council of Siena, 1425, Archivio di Stato di Siena, Consilio generale 123

since only a few years earlier the city's prostitutes were required to wear one like it.

Containment of Jewish life in Siena continued. In 1429 the Jews were allowed to enjoy their festivals, but had to refrain from work on Christian feast days:

> Jews must abstain on Sundays, at Easter, and on the feasts of Our Lady and of all the apostles, from any lending or public business and [must] keep their shops locked without any exception.[88]

The message against Jewish moneylending was visceral, as in this Lent sermon, delivered by Bernardino of Siena in 1430, where he likened the effect of usury to that of an ulcer:

> And if this reduction in wealth for few is dangerous to the state of the city, much greater dangers threaten when they go back to, and unite the wealth and money in, the hands of the Jews. Because then the natural heat of the city, which can be said to be its wealth, does not reach the heart, nor supports it, but by a poisonous flux runs to an ulcer, since all the Jews, and especially moneylenders, are the greatest enemies of Christians.[89]

The Jews were a danger to the body as they were to the body politic, the civic community. Everything about them was dissimulation and a danger to the true spiritual wealth of Christians:

> Spiritual wealth, that is faith and obedience to the ecclesiastical precepts with other spiritual treasures of true Christians, they do not cease to rape, disparage, consume, devour and dissipate with poisoned cajolements, refined friendships, toxic gifts, pretended conversations, deceitful thoughts, and acquired freedoms and favours, dragging with them to hell the unhappy souls of irrational Christians.[90]

PURIFYING CITIES

Many talented preachers had delivered sermons against usury in Europe in earlier centuries, but none possessed such full access to the making of the civic mood as the new type of preacher. Observant branches of the Dominican and Franciscan orders eclipsed their traditional brothers in recruitment and political influence in Italy, Bohemia, and parts of the Empire from the later fourteenth century. Their vision developed into a new business ethic, based on a revolution in the provision of credit through a new type of bank, the *monte di pietà*.[91]

The *monte* was a charitable bank underwritten by the city's rich, and it lent to the poor at low interest. Between the mid fifteenth and into the sixteenth centuries, dozens of such banks were set up across northern and central Italy, inspired by the preaching of both Franciscan and Dominican friars, members of the strict, reformed – Observant – branches of those orders. The responsibility for aiding the poor with subsistence loans now shifted from the Jews to local citizens; it was argued that once this was achieved, the Jews could be expelled.[92] In Urbino, an interesting political alliance led to the creation of the local *monte*. Duke Federico da Montefeltro signed the foundation order in 1468 for the *monte di pietà*, and the local elite gathered in its confraternity of Corpus Domini was to underwrite it, inspired by the preaching of Franciscan friar Domenico da Leonessa (d. 1497). The confraternity commissioned the Flemish painter Justus van Ghent to paint an altarpiece of impeccable orthodoxy, *The Institution of the Eucharist*, for its chapel. This work was accompanied by a *predella* – a lower panel – whose subject was the host-desecration accusation against a Jew of Paris in 1290, as the tale was retold by the Florentine historian Giovanni Villani.[93]

The discourse on credit now inspired fear of contagion and disease, as the words and gestures of talented preachers took hold in Italian cities and, beyond, in imperial cities too.[94] The generation of friars that followed Bernardino, like Antonino of Florence (1389–1459), Bernardino da Feltre (1439–94), and Giovanni da Capistrano (1386–1456),[95] extended the areas of life into which their reform reached. They criticised women for their sartorial habits, bourgeois families for their preparation of trousseaus and marriage festivities, and, crucially, the prevailing ethics of business.[96] Capistrano was licensed to preach throughout the Holy Roman Empire, and against all evils: Jews, heretics, and Hussites; he also hoped to inspire enthusiasm for a crusade against the Turks. In dozens of cities, such preaching emboldened some urban factions to seek out accusations against their Jews, and thus to force emperors and urban councils to acquiesce with the expulsion of their Jews. The discourse of the virtuous city caused the reversal of imperial policies that were centuries old. Such combinations of state action inspired by powerful ecclesiastical or religious actors touched not only Jews, but also other groups – beggars, prostitutes, gypsies.[97]

During the same decades in Iberia, dynastic strife, discontent with royal officials, and a sharpening of attitudes towards Jews were all mobilised by the public discourse delivered by preachers. Disorder worried local authorities, and they tried to contain it with local ordinances. Councillors of the city of Tortosa in 1369 decreed that

> no person of whatever status or condition should throw stones by hand or with a sling ... nor in any other manner nor throw stones at the said Jews nor at the Jewry of the said city nor at its walls ... nor enter that Jewry to do ill.[98]

In dozens of cities in the kingdoms of Castile and Aragon, Jewish communities were all but destroyed in 1391, and the number of 100,000 conversions is probably not exaggerated.[99] Violence began in Seville just before Holy Week (15 March 1391), and by all accounts with an attack on the city's Jews inspired by the local archdeacon and preacher, Ferrant

Martínez.[100] A new ethnic order was born, with thousands of 'new' Christians. Muslims were affected too, as in that very year a royal edict in Catalonia required that Muslims be marked by their clothing.[101]

Iberian cities that had long contained diversity were now confused spaces of mixture and suspicion. Cautious arrangements crafted in earlier decades underwent new civic scrutiny and were found wanting: Remie Constable has analysed the use of urban baths in Iberian cities shared in the fourteenth century by Jews, Muslims, and Christians, according to a rota that separated bathers by sex and religion.[102] Following the mass violence of 1391, such long-standing social practices were no longer sustainable. Bathing became a suspect sign of residual Jewishness, and, for bath-keepers and women, a dangerous zone of lascivious activity. The year 1391 set the tone for the next century, one of suspicion that in every Christian lurked a dangerous stranger, a *converso*. This social ill, played out in cities supervised by ambitious and active monarchs, saw the gradual reversal of policies and the reallocation of space. Cities no longer lived by the *fueros* that had managed diversity; the inquisition began its operations in them in 1478.

Bohemia experienced its own crises, with civil war over religious and ethnic identities fought across its countryside, and, pointedly, sieges of its cities throughout the fifteenth century. The threat of a regional 'heresy' in the form of Hussitism – Christianity as inspired by the Czech theologian and religious leader Jan Hus (1369–1415) – prompted Catholic cities to welcome charismatic preachers in defence of orthodoxy. Czech-speaking citizens who identified with the Hussite cause were imprisoned and executed in Olomouc, Moravia's leading city, in the 1440s. The agitation also affected other tolerated groups, such as the city's well-established Jewish community.[103] The 1450s saw the preaching tours of the Empire of Giovanni da Capistrano, with his message of renewal through purification and reform, and the urban population responded with accusations against Jews. These led to show trials and expulsions: from Wroclaw in 1453; and from Brno, Olomouc, and Znojmo in 1454. This was a world that John Van Engen has recently described as being 'astir' for the variety of religious positions, and for the strong feelings and actions – often violent – that they inspired in fifteenth-century people in their cities.[104]

CITIES OF EXCLUSION

We have observed the growth of mechanisms and motivations for urban exclusion and expulsion. The creation of the Ghetto in Venice in 1516 was an alternative to expulsion, and it was preceded by attempts to resettle Jews, as we saw happen in Siena decades earlier.[105] Such separation occurred in other cities that aimed to maintain their Jews while adhering to attitudes so often promoted in preaching and accepted by urban elites.

Religious difference was a barrier to full integration into the civic life of European cities. But there were lives to be lived in that difference, and this was true of other types of stranger too: Flemings in London, or Swedes in Lübeck.[106] Living in difference involved choices – it was not merely a condition delivered by the authorities. It allowed people to migrate, prosper, and enjoy positions of privilege based on professional expertise and labour while also retaining contacts with other places and traditions held dear. Some habits and practices – accents, hair-styles, bodily routines – long endured. Jews occasionally lived with added markings, more or less shaming, like the requirement to take the humili-ating Jewish Oath, or, for Tuscan Jewish women, to wear gaudy ear-rings.[107] This was life with diversity, which was also life with vulnerability.

Vulnerability was inherent in the lives of strangers who inhabited occupational niches – bankers, merchants, doctors – and who main-tained their own communities of identity, influence, and mutual sup-port. The visibility of such strangers put them at risk at times of political strife and intense economic competition; this was the case with French people and institutions in England throughout the fourteenth and fif-teenth centuries. Townspeople could be animated to move against their neighbours, unless the countervailing power of the law was reliably applied. And thus even long-standing communities of Albanians were expelled from the towns of the Marche in the 1430s and 1440s, as were those deemed to be 'Slavs' in the decades of the 1450s–70s.[108]

The urban sense of purpose in the period of growth had enabled a certain latitude in the incorporation of strangers from nearby, as well as those strangers whom moralists disdained but civic leaders considered valuable, like Jews or Lombards. Yet a shift occurred in these attitudes

3.2. The Ideal City, Urbino, Fra Carnevale, 1445–84?, *La città ideale*, c. 1480–4, Walters Art Museum, Baltimore

once the sense of opportunity was diminished and that of anxiety enhanced. Identities in the city became even more competitive. Some authoritative voices – particularly of the activist preaching reformers – were now allowed to encourage radical thinking about the possibility of exclusion, of the making of pure, cleansed, and safe – new – societies.

In many parts, a vision of pure Christianity triumphed, and it coincided with fantasies about the ideal city: symmetrical, and free of messy humanity (see Figure 3.2).[109]

Yet once the stranger was not safe, no one else was either.

CHAPTER 4

Women: Sometimes Strangers in Their Cities

Because, I, a mestiza,
Continually walk out of one culture
And into another,
Because I am in all cultures at the same time.
Gloria Anzaldúa, *Borderlands* (1987)[1]

THERE, AND NOT THERE

CITIES DEVISED WAYS OF DEALING WITH NEWCOMERS, WELCOMING SOME AND rejecting others, and these attitudes changed over time. Some newcomers arrived from villages or towns close to the city; others from further afield – invited migrants, traded slaves – were less familiar and remained different, in language, appearance, and religion. Yet even among native citizens there were degrees of empowerment: it was not uncommon for a citizen born elsewhere to be barred from the highest civic offices, just as people without property were, and Jews, and women. Women and those men barred from full civic life thus shared some aspects of experience. Their labour was essential to collective thriving, but they were also seen as possessing qualities that justified their exclusion from full participation in urban life and its benefits.

The exclusion of women was underpinned by science, law, and religion, supported by custom, and naturalised in the public sphere through rituals and representations.[2] It was possible for preachers and judges, and even minor officials, to argue that women were deficient in reason, and that because of this weakness they were easily corrupted. Women's bodies were also troubling, even dangerous.

Historians have learned over recent decades to understand that sexual difference is a necessary category of historical analysis.[3] For the ideas and practices attached to sexual difference – what we call gender – were central to the making of social, moral, political, and aesthetic distinctions. In the society we are studying, women with public authority were few and much noticed, sometimes as subjects of scandal. Yet women had authority within households and in the workshops they often managed jointly; in some regions they could gain the freedom of a city and give testimony in court, and there deliberate over issues that affected their lives, such as dowries and probate.[4] But their access to the full array of cultural and social activities generated by cities was limited, and in that sense they were like a stranger or a settled resident in the city, with civic prospects less ample than those available to full citizens. It is useful to think of women in their towns and cities as being a bit like a Fleming in London, or a Tuscan in Venice, or even a Muslim or Jew in Toledo. This chapter, therefore, is not so much a history of women, but rather an exploration of what we find when we think of them as strangers.

Women's lives varied across Europe, yet the underlying logic of gender was so strong that it needed no formal elaboration in urban statutes. Everyone knew what the gendered order meant. In her exploration in *The Book of the City of Women*, written c. 1405, the poet Christine de Pizan has the figure of the Author fall asleep in her study, only to imagine, with the help of the Ladies Reason, Rectitude, and Justice, what an ideal city would be like. The Author turns to Lady Reason:

> Most honourable and worthy lady ... I'd like you to explain to me why women are allowed neither to present a case at a trial, nor bear witness, nor pass sentence.[5]

Here is a question that may have occasionally been raised outside the realms of poetry and rhetoric.

Religious texts recognised women as maiden, wife, or widow (*virgo*, *uxor*, or *vidua*) in sermons and guidance literature that addressed each of these types. Yet women's positions were more diverse than these categories suggest. Many women lived as concubines, live-in partners of members of the clergy, who were expected to live a celibate life. These could be long-standing relationships, but their lack of full legal authority made the female partners vulnerable.[6] Many women lived neither as wives nor as widows, but as single women, often in households headed by women.[7] Single rural women entered service in cities, and some returned to their original communities after a period of work. In parts of England and the Low Countries, they also moved from villages to larger villages that were hubs of the textile industry. The later fourteenth century was probably the most advantageous period for such workers, with high wages and much demand for women's labour in manufacture and domestic service.[8] So *Le Menagier de Paris*, a guidebook from 1392 for a young Parisian housewife, recommended that she pay particular attention in hiring:

> And know that usually such women from foreign parts are guilty of some vice in their country, and that is the cause that forced them to serve away from their place.[9]

Sources that permit an assessment of household size and shape are scarce before the fourteenth century. But once we possess sufficient data, these show households all over Europe in which working women lived together, from York, to Douai, to Florence. We can occasionally glimpse the strong relationships that developed between women living together. Two women of Douai described their lives in a joint will: 'Know all those who are and will be that Jake de France and Liegars de Ghesnaing as companions make their will together.' They left each other those goods accumulated during their relationship.[10]

There developed a difference in the ratio of men to women in urban settings: in northern Europe, women were usually more numerous, some 100 women to 90–5 men.[11] South of the Alps, it was largely the opposite: 110 men to 100 women, where women married at a younger age, and where slavery contributed in many cities – Genoa, Venice, Dubrovnik/ Ragusa, Barcelona – a significant portion of household labour.[12] Seasonal migration affected the sex-ratio for periods at a time, and regimes of agriculture and husbandry did too. In areas of transhumance – the seasonal movement of animals from lowland to highland pastures – men were on the road for months at a time droving their animals, as in parts of Castile in the thirteenth century;[13] or in the Alpine regions, where men from valley communities spent spring to summer with their flocks and herds.[14]

4.1. Simone Martini, Altarpiece of Sant'Agostino Novella, 1324, Pinacoteca Nazionale, Siena

Cities were full of working women, yet when contemporaries imagined these spaces, they conjured a different picture altogether. Ambrogio Lorenzetti's 1337/8 wall-painting of the well-governed city of Siena, which we have already encountered, has women enjoying the good life, dancing in a ring in the public square, or riding out of town for pleasure.[15] They are at peace, and and cannot be seen publicly exerting themselves. Just a decade earlier, in 1324, the great Sienese artist Simone Martini (1284–1344) had depicted women in his altarpiece in honour of the local saint, Sant'Agostino Novello (1240–1309). Martini painted four miracles attributed to Agostino, three of which took place within domestic spaces, and one on a rocky country road (see Figure 4.1).

Agostino's virtue was applied to the protection of children above all. The top-left scene has him swooping down to stop a dog from tearing a child apart;[16] at the bottom left, he arrives just in time to cradle a child and stop his fall from a balcony; at the bottom right, Agostino arrives again – superhero-like – to save a boy who had fallen out of a hammock onto a balcony. In both the bottom left and the bottom right, mother and tender child occupy part of the domestic sphere. At the bottom right, mother ventures out in pious mode, dressed decorously, carrying her child as a votive offering to the church of Sant'Agostino.

Women at dance, women at home with their children, women indoors: this is how male experts in representation chose to depict their cities to themselves.[17]

WOMEN'S WORK IN URBAN SPACES

European cities lived with the difference that was women in their streets, in public, with all the challenges that the presence of women created. As they did in other domains, law-makers anticipated, legislated, and hoped to contain the risks they considered women could pose to individual citizens, and to the city's reputation, its *fama*.[18] For this reason they legislated to control women's property, dress, and conduct. A woman's dowry – which followed her from her natal home and returned to her after her husband's death – was an important civic resource, an element of local wealth. The statutes of Siena of 1309 obliged heirs to and holders of a dead man's estate to satisfy a widow's claim of her dowry within two months of her plea.[19]

Many of those who worked and traded in the city, and who owned property and the means to produce and exchange, were organised by crafts in workshops based in households. A glance at one city's craft composition is instructive: in 1301, Edward I issued ordinances for the city of York, his capital during the Scottish Wars, providing regulations craft by craft. The city had thirty-five bakers, twenty-six taverners, thirty-five cooks, forty-nine butchers, fifty fishmongers, seventy brewers, thirty-seven poulterers, nine fish retailers, and forty-five hostellers.[20] These craft groups were led by men, but in them women – wives, daughters, and hired labourers – worked and bore responsibilities. In workshop-households women also brewed and sold ale.[21] In each craft household there were servants and apprentices to be trained and nurtured by women.

This order of family and work based on the household was affected by the very principle that enabled commerce, that is, the movement of people. Merchants were frequently away on business, often for long periods, and this reality of urban life was exploited to the full by such urban writers as Boccaccio and Chaucer. They imagined the human possibilities, of cuckolded husbands above all. Anticipating the dramas that such mobility enabled, several towns legislated on bigamy, as did Verona in 1327:

> We decree that if someone who has a wife, and she is alive, contracts marriage with another woman, he will be punished by a fine of 100 pounds ... And this same applies to women doing so.[22]

Wives in merchant and artisan households were well-versed in business affairs, often highly literate, and able to handle numbers and accounts. Among the thousands of letters surviving from the correspondence of the Datini Company, which was based in the Tuscan city of Prato, some hundreds of letters were exchanged between Francesco and Margherita Datini, who were married in Avignon in 1376, when he was 41 and she 20. A fortnight's absence produced eleven letters; in that of 26 August 1389, they discussed health, travel plans, the quality of their wine, and plans for future purchases.[23] Their writing style is plain, as was common for merchants' letters; they begin and end with conventional dating and salutation phrases, which Margherita commanded as well as Francesco.[24] Further down the social scale, but well endowed and highly active, was Laureta Bonafazzy of Marseilles, the widow of Peyret, whom we know, thanks to her accounts of 1403–4 (studied by Daniel Smail). Laureta habitually used two systems of account and worked with different currencies in paying wages; she managed a large household of men and women, free people and slaves, through the unceasing seasonal array of work and reward.[25] Women in commercial households were as central to economic and emotional well-being as were the wives of artisans to the flourishing of the workshop.

Given the centrality of households to production, training, and retail, arrangements had to be made for periods when the male head of household was absent, and for his death. In English, Flemish, and some German towns a widow could trade as *femme sole*, *Kauffrau*, or *coopwijf*, as an independent legal entity. In these cities we witness the widespread entry of women into a certain type of citizenship.[26] Both married women and widows could aspire to this status, although they paid an entry fee higher than that paid by men.[27] In Bruges, between 1331 and 1460 women were 10 per cent of new citizens, and 10 per cent in Leiden between 1400 and 1532. And when a new citizen was not a local woman, even if she was married she had to prove her own worthiness.[28] [29] Having a legal persona and civic status meant that a single woman could be taken to court for debt; from the early fourteenth century, so could some married women. In 1388 Mabina Taverner was received as a *comburgensis* of Kilkenny, and thus gained the freedom to buy and sell freely, for the payment of 40d, as long as she lived in the city's suburb of Irestoun. If she wanted to move into the centre of Kilkenny, she would have to pay the city an additional 6s 9d for the privilege.[30] Women were also deemed to belong to their home cities even if marriage had led them to settle elsewhere.[31]

Even where this category of female-citizenship did not exist in law, craftsmen realised that the most effective way of ensuring continuity in production was to allow widows to run the workshop until a male heir might replace her.[32] And so, in Italian cities, where women did not enter citizenship, other concessions for securing their labour and status developed. The shoemakers (*bottai*) of Venice added in 1338 to their statutes of 1271 a provision for the occasion of a craftsman's death:

> Item, if any master of this craft dies and leaves a son of less than 17 years, if the wife wishes to hold the craft for the son, she will act as master, in the position to work and instruct the youths in the craft until one of them is seventeen and knows the craft to work as a master.[33]

In fifteenth-century Buda, the craft was obliged to allow the widow to maintain the butcher's shop, and to appoint a man to do the work on her behalf.[34] Crafts extended some of their social benefits to women, too. The Venetian crockery-making smiths provided in their statutes of 1301 for wives to be buried just like other members of the craft, with the craft's cross and banner.[35]

With the growing demand for labour so evident from the second half of the fourteenth century, we notice greater latitude in the inclusion of women.[36] The Venetian *bottai* allowed women to enter the guild, with one of the journeymen assigned as supervisor.[37] In late fourteenth-century Chester, John the Armourer, an immigrant from the Isle of Man, had become a successful merchant and a member of the confraternity of St Anne. So robust was his professional situation that after his death his widow – designated 'Lady' (*Domina*) – continued to run his business and to enjoy membership of the craft.[38] Guild regulations codified in Vienna in 1430 similarly allowed widows to continue the workshop's activities.[39]

Women worked as servants and as labourers in workshops, and in all stages of the preparation of textiles. In England this is visible in the poll tax returns, where, for example, in Salisbury in 1379, fifty-five women with textile-related names made their own contribution.[40] In Exeter, women were particularly numerous as contracted workers in the workshops of weavers and tailors. It is likely that after the Black Death female apprentices became a more common – if not always an official – category: in 1380/1 William Wymark referred to his employee Joan Blakhay as 'servant and apprentice'.[41] Similarly, when demand for working hands was high, transgressive behaviour was ignored in a useful worker. In 1450, the dean of the spicers' craft in Ghent allowed Beatrice, daughter of the spicer Pieter de Wilde, access to the craft, despite her reputation as having lived with co-worker Christoph van der Hove outside marriage. She in turn agreed to marry Christoph and hire him as a *compagnon* – a labourer in her shop.[42]

Women with distinctive skills in the production of luxury goods of high cost and profit were rewarded with some freedoms that other working women did not enjoy. The survey of the occupations of Paris made for King Louis IX in 1286 by the official in charge of the capital, his *prévôt* Étienne Boileau, shows just how crafts organised women's work. At least nine crafts employed a majority of women, that is, in the crafts of handling silk for the making of exquisite objects. But they were represented by men, even when women held positions of training and supervision.[43]

In another centre of luxury manufacture, Venice, a distinctive category emerged for women in the later fourteenth century: that of public merchant (*mercantessa pubblica*). These were widows registered with the *Arte d'oro battiloro* to work in the lucrative craft of making and working with silver thread, for which Venice was famous. An interesting case of 1395, studied by Paula Clarke, introduces us to the widow Lucia 'ab auro', who both sold gold leaf and made gold thread.[44] She was supplied by a gold beater, Alberto di Francesco, who extended her credit so long as she worked solely with him. Lucia used a female slave, Benevenuta, who stayed on with her even after being freed and ultimately became a partner in the business. Lucia's widowed daughter, Franceschina, continued the business after her mother's death and sold finished head-jewellery to a mercer's wife for retail.

Some well-situated married women also developed their own status of *mercantessa*, such as the Venetian Pasqua Zantani, active in the 1360s, who traded silk with her husband and brother but ran her own silver-thread business. She supervised the men who beat the leaf, hired immigrant women workers, and did business with foreign merchants. Here were networks of working women, underpinned by kinship: Pasqua hired her nieces and nephews, whose marriages she arranged in due course.[45]

Alongside women made rich and influential in guild-related households, there were many more women involved in service, or in the smallest-scale retail.[46] In his poem *Le Dit des rues de Paris* of c. 1280–1300, the poet Guillot described the streetscape of the capital when it was some 200,000-strong. He regularly came across women selling in the streets:

> On King of Sicily street
> I entered, and soon saw Sedile:
> On Renaut-le-Fevre street
> Just where they sell peas and beans.[47]

In much smaller, early fourteenth-century Welsh Ruthin, the borough court recorded fifty-six women with their occupations; thirty-three of fifty-six were described as forestallers – vendors believed to be selling without a licence.[48]

While women of all status in Ruthin sold without licence, those of low status were the repeat offenders, perhaps because they had fewer options to make a living. Such women walked the streets and sold outside the market.[49] In Ghent in 1402 the dean of the fruit-sellers' guild stopped a woman who worked for a guild member from going to market, although she was allowed to help carry his produce to it. She was living with him, so sexual dishonour combined with her marginal status as a petty saleswoman.[50] Access to the market was highly contentious between different types of trader and created occasions for bitterness and strife. The ecclesiastical court of Canterbury dealt in 1423 with a case of defamation in which Elena Somerset was summoned to answer for accusing Agnes, wife of Michael Norton of Oxford, of approaching the wheat market with other legitimate traders while pretending to have the right to trade, against the law.[51]

Women worked in city streets, yet their voices unsettled the makers of urban statutes. Women were best not seen or heard in public, according to urban legislators, who even turned their attention to the participation of women in the age-old rituals of death. The early thirteenth-century statutes of Mantua decreed that 'no woman can or should follow the body of the dead person outside the house or attend the burial in any manner or by any device', although they did allow women to weep in the house of the dead.[52] The San Gimignano statutes of 1255 prohibited the entry or exit of women from the Porta San Giovanni, the southern gate to the city, 'when the dead is being carried to the church or to the grave to be buried'. Nor were they to raise the sound of mourning until the moment of entry into the church for burial.[53]

Women's work was central to any town's well-being, but the shame that women could bring to individuals and communities was also great. So urban statutes decreed penalties – and in some regions rituals – that punished and shamed those who transgressed the marital moral code. Most infamous is the *corada*, a race through the city streets by partners in adultery, as provided for in the statutes of many towns of the Midi, and so colourfully depicted in the illustrations to the statutes of Toulouse and Agen; this was followed by banishment or mutilation.[54] Disfigurement was a life-long reminder of past transgressions and could be incurred for relatively minor crimes. In the town of Gourdon in the Quercy, in 1324, a woman lost her ear – 'perya laurelha' – for the theft of a chicken.[55]

WOMEN AND URBAN COURTS

Access to courts was also a mark of difference. Some groups maintained their own courts, as did the clergy, as well as Jews and Muslims on family and religious matters. Men and women had varying degrees of access to courts. Since women did so much work, cared for young and old, supervised and trained rising craftsmen, and were entitled to a share of inheritance in the form of their dowry, there were occasions – many occasions – when they needed legal redress. In the cities of southern France, women took oaths and delivered testimony. Daniel Smail has found that in Marseilles some 24 per cent of land transactions involved women.[56] Since 'there were no impediments whatsoever, either legal or customary, on the testimony of women', they made up 21 per cent of witnesses in cases between 1323 and 1416.[57] In Welsh Ruthin, married and unmarried women rarely used men to bring pleas to the borough court and frequently appeared as litigants, although they only infrequently brought suits for violent crimes.[58] In England, the patterns by which Jewish women were involved in litigation mirrored those of Christian women: they were a minority of litigants, and were usually involved as wives or widows.[59] In ecclesiastical courts, women participated as effective witnesses and plaintiffs, with a distinctive style of narrating testimony and anchoring memory.[60]

The participation of women as plaintiffs or witnesses diverged vastly across Europe. In Sassari, the statutes of 1316 made it clear that two women witnesses should count as one man.[61] Some communities considered courts to be unsuitable spaces for women. The statutes of c. 1403 for the city of Buda made the provision that 'If she is a married woman of good standing, she should swear in her own house'; but if she was a *fragnerin* – a small trader, a pedlar – then she should appear in the town hall.[62] Similarly, the 1439 statutes of Montebuono established that if a woman's testimony was necessary in a legal case, the vicar or notary should examine her outside the commune's palace, or city hall (*extra palatium communis*); wherever that may be, she should be accompanied by a man.[63]

Involvement in trade meant working with credit, and many women did just that, wives working alongside their husbands and widows continuing an established business. When, in Bergamo in 1338, Flora, the widow of an immigrant to the city, prepared to make her will, she made provision for her relatives, but she also left for the poor of her neighbourhood flour, vegetables, and chickpeas – not hard, she specified, but nicely prepared in olive oil. All this was done in restitution for her work as a lender of money at interest, to ease her conscience and make amends.[64] Most women probably did business in what William Chester Jordan has called the 'domestic' part of the loan market. As we have seen, Sharon Farmer has suggested that female silk-workers of Paris may have preferred to borrow from Jewish lenders, men and women settled as families, rather than from the Lombards, who lived as expatriates, often in male households.[65] Hannah Meyer's research on England shows that women lenders were numerous and provided loans as large as men did, and as individuals as well as alongside their husbands.[66]

Women also appeared in courts as expert witnesses. Sexual health was so closely associated with childbirth that midwives were often called to give testimony in ecclesiastical courts regarding the dissolution of uncon-summated marriages.[67] In cases where proof of majority was required, the evidence of the wet-nurse who had nourished the applicant was useful. And so the archives of Valencia, for example, offer cases aplenty of wet-nurses – usually the wives of artisans – providing details of the circumstances that had led to their employment, and to the development of a strong relationship between carer and nursling.[68] Midwives were considered reliable witnesses to birth in other contexts too. When in 1358 the Trevisan Giacomo Roncinelli, resident in Venice, decided to register his son's birth and thus secure the boy's citizenship, he sent the midwife Maddalena, another Trevisan immigrant, to summon the notary.[69] Women assisted at the most momentous events of the life-cycle.

WOMEN'S RELIGIOUS PLACES

Women knew their urban environment well, and some used it creatively to push against prevailing expectations. Those who were eager to experi-ence an enhanced religious life in their hometowns influenced the urban religious landscape. While the first millennium of Christian life saw the search for religious perfection above all in rural and solitary settings, away from city life and its temptations, the period of urban growth also saw religious change. New religious orders engaged with cities, and with the sins these generated.[70] This prompted the develop-ment of a style of preaching suited to merchants and bankers, and to more literate laypeople, and the creation of an imaginary to fit the bustle, competition, and volatility of urban life.[71] In the early thirteenth century, Francis of Assisi (1181/2–1226) exemplified this perfectly in his rejection of the career set out for him by his family: study of law, mercantile practice, marriage, and civic life.[72] While the friars attracted interested women, they refused to accept them into their orders as equals, offering what seemed in cities like highly conservative institutions, Franciscan or Dominican convents. This was the fate of Clare of Assisi (1194–1253), a high-born woman who had to accept she could not follow Francis. She lived as head of the community in San Damiano in Assisi: in the city, but enclosed behind convent walls. Ultimately, the Franciscans developed a compromise, a form of enhanced religious living in cities – the Third Order – open to lay men and women, but associated with women above all.[73]

Women carved out a city space in search of goals in religion, rejecting the married life planned for them. Inspired by Franciscans, Angela da Foligno (1248–1309) turned her bedroom into a 'cell' and travelled the roads between Umbrian cities as a pilgrim.[74] Most spectacular was Siena's Caterina Benincasa (1347–80) – the future St Catherine of Siena – a dyer's daughter who rose to European fame for her visions and suggestions for ending the schism in the church.[75]

In northern European cities, in Flanders and Brabant above all, women who came to be known as beguines – *begijnen* – seized more control of the shape of religious innovation. As Walter Simons has shown so well, in large centres – Bruges, Louvain, Ghent – and many smaller centres too, groups of women, unmarried as well as widowed, lived together supported by their labour and donations from admirers. When size allowed, they crafted parish-like enclaves in the city, safe and self-sufficient.[76] Women understood well the rules of urban living, and carefully shaped religious lives so as to threaten the gendered order very little: they did not preach, they did works of charity, and they worked above all in textiles, from combing to cutting, and in tailoring too.[77] Women in dozens of beguine communities managed their own affairs, thanks to their command of writing and management skills. In some of the larger houses, they copied and illuminated books, and in some cases – such as St Elisabeth of Ghent – they even trained orphan girls in the craft.[78] Such women were so embedded in local life that when Pope Clement V attempted to disband them in a decree of 1311, local bishops, as well as the count of Flanders, resisted the decree and offered support to these inoffensive beacons of virtuous feminine urban living.[79]

WOMEN ABOUT THE CITY

City spaces were highly coded and characterised not by utter separation between groups, but by what we might call zoning. All cities, and especially those with many visitors and newcomers, were full of signs and markings, with church towers, and shop- and house-signs.[80] Townfolk usually lived among people similar to them by occupation, status in canon law, ethnic origin, and religion. Yet they were never too far from those who were different.

Just how protected elite women, the wives of citizens or of privileged foreigners, were is made clear in the *Mesnagier de Paris*, with its instructions for a young wife. It teaches her not only how to cook for an assortment of possible occasions and for people of widely differing ranks, but also how to behave prudently in the city. The young woman would have to go out into the world, to attend mass and to supervise the purchase of food, and she did so being modestly dressed and accompanied by a maid.[81] Indeed, communal statutes protected such privileged women by assigning higher fines to those who violated them. The statutes of Auragne in southwest France of 1255 laid down a fine of 30s toulousain for 'knowing a woman carnally' against her will; but if she was 'noble, of good extraction, and of good conduct', the fine would be determined by the court.[82] Women were set apart, some for respect, others for disdain. One can imagine such a married woman exiting her home in the company of a servant and receiving the polite greeting of that flâneur, Guillot, author of *Le Dit des rues de Paris*:

> I spy a woman in a doorway
> who carries herself very nobly;
> I greet her simply,
> and she me, by St. Louis!![83]

There was an urban visual language – a semiotic system – which informed and guided every inhabitant.

While the church had a long history of regulating clerical garb, and with particular intensity in periods of reform, regulation of laypeople's dress came only later into urban statutes. By the late thirteenth century, sumptuary legislation became apparent in southern French and in Italian towns, restricting in particular the use of silks and furs in various combinations. In Montpellier in 1273, wearing silk was limited to women's inner garments:

> Item, we declare that no woman may wear silk garments; women may wear *cendal* [silk cloth] as a lining of their garments, but not on the exterior.[84]

What began as control of waste and display developed into a system of hierarchical distinction, with particular fabrics, lengths, and decorations assigned by status and gender to clerical and lay persons. By the fifteenth century, Jewish women in many Italian cities had to wear the conspicuous earrings that respectable Christian women did not, as a sign of their concupiscence.[85]

However well-marked and covered women were, they were never quite safe. Unwanted attention from strangers was a frequent experience that emerges vividly from the legal records. Those of the small town of Gourdon in the Quercy show that women were occasionally presented to court for theft, but only rarely for graver crimes. The offences usually took place in the course of an interaction between neighbours. Women suffered the type of harassment that so often casts the victim as the perpetrator. So in 1320, Bona, a Jewish woman, was tried for throwing a stone at Peyre de Farganel, the son of a citizen. She answered for herself effectively in court that Peyre had first thrown stones at her, repeatedly, and she was supported in this by three female witnesses, Christian women. First, Peyrona reported that she had seen Peyre:

> He threw a stone at the said Jewess once, and it did not hurt her. Then he did so again with a stone, and hit her leg, and when he hit her, the said Jewess took a stone and threw it at the said Peyre.

The witness Galharda added that a great deal of chatter accompanied the exchange: 'apres gran re de paraulas'.[86] Alas, we do not know the outcome of the trial.

Living in a neighbourhood offered support and safety, but also pitted neighbours against each other, with angry words and covetous glances at the possessions of those living next door. The 1316 statutes of Sassari in Sardinia expected violence to erupt not only between men and women, but also with women on the offensive, as in the clause 'Of women who beat men' ('De mulieribus percussientibus homines'), a grave breach of ordered authority, with differing fines depending on whether the victim was a free man or a slave.[87] The statute included a clause about violence between women that left a scar:

> If any woman will hit another woman with a metal bar, a stone or a stick, or
> any other thing, and draw blood, if the strike was on the face, so that a
> mark remained, she will be judged by the podestà.

There was a sliding scale of substantial fines, for free women and unfree, and for facial or other injuries.[88] A case from 1388 in Dijon notes the marking caused by Péronete, wife of Jacquot le Pitoul, who threw a handful of hot lime on the face of the wife of Suleiman the Jew, leaving her marked with blisters.[89] Violence between women – like that between men – was sometimes inspired by drinking and often took place in drinking places, as the many instances of violence between Flemish women in the taverns of eastern England attest.[90]

Neighbours might offer each other helpful testimony in court, but they might also exchange angry words. Around 1315 in Gourdon, Stephanus complained of the theft of an axe, a pan, a chest, some cloth, and a tripod. When asked whether he knew who did it – 'quis hoc fecerat' – he said he believed that Guglielma Nadala had done it, a woman who often fetched water for him and tended to his house. When summoned, Guglielma said he had allowed her to take the items, and that she had pawned them to a Jew of the town for 5 *solidos* of Cahors.[91] Women accused each other of small thefts, like that of some flour, which the wife of Helias Boichel was suspected of taking. In her defence, she claimed that she had run into the house, since she 'heard the child of the said R crying, and [so] she entered into the house of the said R'.[92] The poor especially lived in close proximity, which meant mutual help was close by – but so were opportunities for tension, frustration, and enmity.[93]

WOMEN AT RISK

Away from their neighbourhood, on the road, all people were at greater danger. So travellers to and from cities tried to organise into groups and to pace their movement between safe havens, where shelter was available, as did Chaucer's Canterbury pilgrims.[94] Women – like Jews and priests – did not usually bear arms, and without obvious protectors they suffered insult and abuse. That great English traveller Margery Kempe (1373–1438) described how exposed she felt when her companions left her on the road, on her own:

> The night fell upon her, and she was right heavy, for she was alone. She knew not with whom she might rest on that night nor with whom she would go the next day. There came priests of that country [Germany] to her where she was at hostel. They called her English 'sterte' and spoke many lewd words unto her ... She had much dread for her chastity and was in great heaviness.[95]

Poor people were particularly vulnerable, and women feared rape and dishonour. The author of *Sefer Hasidim*, an early thirteenth-century book written in Regensburg for the guidance of pious Jewish lives, suggested that a woman traveller who

> hears she may be injured by Christians, and fears they may sleep with her, can dress like a nun so they may think she is a nun and not sleep with her. And if she hears that the enemies of Israel may hurt her she can also dress as a nun and say she is Christian.[96]

By the later fourteenth century, what had earlier been seen as useful migration was now often treated as vagrancy. In the town of Manosque in these decades, all thirty-two cases of people recorded in court as vagabonds involved women as the defendants, and their involvement in court cases had often to do with adultery.[97] Where ethnic difference combined with recent migration, we find women being suspects of prostitution. Indeed, in early fourteenth-century Ruthin, all those presented to the borough court for prostitution were Welsh women.[98] Many Flemish women in fourteenth-century English towns were presented to borough courts for prostitution and for keeping brothels. In Great Yarmouth,

Flemish men and some women, were frequently fined for the illegal sale of beer and for keeping a 'disreputable house' (*mauvais hostel*).[99] Given that brewing and tavern work employed many Flemish women in England, a vicious circle of work, poverty, alcohol, and sex emerges for women deemed foreign, even when they were settled and at work; and the punishment was banishment from the town or city to its suburbs – or beyond.

A group about whose lives we know very little but which was increasingly part of European urban life were Black African female slaves, and freed slaves. Such slaves were usually domestic servants, living in close proximity with family members, and ultimately manumitted, baptised, and renamed.[100] The Florence *catasto* of 1427 recorded 360 female slaves, about 1 per cent of the population; in Genoa it was 4–5 per cent in the 1380s.[101] Freed slaves of either sex remained poor, and thus vulnerable, even after baptism. Like other social groups of difference, they created their own networks, like the confraternity in fifteenth-century Valencia.[102] Black Africans became familiar strangers in European cities in later medieval Europe.[103]

Urban ordinances and statutes regularly dealt with the presence of those considered 'common women'.[104] In areas with large numbers of slaves – Iberian and Italian cities – urban codes instructed locals not to encourage their slaves to sell themselves for sex.[105] Statutes of northern and central Italian communes frequently addressed the subject of prostitution. Prostitutes were treated as a nuisance; religious houses, like the college of San Salvatore in early thirteenth-century Bologna, sought to distance such women from their compounds, just as they sought to control the building of dovecotes or drains.[106] In Siena, the statute of 1309 explained that prostitutes should keep away from the area around the convent of the Servite friars.[107] In London, 'all common harlots, and all women reputed as such, should have and use hoods of ray only', a striped hood, according to ordinances of 1351 and 1382.[108] The statutes of Buda also required around 1403 that prostitutes wear a yellow stripe as broad as a hand on their headgear.[109]

The York Ordinances of 1301, as we have seen, were granted by King Edward I for the regulation of the city's work, craft by craft. The situation of prostitutes there is highly revealing of habits of thought. Following the rubric on hostellers and landlords comes one on 'Pigs and prostitutes':

'No one shall keep pigs which go in the streets by day or night, nor shall any prostitutes stay in the city.' The drafter was thinking about nuisances to the city: dirty and noisy streets, and so from pigs to prostitutes. He stated:

> If anyone finds a pig in the streets he may kill it.

And seamlessly to:

> If any prostitute keeps a brothel and resides in the city, she is to be taken and imprisoned for a day and a night.

And to encourage enforcement, he added:

> The bailiff who takes her shall have the roof timbers and the door of the building in which she lodged. Nonetheless, he who rents out houses to prostitutes shall lose the rent of such a house for one term.[110]

Similarly, in 1331 in Bergamo, both the prostitute and the person who gave her lodging were targeted:

> that no public prostitute should stand or stay nor live in the city or within the walls of the city of Bergamo, or incur a fine at the Vicarius' discretion. And no one within the walls of the city should rent or give free to those prostitutes or to their people any house to be in and reside in, or incur a fine of 100 imperial solidi for each and every infraction.[111]

Prostitution was a constant presence in urban life, often located in areas associated with other nefarious, yet necessary, activities, like money-lending. The Parisian poet Guillot saw women for sale wherever business was done. And where there were students, there was sex:

> Nearby is the Rue des Ecoles
> There Lady Nicole lives.
> In that street it appears
> That hay and straw are sold together.[112]

By the later fourteenth century, prostitution was at the heart of campaigns for the reform of civic life. When the Emperor Charles IV had his capital, Prague, expanded to create the New Town, the old wall was removed, thus situating the city's Venice brothel at the centre of the new urban space. David Mengel has shown that the religious reforms of preacher Jan Milič of Kroměřiž (d. 1374), led to the transformation of the brothel into a centre for preaching and pastoral care – New Jerusalem.[113] Care for prostitutes – usually by providing them with dowries and arranging marriages – was a branch of charitable work that became more prominent in late medieval cities.[114] The language in which the discussion of prostitution was expressed became increasingly moralised, heavy with condemnation and disgust.

Hand in hand with these harsher attitudes came the creation of urban brothels in cities, whose supervision was farmed out to individuals – to men as well as women. Venice did this with the opening of its Casteletto in 1360, in the Rialto – the hub of moneylending too.[115] In fifteenth-century Camerino, in the Macerata, women of ill-fame – *male fame* – were obliged to stay at least twenty houses away from the Franciscan convent, other religious institutions, or any church, and this was to be checked by the local podestà and captain. Such women were truly outlawed. The statute goes on to say that 'anyone can offend them without punishment or fine'.[116] In the court records of the Châtelet of late fourteenth- and fifteenth-century Paris, prostitutes were frequently presented for theft from clients, often theft occasioned by their sex-work.[117] Prostitutes were regarded with suspicion above all.

***

Public discourse in many cities of the later fourteenth and fifteenth centuries included ambitious programmes for moral reform to which town councils in Italian cities, in Iberian ones, and throughout the Empire responded. Those most exposed bore the brunt of the anxiety and mistrust that inspired this response. The groups that lived in some strangerhood – prostitutes, beggars, Jews, homosexuals, troublesome hawkers of food, and, from the 1420s, those who came to be called Gypsies, Bohemians, or Egyptians – were marked, excluded from public spaces, and sometimes expelled.[118] Most women remained in families and homes, yet also in a state of troubling strangeness, in cities that needed them and, often, cherished them, but by whose officials and their rules they were also scrutinised, constrained, and disciplined.

Conclusion

Is it lack of imagination that makes us come
to imagined places, not just stay at home?
Or could Pascal have not been entirely right
about just sitting quietly in one's room?

Continent, city, country, society:
the choice is never wide and never free.
And here, or there ... No. Should we have stayed at home,
wherever that may be?

From Elizabeth Bishop, *Questions of Travel* (1956)[1]

T HE WILES LECTURES THAT UNDERPIN THIS BOOK WERE INSPIRED BY the sight of hundreds of thousands of refugees walking across Europe, which led me to create a lecture on townswomen. Every project of research is a journey of unexpected discoveries, and so this has been. We began with an appreciation of the urban landscape of Europe after 1000, with its areas of extensive and long-standing urbanisation in the south and the wave of new foundations north of the Alps. We have witnessed communities of strangers coming together in tentative sworn associations to create communes and appoint officials. Cities won freedoms from local rulers, and with these came responsibilities; so they developed rules and procedures to ensure the safety and flourishing of their communities. And since growing commerce and manufacture required both skilled and less-skilled workers, and attracted those who sought the opportunities of urban life, rules about entry and settlement soon had to be formulated, stated, and enforced. Those who lived in towns and cities reflected a great deal on the arrival of newcomers and the settlement of strangers. The reception of new residents was an act of trust, carefully considered, and always conditional. Town councils and magistrates recognised that the movement of people into their communities was an utter necessity, but also a risk.

The procedures they devised have left ample materials to study, the rich literature of urban statutes that formed the basis for much of the discussion in Chapter 2. The word foreign *forinsecus* or *extraneus* was used for traders who came from a neighbouring town or village to sell in the urban market, and whose presence was limited to that exchange. But some such foreigners developed local contacts, and so earned a reputation. A good name was essential if they ever wished to extend their stay and settle, since the process required a local to vouch for them. A period of residence was a necessary qualification if they wished to go further and attain full integration, to become citizens: *civis, poorter,* or *burgher.* We have seen that applicants were variously required to prove their religious probity, to have freed themselves from duties to other lords, to buy property, or to build a house for their settled family. Large cities in northern Europe allowed some women – wives and widows – to become citizens, although they were never citizens in the fullest sense that men were.

Most people never became citizens, nor was it expected that they would. The majority of migrants moved from village to town, and they became domestic servants, or workers in workshops. Those who had trained could proceed and become members of guilds, and so enter the represented citizenry, the civic sphere of office-holding and business contacts. This study has, therefore, touched upon them very little. Research about their experiences is possible from the later part of our period, and only in some regions.[2]

At the other end of the social scale and the hierarchy of wealth were those newcomers we have called 'desirable strangers', individuals and groups sought out by cities for their ability to provide essential expert services: bankers, physicians, notaries, magistrates, teachers, miners, silk manufacturers, or ship-makers. We have seen that the attraction of such settlers was often a priority pursued by kings and territorial rulers, who offered charters of protection and distinctive arrangements for safe and profitable relocation. Where cities operated under royal or seigneurial legislation, their choices about the settlement of strangers were determined by law; the more autonomous urban communities have left us the products of local deliberation in the form of their statutes.

'Desirable strangers' tended to create communities or enclaves within the city characterised by language, bolstered by kinship, and marked by distinctive professional networks of knowledge or credit. Here we note two types of settlement: a largely male group of traders who might stay for long periods, but who were not settled in family households, like the Lombards in Paris; or a distinctive and permanent group, like the Jews of Siena or the Flemings of London, settled in families, associated with particular trades, making an enduring spatial imprint on the city through a variety of placenames and their communal buildings. Jews in Cologne or Germans in Riga settled there for generations, their communities often reinforced by new arrivals. In both cases, marks of identity were attached to the groups – ranging from appearance, through accent, to religion – and their difference could be lived with relative safety for long periods of time.

Religious difference was an aspect of existence whose effects varied across the year and over time: Lent and Easter often inspired heightened awareness and acts of aggression against Jews; periods of military conflict between England and France threatened the lives and property of French aliens in England – those living in households and even those in religious institutions; war between the papacy and Florence saw the destruction of that well-established Tuscan community in Avignon in 1376. In each of these cities and kingdoms families assessed their well-being, and for some – like the Jews of Europe – this sometimes meant upping sticks and moving on, as we have seen in the case of the small Jewish community led by Izaac towards settlement in Gourdon in the Quercy in 1263.

In some cities, newcomers arrived in the aftermath of conquest and regime change. We have noted the peculiar composition of cities like Riga and Buda, or regional centres like Ruthin, where groups lived side by side and yet apart, with varying rights and access to political influence. New rulers or conquerors, in Sicily and England, Iberia and Outremer, confronted existing diversity and attempted to control and contain – not abolish – it, while also cultivating the political and cultural authority of

Christian royal governance. Our story has some clear lineaments that follow the logic of economic and demographic change, but it also deserves a set of regional histories. I hope this short book will help historians conceptualise future research and discovery as to what Europeans shared – and how they diverged – in the treatment of newcomers and in living with neighbours marked by difference.

All these activities were made possible by a combination of economic opportunities, demographic realities, and discursive frames of reference. That is to say that the aspirations of would-be newcomers and those of settled townspeople were understood, represented, and communicated within existing – and evolving – frames of language, law, and religious lore. Ideas about citizenship were anchored in Roman law, and the common good developed as a useful concept for urban cooperation. It is hard to assess just how much the biblical tenet 'But thou shalt love thy neighbour as thyself' (Leviticus 19:18)[3] inspired the treatment of strangers: Christian charity is never invoked in the crisp formulations of urban statutes dealing with *forinseci* or *extranei*. And when the acts of mercy were put into visual and material forms, they imagined the 'stranger' as a passing pilgrim, and always poor.

It is accordingly also evident that when the sense of well-being and opportunity was less robust among those who formed the citizenry and leadership, attitudes to newcomers changed. We hinted at the ways this worked in various European regions. Some reconsideration of the terms of entry is evident already in the early fourteenth century, when demographic pressure bore down on both countryside and cities, and to a greater extent following the Black Death, and in its long aftermath. City leaders, guild members, and even confraternities all sought ways of protecting themselves. Yet cities also sought to bring in new citizens who would make a contribution to the fiscal commitments that kept cities safe and comfortable. A greater degree of differentiation is evident between townspeople, all of which were now more closely monitored. This was achieved by the requirement of distinctive – and frequent – oaths, by more differentiated official documentation, and through the labelling of urban group in terms of perceived lifestyle and morality. Some of the labour of social distinction was handed over to professional preachers and castigators, who made it their mission to identify sins within the city, name and shame groups, and define the common good anew, as a striving for moral purity. In such cases, as Chapter 3 has shown, religious moral discourse built on existing ideas in criticising luxury and lasciviousness, alongside the polluting presence of Jews.

That chapter examined the Jews not as a group to be treated apart, but rather as a revealing case of embedded difference in the city. Jews were never treated as strangers in the sources I have studied, never *forinseci* or *extranei* (except when Jews were newcomers from elsewhere, and were thus to be distinguished from local Jews), and yet they did maintain aspects of difference, just as other communities in cities did. It is that vulnerable belonging that is so interesting to witness, and it makes the stories of expulsion and episodic violence all the more tragic, as neighbours turning against neighbours always is.

If townspeople as a whole lived together – settled and familiar – while retaining marks of difference that occasionally justified their exclusion from some aspects of political and civic life, women experienced this too. How useful is it to think of women as strangers in their urban communities? Chapter 4 is an attempt to do just that, as it traces aspects of difference attached to women in the communities of their birth, where they nurtured families, and offered essential work and expertise. Again, the regions of Europe, each with its own social and economic arrangements, offered women differing degrees of integration, with the possibility of entry into (a form of) citizenship in German, English, and Flemish towns. Here women are not unlike Jews in their utter embeddedness, integration into work routines, and even closeness to citizen status, and yet they were excluded from deliberation and authority. What is also similar is the sense of physical danger they often sensed, and the recurrent attempts to 'purify' cities of the sight and sound of them.

All the arrangements we have studied are associated with the confident assertion of the common good by prominent men, enabled and intellectually informed by experts in law, rhetoric, commerce, and religion. The treatment of strangers – expansive or restrictive – is part of the work of politics, where propertied and economically active Christian men took decisions about the common good and determined the rules by which all others lived. This may be an obvious observation, yet it also leads us to understand better how exclusion and separation are never about a sole group and its attributes, but are related to a vision of power and privilege that affected everyone. Therefore, thinking about strangers, or those estranged from the city's image of itself, is so revealing about the fundamental values and forms of practice that cities accepted and tolerated. Here I am reminded of the words of Heleni Porfyriou: 'We are all strangers, but only some of us are aware of this.'[4] Another way of thinking of the condition of stranger is as always a neighbour, always with us. And we may go further, with Emmanuel Levinas, and see ourselves defined, deeply bound, and ultimately hostages of the other, who is our neighbour:

> To be reduced to having recourse to me is the homelessness or strangeness of the neighbour. It is incumbent on me.[5]

***

The ideas and practices we have examined here, and which we have observed as they changed over time, were soon challenged by the global reconfiguration of European states and the lives their people lived.[6] As Europeans travelled more widely, conquered lands, and converted people in Africa, Asia, and the Americas, all questions of identity and belonging were challenged anew. Ideas about Christian cohesion that had defined Europe for so long were now also lost, as large parts broke their ties to traditional religion, its rituals, and its ethics.[7] Questions of social obligation, of the duties one owed to others, were being re-examined and redefined. When a Poor Law was introduced in 1531 by Emperor Charles V to his domains in the Low Countries, the Dominicans of Ypres responded swiftly. The new law prohibited begging, they argued, but it also targeted 'peaceful migrants [who] should be received as a profit to the city'.[8] The Flemish humanist Christianus Cellarius (d. 1554) composed two orations, one in favour of helping the indigent refugee, and the other against. In the former he asks:

> Do you want all these to go back to their country? What country?...
> Where shall the miserable woman go?...

The argument against is kindly, but it sets as a priority helping the local needy, rather than letting in the stranger:

> I do not command you to go back to your own country, woman, since you have none [*quandoquidem nulla est*]. I would rather persuade you to seek food by manual labour . . . Forgive us that we supply you with food for a few days rather than your whole life.[9]

The discourse on foreign beggars that guided the new imperial law was based on a tradition developed in the fifteenth century and perfected at the University of Salamanca. No foreign beggars were to be supported, and local ones only when they were documented; pilgrims should not stray from the pilgrimage route; and the respectable poor were to be treated within hospitals.[10] Here is an Iberian version of the reforming theologies we saw preached in Tuscany by Bernardino of Siena in the fifteenth century; here is the exclusion and separation of social groups, now transmitted across Europe by the Catholic Habsburg rulers.

William Shakespeare looked back at this period from the 1590s in his play *The Book of Sir Thomas More*. He imagined the feelings of Thomas More (1478–1535), then under-sheriff of London, as he witnessed the bloody riots against foreigners that broke out on May Day 1517, when the houses and goods of Spanish, Italian, Hanseatic, and Flemish 'strangers' in London were sacked:

> Imagine that you see the wretched strangers,
> Their babies at their backs and their poor luggage,
> Plodding to the ports and coasts for transportation,
> And that you sit as kings in your desires.
> Authority quite silent by your brawl,
> And you in ruff of your opinions clothed;
> What had you got? I'll tell you: you had taught
> How insolence and strong hand should prevail,
> How order should be quelled; and by this pattern
> Not one of you should live an aged man,
> For other ruffians, as their fancies wrought,
> With self same hand, self reasons, and self right,
> Would shark on you, and men like ravenous fishes
> Would feed on one another.[11]

Care for strangers – through good times and hard – is not only an expression of our better selves. Our treatment of them has consequences – in Shakespeare's words again: 'you had taught/ How insolence and strong hand should prevail'.

Notes

1 CITIES AND THEIR STRANGERS

1 Simona Cerutti, *Étrangers: Étude d'une condition d'incertitude dans une société d'Ancien Régime*, Monrouge, 2012, pp. 11–24.

2 *Les Statuts municipaux de Marseille*, ed. Régine Pernoud, Monaco and Paris, 1949, no. 18, p. 200 (also no. 21, p. 202).

3 On the transformation of urban life in the early medieval centuries, see Chris Wickham, *Framing the Early Middle Ages: Europe and the Mediterranean, 400–800*, Oxford, 2005, pp. 591–670. For essays that address the experiences of particular regions, see John Rich (ed.), *The City in Late Antiquity*, London, 1992, and on immigration in the Roman world, Catharine Edwards and Greg Woolf (eds.), *Rome the Cosmopolis*, Cambridge, 2003.

4 On Henri Pirenne's ideas and work, see Walter Prevenier, 'Henri Pirenne (1862–1935)', in *French Historians 1900–2000: New Historical Writing in Twentieth-Century France*, ed. Philip Daileader and Philip Whalen, Chichester, 2010, pp. 486–500.

5 Adriaan Verhulst, *The Rise of Cities in North-West Europe*, Cambridge, 1999, pp. 68–118; see also Jacques Heers, *La Ville au Moyen Âge en Occident: Paysages, pouvoirs et conflits*, Paris, 1990, pp. 96–145. On urban growth and its relation to Roman and early medieval features of settlement, see the essays in Richard Hodges and Brian Hobley (eds.), *The Rebirth of Towns in the West AD 700–1050*, London, 1988. On the role of the Roman heritage for towns, see Frans Theuws and Arnoud-Jan Bijsterveld, 'Early Town Formation in the Northern Low Countries: Roman Heritage, Carolingian Impulses, and a New Take-Off in the Twelfth Century', in *Town and Country in Medieval North-Western Europe: Dynamic Interactions*, ed. Alexis Wilkin, John Naylor, Derek Keene, and Arnoud-Jan Bijsterveld, Turnhout, 2015, pp. 87–118; esp. pp. 87–91.

6 Peter Johanek, 'Merchants, Markets and Towns', in *The New Cambridge Medieval History*, vol. III, ed. Timothy Reuter, Cambridge, 1999, pp. 64–94, and Marc Boone, 'Medieval Europe', in *The Oxford Handbook of Cities in World History*, ed. Peter Clark, Oxford, pp. 221–39; as well as David Nicholas, *Urban Europe, 1100–1700*, Basingstoke, 2003. For an overview, see Steven A. Epstein, *An Economic and Social History of Later Medieval Europe, 1000–1500*, Cambridge, 2009, chapters 1–5, and Michael M. Postan, *The Medieval Economy and Society: An Economic History of Britain in the Middle Ages*, Harmondsworth, 1972, chapters 11–12.

7 Robert Bartlett, *The Making of Europe: Conquest, Colonization and Cultural Change, 950–1350*, London, 1993, offers an overview of the political as well as religious expansion.

8 For an extremely interesting analysis of the interaction of a city and its surroundings, see Chris Wickham, *Medieval Rome: Stability and Crisis of a City, 900–1500*, Oxford, 2015, chapter 2.

9 On the proportions and sizes of urban populations, see Giorgio Chittolini, 'Urban Populations, Urban Territories, Small Towns: Some Problems of the History of Urbanization in Northern and Central Italy (Thirteenth–Sixteenth Centuries)', in *Power and Persuasion: Essays on the Art of State Building in Honour of W. P. Blockmans*, ed. Peter Hoppenbrouwers, Antheun Janse, and Robert Stein, Turnhout, 2010, pp. 227–41; at pp. 233–5.

10 On the involvement of lords in town creation, see Peter Johanek, 'Seigneurial Power and the Development of Towns in the Holy Roman Empire', in *Lords and Towns in Medieval Europe: The European Historic Towns Atlas Project*, ed. Anngret Simms and Howard B. Clarke, Farnham, 2015, pp. 117–54.

11 On the centrality of the oath to civic life, see Paolo Prodi, *Il sacramento del potere: Il giuramento politico nella storia costituzionale dell'Occidente*, Bologna, 1992, and Otto G. Oexle, 'Gilde und Kommune: Über die Entstehung von "Einung" und "Gemeinde" als Grundformen des Zusammenlebens in Europa', in *Theorien kommunaler Ordnung in Europa*, ed. Peter Blickle, Munich, 1996, pp. 75–97. On the role of merchant guilds in town formation, see Verhulst, *The Rise of Cities*, pp. 123–5. And for a sober assessment of the meaning of such oath-taking, see Susan Reynolds, *Kingdoms and Communities in Western Europe, 900–1300*, 2nd edn, Oxford, 1997, pp. xli–xlv.

12 'facta itaque conspiratione quam communionem vocabant', Reynolds, *Kingdoms and Communities*, p. 176.

13 For an illuminating discussion of urban plots, see Jerzy Piekalski, *Prague, Wrocław and Krakow: Public and Private Space at the Time of the Medieval Transition*, trans. Anna Kinecka, Wrocław, 2014, chapter 4.

14 Plato, *Laws*, ed. Michael Schofield and trans. Tom Griffith, Cambridge, 2016, V.737e, p. 184.

15 *Pommersches Urkundenbuch*, vol. I, ed. Klaus Conrad, Cologne, 1970, no. 308a, pp. 374–6; at p. 375.

16 On forms of citizen participation in urban government, see Thierry Dutour, 'Le Consensus des bonnes gens: La participation des habitants aux affaires communes dans quelques villes de la langue d'oïl (XIIIe –XVe siècle)', in *Le Pouvoir municipal: De la fin du Moyen Âge à 1789*, Rennes, 2010, pp. 187–208.

17 For an interesting collection of essays on the legacy of the concept of the medieval city, see Peter Johanek and Franz-Joseph Post (eds.), *Vielerlei Städte: Der Stadtbegriff*, Cologne, 2004.

18 Hendrik Dey, 'From "Street" to "Piazza": Urban Politics, Public Ceremony, and the Redefinition of *platea* in Communal Italy and Beyond', *Speculum* 91 (2016), 919–44. On space in the historical analysis of city life, see Peter Arnade, Martha Howell, and Walter

Simons, 'Fertile Spaces: The Productivity of Urban Space in Northern Europe', *Journal of Interdisciplinary History* 32 (2002), 515–48. On the political implications of the power to build in a late medieval city, see Patrick Boucheron, *Le Pouvoir de bâtir: Urbanisme et politique édilitaire à Milan (XIVe–XVe siècles)*, Rome, 1998.

19 Nicholas, *Urban Europe, 1100–1700*, figure 1.3, pp. 19–20.

20 Peter Biller, *The Measure of Multitude: Population in Medieval Thought*, Oxford, 2000, p. 223.

21 On Champagne's fairs, see Elizabeth Chapin, *Les Villes de foires de Champagne des origines au début du XIVe siècle*, Paris, 1937.

22 Ulrich Müller, 'Network of the Centres – Centres of the Networks? The Relations between "Hanseatic" Medieval Towns and Their Surroundings/Hinterlands', in *Town and Country in Medieval North Western Europe: Dynamic Interactions*, ed. Alexis Wilkin, John Naylor, Derek Keene, and Arnoud-Jan Bijsterveld, Turnhout, 2015, pp. 145–87; for a useful orientation, see Justyna Wubs-Mrozewicz, 'The Hanse in Medieval and Early Modern Europe: An Introduction', in *The Hanse in Medieval and Early Modern Europe*, ed. Justyna Wubs-Mrozewicz and Stuart Jenks, Leiden, 2013, pp. 1–35. On the mechanisms that supported trust within the Hanse sphere, see Mika Kallioinen, 'Inter-communal Institutions in Medieval Trade', *Economic History Review* 70 (2017), 1131–52.

23 Cities also associated for the purpose of mutual protection and the promotion of regional peace: see Pierre Monnet, 'Villes et territoires dans l'Empire à la fin du Moyen Âge: Pour une approche régionale entre villes, principautés et royauté en Allemagne', in *La Cité médiévale en débat*, ed. Amélia Aguiar Andrade and Adelaide Millán da Costa, Lisbon, 2013, pp. 71–88, and Gianluca Raccagni, *The Lombard League 1164–1225*, Oxford, 2010.

24 Anu Mänd, *Urban Carnival: Festive Culture in the Hanseatic Cities of the Eastern Baltic, 1350–1550*, Turnhout, 2005.

25 For the classical origins of the term, see Greg Woolf, 'Cosmopolis: Rome as World City', in Edwards and Woolf (eds.), *Rome the Cosmopolis*, pp. 1–20.

26 Olivia Remie Constable, *Housing the Stranger in the Mediterranean World: Lodging, Trade, and Travel in Late Antiquity and the Middle Ages*, Cambridge, 2003, p. 7.

27 Ibid., pp. 315–28; on the *funduq* in other cities, see pp. 332–7. See the Introduction for the discussion of the early history of *funduqs*.

28 Antonio Ivan Pini, 'Nazioni mercantili, "societates" regionali e "nationes" studentesche a Bologna nel Duecento', in *Comunità forestiere e 'nationes' nell'Europa dei secoli XIII–XVI*, ed. Giovanna Petti Balbi, Naples, 2001, pp. 23–40; esp. pp. 28–32; Carsten Jahnke, 'The City of Lübeck and the Internationality of Early Hanseatic Trade', in *The Hanse in Medieval and Early Modern Europe*, ed. Justyna Wubs-Mrozewicz and Stuart Jenks, Leiden, 2013, pp. 37–58; at p. 47.

29 *Libro della comunità dei mercanti lucchesi in Bruges*, ed. Eugenio Lazzareschi, with a preface by Armando Sapori, Milan, 1947, pp. 132–3, 93–4. On the experience of Hanse merchants in London, see Derek Keene, 'Du Seuil de la Cité à la formation d'une économie morale: L'Environnement hanséatique à Londres entre XIIe et XVIIe siècle', in *Les*

Étrangers dans la ville: Minorités et espace urbain du bas Moyen Âge à l'époque moderne, ed, Jacques Bottin and Donatella Calabi, Paris, 1999, pp. 409–24.

30 For an illuminating example of the operation of papal patronage of exiled merchants, see the case of Petrarch's father, in Barbara Bombi, 'The "Babylonian captivity" of Petracco di ser Parenzo dell'Incisa, Father of Francesco Petrarca', *Historical Research* 83 (2010), 431–43.

31 Sharon Farmer, *The Silk Industries of Medieval Paris: Artisanal Migration, Technological Innovation, and Gendered Experience*, Philadelphia, 2016, pp. 139–57.

32 On regional networks of monastic houses, see Tjamke Snijders, 'Near Neighbours, Distant Brothers: The Inter-Monastic Networks of Benedictine Houses in the Southern Low Countries (900–1200)', in *Medieval Liège at the Crossroads of Europe: Monastic Society and Culture, 1000–1300*, ed. Steven Vanderputten, Tjamke Snijders, and Jay Diehl, Brepols, 2017, pp. 69–108.

33 For the case of military orders, see Jochen Burgtorf and Helen Nicholson (eds.), *International Mobility in the Military Orders (Twelfth to Fifteenth Centuries): Travelling on Christ's Business*, Cardiff, 2006 (see especially articles by Burgtorf, Hunyadi, Nicholson, and Vogel).

34 For an interesting recent study of the early modern Sephardi networks through the term or concept of diaspora, see Francesca Trivellato, *The Familiarity of Strangers: The Sephardic Diaspora, Livorno, and Cross-Cultural Trade in the Early Modern Period*, New Haven, CN, 2009. See also the essays in *Atlantic Diasporas: Jews, Conversos, and Crypto-Jews in the Age of Mercantilism, 1500–1800*, ed. Richard L. Kagan and Philip D. Morgan, Baltimore, MD, 2009.

35 On the influence of the friars upon social relations in Tuscan cities, see Katherine Ludwig Jansen, *Peace and Penance in Late Medieval Italy*, Princeton, 2018.

36 Alison Cornish, '*Translatio Galliae*: Effects of Early Franco-Italian Literary Exchange', *Romanic Review* 97 (2006), 309–30.

37 Marco Polo, *Il milione*, ed. Ruggero M. Ruggieri, Florence, 1986. Marco Polo's writings have inspired a modern meditation on cities: Italo Calvino, *Le città invisibili*, Milan, 1972 [translated into English as *Invisible Cities*, trans. William Weaver, London, 1974].

38 Gerhard Fouquet, '"Kaufleute auf Reisen": Sprachliche Verständigung im Europa des 14. und 15. Jahrhunderts', in *Europa im späten Mittelalter: Politik – Gesellschaft – Kultur*, ed. Rainer C. Schwinges, Christoph Hesse, and Peter Moraw, Munich, 2006, pp. 465–87, and Robert Peters, 'Das mittelniederdeutsche als Sprache der Hanse', in *Sprachkontakt in der Hanse: Aspekte des Sprachausgleichs im Ostsee- und Nordseeraum*, ed. Per Sture Ureland, Tübingen, 1987, pp. 65–88, esp. table on p. 81.

39 Consideration of the common good goes back to Aristotle's *Ethics*, as the 'supreme good', M. S. Kempshall, *The Common Good in Late Medieval Political Thought*, Oxford, 1999, pp. 26–8. See, for the Low Countries, Marc Boone and Jelle Haemers, 'The "Common Good": Governance, Discipline, and Political Culture', in *City and Society in the Low Countries (1100–1600)*, ed. Bruno Blondé, Marc Boone, and Anne-Laure Van Bruaene, Cambridge, 2018, pp. 93–127.

40 In their introduction the editors called the 'common good' a 'semantic chameleon', Élodie Lecuppre-Desjardin and Anne-Laure Van Bruaene (eds.), 'Introduction', in their *De Bono Communi: The Discourse and Practice of the Common Good in the European City (13th–16th Centuries)*, Turnhout, 2010, pp. 1–9; at p. 3. On the royal use of the concept of the common good, see, ibid., Albert Rigaudière, 'Donner pour le Bien Commun et contribuer pour les biens communs dans les villes du Midi français du XIIIe au XVe siècle', pp. 11–53; and on the expression in Italian communes through works on rhetoric and government, see, ibid., Andrea Zorzi, 'Bien Commun et conflits politiques dans l'Italie communale', pp. 267–90. See the analysis of a work from fifteenth-century Ghent in Jan Dumolyn, 'Une Idéologie urbaine "bricolée" en Flandre médiévale: Les *Sept Portes de Bruges* dans le manuscrit Gruuthuse (début du XVe siècle)', *Revue belge de philologie et d'histoire* 88 (2010), 1039–84.

41 *Isidore of Seville's Etymologies*, vol. II, trans. Priscilla Throop, Charlotte, VT, 2005, pp. XV.2.1; 'Civitas est hominum multitudo societatis vincula adunata, dicta a civibus, id est ab ipsis incolis urbis [pro eo quod plurimorum consciscat et contineat vitas]. Nam urbs ipsa moenia sunt, civitas autem non saxa, sed habitatores vocantur', Isidore of Seville, *Etimologiarum sive originum libri XX*, vol. II, trans. W. M. Lindsay, Oxford, 1911, 15:2.1.

42 'Des lor comencerent a fonder maison, & villes fermer & forteresse, & clore le de murs & de fosses. & de lors comencerent a establir ses costumes & sa loi & les droit, qui estoient comuns por trestut li borgiois de la ville. Por ce dit Tuilles que cités est uns asenblement de jens a abiter en un luec & vivre a une loy', Brunetto Latini, *Li livre dou Tresor*, ed. Spurgeon Baldwin and Paul Barrette, Tempe, AZ, 2003, Book III, c. 73, pp. 362–4; at p. 363. The translation, from Brunetto Latini, is from *The Book of Treasure (Li Livres dou Tresor)*, trans. Paul Barrette and Spurgeon Baldwin, New York, 1993, c. 73, p. 351.

43 Patrick Lantschner, *The Logic of Political Conflict in Medieval Cities: Italy and the Southern Low Countries, 1370–1440*, Oxford, 2015, p. 8. On the moral dimension in writing about urban life, see Pierre Monnet, 'Villes et citoyenneté: En guise d'introduction', in *Religion et pouvoir: Citoyenneté, ordre social et discipline morale dans les villes de l'espace Suisse (XIVe–XVIIIe siècles)*, ed. Mathieu Caesar and Marco Schnyder, Neufchâtel, 2014, pp. 11–33. On the distinction between private and communal responsibilities within the discussion of the common good, see Peter von Moos, '"Public" et "privé" à la fin du Moyen Âge: Le "bien commun" et la "loi de conscience"', *Studi Medievali* 3rd series, 41 (2000), 505–48.

44 'Menius: Worumme sal mans eyne stad heysen, und welchis sal man eyne stat heissen?'; Gayus: Is heist eyne stat, das das volk, das dorynne wonit, steticlich in eynir eynunge stehen sal und dem rechten beystehen', in *Das Liegnitzer Stadtrechtsbuch des Nikolaus Wurm: Hintergrund, Überlieferung und Edition eines schlesischen Rechtsdenkmals*, ed. Hans-Jörg Leuchte, Sigmaringen, 1990, p. 24. On Wurm and the tradition within which he operated, see Eberhard Isenmann, *Die deutsche Stadt im Spätmittelalter, 1250–1500: Stadtgestalt, Recht, Stadtregiment, Kirche, Gesellschaft, Wirtschaft*, Stuttgart, 1988, pp. 411–38. Reference to the common good developed in German towns later than in the Low

Countries and Italy: see Pierre Monnet, 'Bien Commun et bon gouvernement: Le traité politique de Johann von Soest sur la manière de bien gouverner une ville (*Wye men wol eyn statt regyrn sol, 1495*)', in *De Bono Communi: The Discourse and Practice of the Common Good in the European City (13th–16th Centuries)*, ed. Élodie Lecuppre-Desjardin and Anne-Laure Van Bruaene, Turnhout, 2010, pp. 89–106; also, Jan Dumolyn, 'Urban Ideologies in Later Medieval Flanders: Towards an Analytical Framework', in *The Languages of Political Society: Western Europe, 14th–17th Centuries*, ed. Andrea Gamberini, Jean-Philippe Genet, and Andrea Zorzi, Rome, 2011, pp. 69–96. Edith Ennen, similarly, opened her important book on European cities with the question 'Was ist eine Stadt?', *Die europäische Stadt*, Göttingen, 1972, p. 11.

45 Carol Symes, *A Common Stage: Theater and Public Life in Medieval Arras*, Ithaca, NY, 2007, chapter 1.

46 Albertanus of Brescia, *Liber de doctrina dicendi et tacendi: La parola del cittadino nell'Italia del Duecento*, ed. Paola Navone, Florence, 1998. For Welsh contributions to the praise of cities, see Helen Fulton, 'The *encomium urbis* in Medieval Welsh Poetry', *Proceedings of the Harvard Celtic Colloquium* 26 (2006), 54–72.

47 Martine Veldhuizen, *Sins of the Tongue in the Medieval West: Sinful, Unethical, and Criminal Words in Middle Dutch (1300–1550)*, Turnhout, 2017.

48 Serena Ferente, 'The Liberty of Italian City-States', in *Freedom and the Construction of Europe*, vol. I: *Religious Freedom and Civil Liberty*, ed. Quentin Skinner and Martin van Gelderen, Cambridge, 2013, pp. 157–75; esp. pp. 157–63. For an overview, see Knut Schulz, *'Denn sie lieben dies freiheit so sehr...': Kommunale Aufstände und Entstehung des europäischen Bürgertums im Hochmittelalter*, Darmstadt, 1992.

49 For a penetrating analysis of the impact of medieval cities on their surroundings, see Richard C. Hoffmann, 'Footprint Metaphor and Metabolic Realities: Environmental Impacts of Medieval European Cities', in *Natures Past: The Environment and Human History*, ed. Paolo Squatriti, Ann Arbor, MI, 2007, pp. 288–325; Bernd Herrmann, 'City and Nature and Nature in the City', in *Historians and Nature: Comparative Approaches to Environmental History*, ed. Ursula Lehmkuhl and Herrmann Wellenreuther, New York and Oxford, 2007, pp. 226–56. On legislation, Denis Clauzel, Isabelle Clauzel-Delannoy, Laurent Coulon, Bertrand Haquette, and others, 'L'Activité legislative dans les villes du Nord de la France à la fin du Moyen Âge', in *'Faire bans, édictz et statuz': Légiférer dans la ville médiévale*, ed. Jean-Marie Cauchies and Eric Bousmar, Brussels, 2001, pp. 295–329.

50 Barbara Rouse, 'Nuisance Neighbours and Persistent Polluters: The Urban Code of Behaviour in Late Medieval London', in *Medieval Urban Culture*, ed. Andrew Brown and Jan Dumolyn, Turnhout, 2017, pp. 75–92.

51 Michael Kucher, 'The Use of Water and Its Regulation in Medieval Siena', *Journal of Urban History* 31 (2005), 504–36, and Duccio Balestracci, Laura Vigni, and Armando Costantini, *Memoria dell'acqua: I bottini di Siena*, Siena, 2006. On Pavia's water policy, see Laura Bertoni, *Pavia alla fine del duecento: Una società urbana fra crescita e crisi*, Bologna, 2013, pp. 114–19.

52 On Siena's guilds, see Valentina Costantini, 'Corporazioni cittadine e popolo di mercanti a Siena tra Due e Trecento: Appunti per la ricerca', *Bullettino Senese di Storia Patria*

120 (2013), 98–133; also her 'On a Red Line across Europe: Butchers and Rebellions in Fourteenth-Century Siena', *Social History* 41 (2016), 72–92.

53 For a full contextualisation of the frescoes, see Patrick Boucheron, *The Power of Images: Siena, 1338*, trans. Andrew Brown, Cambridge, 2018. On the intellectual roots of the political ideas expressed, see Quentin Skinner, 'Ambrogio Lorenzetti: The Artist as Political Philosopher', *Proceedings of the British Academy* 72 (1986), 1–56; Nicolai Rubinstein, 'Political Ideas in Sienese Art: The Frescoes by Ambrogio Lorenzetti and Taddeo di Bartolo in the Palazzo Pubblico', *Journal of the Warburg and Courtauld Institutes* 21 (1958), 179–207. For an analysis of the vantage points developed by Lorenzetti, and their political meanings, see Andrea Brogi and Francesca Bianciardi, *Nella Siena ritrovata di Ambrogio Lorenzetti*, Siena, 2005.

54 On the ethics of government, see John Sabapathy, *Officers and Accountability in Medieval England, 1170–1300*, Oxford, 2014.

55 For these lines, see Boucheron, *The Power of Images*, p. 144, and, about them, pp. 87–8.

56 R. R. Davies, *Domination and Conquest: The Experience of Ireland, Scotland and Wales, 1100–1300*, Cambridge, 1990.

57 Vincenzo D'Alessandro, 'Immigrazione e società urbana in Sicilia (secoli XII–XVI): Momenti e aspetti', in *Communità forestiere e 'nationes' nell'Europa dei secoli XIII–XVI*, ed. Giovanna Petti Balbi, Naples, 2001, pp. 165–90; esp. pp. 168–70.

58 Olha Kozubska-Andrusiv, '"propter disparitatem linguae et religionis pares ipsis non esse...": "Minority" Communities in Medieval and Early Modern Lviv', in *Segregation – Integration – Assimilation: Religious and Ethnic Groups in Medieval Towns of Central and Eastern Europe*, ed. Derek Keene, Balász Nagy, and Katalin Szende, Farnham, 2009, pp. 51–66; pp. 52–3.

59 On the legal underpinning for settlement, see Katalin Szende, '*Iure Theutonico*? German Settlers and Legal Frameworks for Immigration to Hungary in an East–Central European Perspective', *Journal of Medieval History* 45 (2019), 1–20; esp. 10–18.

60 For the Butchers, see *Zunftbuch und Privilegien der Fleischer zu Ofen aus dem Mittelalter*, ed. István Kenyeres, Budapest, 2008.

61 On this post, see William Chester Jordan, *Men at the Center: Redemptive Governance under Louis IX*, Budapest, 2012, pp. 38–43.

62 Farmer, *The Silk Industries of Medieval Paris*, pp. 147–9.

63 Marcin Starzyński, *Das mittelalterliche Krakau: Der Stadtrat im Herrschaftsgefüge der polnischen Metropole*, trans. Christian Prüfer and Kai Witzlack-Makarevich, Vienna, 2015, esp. pp. 19–30.

64 For some reflections on the historical use of the term, see Geoffrey Hosking, *Trust: Money, Markets and Society*, London, 2010. For definitions and some useful categories, see Niklas Luhmann, *Trust and Power*, revised translation by Christian Morner and Michael King, based on translation by Howard Davies, John Raffan, and Kathryn Rooney, Cambridge, 2017, pp. 3–114. For a discussion of trust in medieval cities, with a heavy emphasis on urban 'anonymity', see Thierry Dutour, *Sous l'Empire du bien: 'Bonnes gens' et pacte social (XIIIe–XVe siècle)*, Paris, 2015, pp. 117–47, and, for the Italian context, see Paolo Prodi (ed.), *La fiducia secondo i linguaggi del potere*, Bologna, 2007.

65 On techniques of identification of commercial goods, see Reinhold C. Mueller, 'Merchants and Their Merchandise: Identity and Identification in Medieval Italy', in *Gens de passage en Méditerranée de l'antiquité à l'époque moderne: Procédures de contrôle et d'identification*, ed. Claudia Moatti and Wolfgang Kaiser, Paris, 2007, pp. 313–44.

66 On the ecological effects of feeding cities, see Hoffmann, 'Footprint Metaphor and Metabolic Realities', pp. 296–304. On the effect of urban demand on the maintenance of woods, see Richard Keyser, 'The Transformation of Traditional Woodland Management: Commercial Sylviculture in Medieval Champagne', *French Historical Studies* 32 (2009), 353–84. On feeding the Low Countries, see Stéphane Curveiller, 'Les Relations d'une ville du littoral flamand et de son hinterland: Dunkerque et Bergues au Moyen Âge', in *La Ville au Moyen Âge*, vol. I: *Ville et espace*, ed. Noël Coulet and Olivier Guyotjeannin, Paris, 1998, pp. 213–31, and Richard Unger, 'Feeding Low Countries Towns: The Grain Trade in the Fifteenth Century', *Revue belge de philologie et d'histoire* 77 (1999), esp. 329–58; at 329–31. On the interrelationship between cities and the territories around them, see Denis Menjot, 'La Ville et ses territoires dans l'Occident médiéval: Un système spatial. État de la question', in *La ciudad medieval y su influencia territorial*, ed. Beatriz Arízaga Bolumburu and Jesús Ángel Solórzano Telechea, Nájera, 2007, pp. 451–92.

67 Bruce M. S. Campbell, James A. Galloway, Derek Keene, and Margaret Murphy, *A Medieval Capital and Its Grain Supply: Agrarian Production and Distribution in the London Region c. 1300*, London, 1993. For some interesting ideas about the effect of urban life on rural communities, see Jane Jacobs, *The Economy of Cities*, London, 1969, chapter 1.

68 As suggested in James Davis, *Medieval Market Morality: Life, Law and Ethics in the English Marketplace, 1200–1500*, Cambridge, 2012, pp. 279–84.

69 "בני אדם שמהלכים בארץ למצוא מקום לגור ביי่שובי הארץ שם יעיינו באותה העיר מה עניין הגוים אם גדורים בעריה. אם יזורו יהודים באותה העיר גם בניהם ובנותיהם יהיו עושים כיוצא בהם כאותם גוים כי כל עיר ועיר כמנהג הגוים כן מנהג היהודים שעמהם" in *Das Buch der Frommen*, ed. Jehuda Wistinetzki, Frankfurt, 1924, repr. Jerusalem, 1969, c. 1301, p. 321. See also comments in Ephraim Shoham-Steiner, '"For in every city and town the manner of behaviour of the Jews resembles that of their non-Jewish neighbours": The Intricate Network of Interfaith Connections – A Brief Introduction', in *Intricate Interfaith Networks in the Middle Ages: Quotidian Jewish–Christian Contacts*, ed. Ephraim Shoham-Steiner, Turnhout, 2016, pp. 1–32; at pp. 3–4.

70 For chains, see *Statuta comunis et populi civitatis Camerini (1424)*, ed. Fabrizio Ciapparoni, Naples, 1977, Lib. 1, rubric 176, p. 52. Cairo Montenotte, near Genoa, outlawed entry – of humans or beasts – except through its gates: 'nullus debet intrare, vel exire de Castro vel de Burgo Carij nisi per portam, nec bestias aliquas extrahere, vel ducere', *Statuta, capitula, sive ordinamenta communis Carij*, C.LXXVI: www.cairomontenotte.com/biblioteca/scorzoni/b-1.html c. 49.

71 John Cherry, 'Seals of Cities and Towns: Concepts of Choice', in *Medieval Coins and Seals: Constructing Identity, Signifying Power*, ed. Susan Solway, Turnhout, 2015, pp. 283–95; at pp. 284–5.

72 Albert Rigaudière, 'Municipal Citizenship in Jacobi's *Practica aurea libellorum*', in *Privileges and Rights of Citizenship: Law and the Juridical Construction of Civil Society*, ed. Julius Kirshner and Laurent Mayali, Berkeley, CA, 2002, pp. 1–25; at pp. 12–13, 15–16.

73 Ibid., pp. 11–12. See also, on walls, Kathryn Reyerson, 'Urban Sensations: The Medieval City Imagined', in *A Cultural History of the Senses in the Middle Ages*, ed. Richard G. Newhauser, London, 2016, pp. 45–65; at pp. 47–50. In some regions, like East Anglia, many towns had no walls: Bärbel Brodt, *Städte ohne Mauern: Stadtentwicklung in East Anglia im 14. Jahrhundert*, Paderborn, 1997.

74 As in Bruges: see Wim De Clercq, Roland Dreesen, Jan Dumolyn, Ward Leloup, and Jan Trachet, 'Ballasting the Hanse: Baltoscandian Erratic Cobbles in the Later Medieval Port Landscape of Bruges', *European Journal of Archaeology* 20 (2017), 710–36; at 710–12.

75 Camille Serchuk, 'Paris and the Rhetoric of Town Praise in the *Vie de St. Denis* Manuscript (Paris Bibliothèque Nationale de France, ms 2090–2)', *Journal of the Walters Art Gallery* 57 (1999), 35–47; see figures 1, 3, 6–8. Christine Bousquet-Labouérie, 'L'Image de la ville dans les *Grandes Chroniques de France*: Miroir du prince ou du pouvoir urbain?', in *La Ville au Moyen Âge*, vol. II: *Sociétés et pouvoirs dans la ville*, ed. Noël Coulet and Olivier Guyotjeannin, Paris, 1998, pp. 247–60.

76 'Et est notoire cose que les portes sunt de le nécessité de la ville … si que se les portes fussent ostées, li boine gent de la ville seroint en péril de estre mourdri par nuit et de desrobeir leur avoir', as cited by Walter Prevenier, '*Utilitas communis* in the Low Countries (Thirteenth–Fifteenth Centuries): From Social Mobilisation to Legitimation of Power', in *De Bono Communi: The Discourse and Practice of the Common Good in the European City (13th–16th Centuries)*, ed. Elodie Lecuppre-Desjardin and Anne-Laure Van Bruaene, Turnhout, 2010, pp. 205–16; at p. 206.

77 Osvaldo Cavallar, 'Regulating Arms in Late Medieval and Renaissance Italian City-States', in *Privileges and Rights of Citizenship: Law and the Juridical Construction of Civil Society*, ed. Julius Kirshner and Laurent Mayali, Berkeley, CA, 2002, pp. 57–126.

78 On the vocabulary of urban status, see Hans Andersson, *Urbanisierte Ortschaften und lateinische Terminologie: Studien zur Geschichte des nordeuropäischen Städtewesens vor 1350*, Gothenburg, 1971.

79 On these terms, see Cinzio Violante, *La società milanese nell'età precomunale*, Bari, 1953, Appendix II, pp. 252–8; and, for England, Bart Lambert and W. Mark Ormrod, 'Friendly Foreigners: International Warfare, Resident Aliens and the Early History of Denization in England, c. 1250–c. 1400', *English Historical Review* 130 (2015), 1–24; esp. 8–14.

80 Marino Berengo, *L'Europa della città: Il volto della società urbana europea tra medioevo ed età moderna*, Turin, 1999, pp. 181–201. On Siena, see William M. Bowsky, 'Medieval Citizenship: The Individual and the State in the Commune of Siena, 1287–1355', *Studies in Medieval and Renaissance History* 4 (1967), 193–243; at 197–8. For an interesting survey of citizenship as a civic idea, see Maarten Prak, *Citizens without Nations: Urban Citizenship in Europe and the World, c. 1000–1789*, Cambridge, 2018.

81 '[S]e saranno più fratelli carnali et alcuno di loro diventarà cittadino et ne la città di Siena continualmente abitarà, la sua abitatione et cittadinanza a' fratelli e' quali rimangono nel contado, no possa fare', *Il costituto del Comune di Siena, volgarizzato nel MCCCIX–MCCCX*, vol. II, ed. Mahmoud Salem Elsheik, Siena, 2002, Dist. V, c. LIII, p. 174.

82 On categories of citizenship, see Giuliana Albini, '"Civitas tunc quiescit et fulget cum pollentium numero decoratur": Le concessioni di cittadinanza in età viscontea tra

pratiche e linguaggi politici', in *The Languages of Political Society: Western Europe, 14th–17th Centuries*, ed. Andrea Gamberini, Jean-Philippe Genet, and Andrea Zorzi, Rome, 2011, pp. 97–120.

83 Julius Kirshner, '*Civitas sibi faciat civem*: Bartolus of Sassoferrato's Doctrine on the Making of a Citizen', *Speculum* 48 (1973), 694–713; esp. 694–703.

84 Joseph Canning, *The Political Thought of Baldus de Ubaldis*, Cambridge, 1987, pp. 169–84.

85 *The People of Curial Avignon: A Critical Edition of the Liber Divisionis and the Matriculae of Notre Dame la Majour*, ed. Joëlle Rollo-Koster, Lewiston, NY, 2009, p. 28.

86 Giacomo Todeschini, '*Intentio e dominium* come caratteri di cittadinanza: Sulla complessità della rappresentazione dell'estraneo fra medioevo e modernità', in *Cittadinanze medievali: Dinamiche di appartenenza a un corpo comunitario*, ed. Sara Menzinger, Rome, 2017, pp. 229–45. See also, for fourteenth-century debates on the moral nature of citizenship, Janet Coleman, 'Negotiating the Medieval in the Modern: European Citizenship and Statecraft', *Transactions of the Royal Historical Society* 22 (2012), 75–93.

87 For further discussion of citizenship, see Chapter 2 below.

88 On the process in England, see Lambert and Ormrod, 'Friendly Foreigners', and W. Mark Ormrod, Bart Lambert, and Jonathan Mackman, *Immigrant England, 1300–1550*, Manchester, 2019, esp. pp. 24–9. Some 66,000 denization letters have survived, and they form the archives on which the AHRC-supported project 'England's Immigrants, 1330–1550' is based, under the leadership of Mark Ormrod: www.englandsimmigrants.com/

89 Bernard d'Alteroche, 'L'Évolution de la notion et du status juridique de l'étranger à la fin du Moyen Âge (XIe–XVe siècle)', *Revue du Nord* (2002), 227–45, esp. 231–45.

90 See the declaration by Philip V of 1318, described ibid., p. 234.

91 On France, see Jacques Dupâquier and others, *Historie de la population française*, vol. I, Paris, 1988, pp. 268–311.

92 '[S]ecundum quod pormitebant [sic] et secundum quod ordinatum fuerat per commune', Albini, '"Civitas tunc quiescit et fulget cum pollentium numero decoratur"', p. 98, n. 8.

93 The opposition between the European city, born in the Middle Ages, and the 'Asiatic' one is both explicit and implicit throughout Max Weber, *The City*, trans. Don Martindale and Gertrud Neuwirth, New York, 1958, and esp. in chapters 1 and 2. On European views of the eastern city, see Michael Gilsenan, *Imagined Cities of the East: An Inaugural Lecture Delivered before the University of Oxford on 27 May 1985*, Oxford, 1986; also André Raymond, 'Islamic City, Arab City: Orientalist Myths and Recent Views', *British Journal of Middle Eastern Studies* 21 (1994), 3–18; and Patrick Lantschner, 'Fragmented Cities in the Later Middle Ages: Italy and the Near East Compared', *English Historical Review* 130 (2015), 546–82; 548–9. On theories of urban foundations, see Hugh Kennedy, 'How to Found an Islamic City', in *Cities, Texts and Social Networks, 400–1500*, ed. Caroline Goodson, Anne E. Lester, and Carol Symes, Farnham, 2010, pp. 45–63.

94 On the intellectual lineages of such reflection on medieval cities in the early twentieth century, see Marc Boone, 'Cities in Late Medieval Europe: The Promise and Curse of Modernity', *Urban History* 39 (2012), 329–49.

95 Jacques Le Goff, *Time, Work and Culture in the Middle Ages*, trans. Arthur Goldhammer, Chicago, 1982; and his *The Birth of Purgatory*, trans. Arthur Goldhammer, Chicago, 1984. Le Goff's theses have inspired much research and scrutiny, and have been reformulated, but they still offer influential approaches to the study of medieval cities.

96 Ian P. Wei, *Intellectual Culture in Medieval Paris: Theologians and the University, c. 1100–1330*, Cambridge, 2012, chapter 6. See, on the link between commercialisation and charity, Adam J. Davis, *The Medieval Economy of Salvation: Charity, Commerce, and the Rise of the Hospital*, Ithaca, NY, 2019.

97 See the discussion of presentism in the forum assembled in the Viewpoint section of *Past and Present* 234 (2017), 213–89; esp. Miri Rubin, 'Presentism's Useful Anachronisms', 236–44.

98 On dialogue with the past, see Paul Strohm, *Theory and the Premodern Text*, Minneapolis, 2000, esp. 'What Can We Know about Chaucer That He Didn't Know about Himself?', pp. 165–81.

99 On the effect of perceived well-being on political and social attitudes in modern France, see Robert Castel, *La Montée des incertitudes: Travail, protections, statut de l'individu*, Paris, 2009. On historical discussions of trust, see László Kontler and Mark Somos (eds.), *Trust and Happiness in the History of European Political Thought*, Leiden, 2017.

100 For a classic, critically rich exploration of space, see Doreen Massey, *Space, Place, and Gender*, Minneapolis, 1994; on 'home', see the General Introduction.

101 The Italian scholarship on cities and strangers is particularly rich, as the notes that follow and the Bibliography show. For some recent scholarship on migration and the arrival of strangers in cities, which I have found useful, see Cédric Quertier, Roxane Chilà, and Nicolas Pluchot (eds.), *'Arriver' en ville: Les migrants en milieu urbain au Moyen Âge*, Paris, 2013; Donatella Calabi and Paola Lanaro (eds.), *La città italiana e i luoghi degli stranieri XIV–XVIII secolo*, Rome, 1998; Simonetta Cavaciocchi (ed.), *Le migrazioni in Europa secc. XIII–XVIII: Atti della Venticinquesima Settimana di Studi, 3–8 maggio 1993*, Florence, 1994; *Stranieri e forestieri nella Marca dei secc. XIV–XVI: Atti del Convegno di Studi Maceratesi*, Macerata, 1996; Reinhold C. Mueller, *Immigrazione e cittadinanza nella Venezia medievale*, Rome, 2010; and Bottin and Calabi (eds.), *Les Étrangers dans la ville*.

102 For Hungary, the surviving material, archival and archaeological, has now been brought together in Katalin Szende, *Trust, Authority, and the Written Word in the Royal Towns of Medieval Hungary*, Turnhout, 2018.

103 Gérard Noiriel, *Le Creuset français: Histoire de l'immigration, XIXe–XXe siècles*, Paris, 1988, printed in English as *The French Melting Pot: Immigration, Citizenship, and National Identity*, trans. Geoffroy de Laforcade, Minneapolis, 1996. See also Gérard Noiriel, *Immigration, antisémitisme et racisme en France (XIXe–XXe): Discours publics, humiliations privées*, Paris, 2007.

104 Oscar Handlin, *The Uprooted: The Epic Story of the Great Migrations That Made the American People*, New York, 1951, p. 1. See also a different approach in Herbert J. Gans, *Urban Villagers: Group and Class in the Life of Italian-Americans*, New York, 1962.

105 Erik Mathison, *The Loyal Republic: Traitors, Slaves, and the Remaking of Citizenship in Civil War America*, Chapel Hill, NC, 2018, esp. Introduction and chapter 1; Stephen

Kantrowicz, *More than Freedom: Fighting for Black Citizenship in a White Republic, 1829–1889*, New York, 2012, chapter 1.

106 Patrick Lantschner has rightly warned against over-reliance on structures and institutions, and that includes the statutes they formulated, as indicators of the reality of urban life: Lantschner, 'Fragmented Cities', 564–5.

107 The concept is explored in several contexts throughout Gilles Deleuze and Félix Guattari, *A Thousand Plateaus: Capitalism and Schizophrenia*, trans. Brian Massumi, London, 2013; see definition at pp. 7–8. It is most effectively introduced in Ben Jervis, *Assemblage Thought and Archaeology*, London, 2018, especially in chapter 1. On the uses of *assemblage* in geography, see Martin Müller, 'Assemblages and Actor-Networks: Rethinking Socio-Material Power, Politics and Space', *Geography Compass* 9 (2015), 27–41.

108 Central to thinking about social categories in their contingent fluidity is Bruno Latour, *Reassembling the Social: An Introduction to Actor-Network-Theory*, Oxford, 2005.

109 For an exploration of the emotions in an urban context, see Elodie Lecuppre-Desjardin and Anne-Laure Van Bruaene (eds.), *Emotions in the Heart of the City (14th–16th Century)*, Turnhout, 2005.

110 See the question posed in Patrick Gilli and Enrica Salvatori, 'Introduction: L'Autonomie et l'identité de la ville: Une question sociale?', in *Les Identités urbaines au Moyen Âge: Regards sur les villes du Midi français. Actes du colloque de Montpellier 8–9 décembre 2011*, Turnhout, 2014, pp. 1–5, and other articles in the collection. On civic religion, see André Vauchez (ed.), *La Religion civique à l'époque médiévale et moderne (chrétienté et islam)*, Rome, 1995.

111 See Jervis, *Assemblage Thought*, chapter 4, on 'Assemblage Urbanism'.

112 On the design of medieval cities, see Keith D. Lilley, *City and Cosmos: The Medieval World in Urban Form*, London, 2009.

113 On the internal division of Metz, see Robert Lug, 'Politique et littérature à Metz autour de la Guerre des Amis (1231–1234): Le témoignage du Chansonnier de Saint-Germain-des-Prés', in *Lettres, musique et société en Lorraine médiévale: Autour du Tournoi de Chauvency (Ms. Oxford Bodleian Douce 308)*, ed. Mireille Chazan and Nancy Freeman Regalado, Geneva, 2012, pp. 451–83, at pp. 458–63.

114 Roberta Gilchrist, *Norwich Cathedral Close: The Evolution of the English Cathedral Landscape*, Woodbridge, 2015, esp. chapters 3 and 6.

115 'As conglomerations of multiple political units and bases of organization – urban government, neighbourhood organizations, guilds, ecclesiastical institutions, and political associations, as well as external agencies – cities gave rise to a polycentric order in which political relations were often multi-faceted and shifting', Lantschner, *The Logic of Political Conflict in Medieval Cities*, p. 2. On conflict in towns of a zone of conquest, see Spencer Dimmock, 'Social Conflict in Welsh Towns c. 1280–1530', in *Urban Culture in Medieval Wales*, ed. Helen Fulton, Cardiff, 2012, pp. 117–35.

116 Sanjay Subrahmanyam, *Three Ways to Be Alien: Travails and Encounters in the Early Modern World*, Waltham, MA, 2011; see also Cerutti, *Étrangers*, chapter 2.

117 William C. Jordan, *The Great Famine: Northern Europe in the Early Fourteenth Century*, Princeton, 1996.

118 Bruce M. S. Campbell, *The Great Transition: Climate, Disease and Society in the Late Medieval World*, Cambridge, 2016.

119 Samuel K. Cohn, Jr, *Lust for Liberty: The Politics of Social Revolt in Medieval Europe, 1200–1425: Italy, France, and Flanders*, Cambridge, MA, 2006, pp. 58–70. On the effect of such developments on the language of politics, see Jan Dumolyn and Jelle Haemers, '*Takehan, Cokerulle*, and *Mutemaque*: Naming Collective Action in the Later Medieval Low Countries', in *The Routledge History Handbook of Medieval Revolt*, ed. Justine Firnhaber-Baker and Dirk Schoenaers, London, 2017, pp. 39–54.

120 Hartmann Schedel, *Chronicle of the World: The Complete and Annotated Nuremberg Chronicle of 1493*, intro. Stephan Füssel, Cologne: Taschen, 2001. On the pervasive use of cityscapes in Netherlandish art of the fifteenth and sixteenth centuries, see Katrien Lichtert, Jan Dumolyn, and Maximiliaan P. J. Martens, 'Images, Maps, Texts: Reading the Meanings of the Later Medieval and Early Modern City', in *Portraits of the City: Representing Urban Space in Later Medieval and Early Modern Europe*, ed. Katrien Lichtert, Jan Dumolyn, and Maximiliaan P. J. Martens, Turnhout, 2014, pp. 1–8.

2 STRANGERS INTO NEIGHBOURS

1 W. H. Auden, *The Shield of Achilles*, London, 1955, at p. 67.

2 For a useful introduction to the distribution and types of towns and cities, see Nicholas, *Urban Europe 1100–1700*, chapter 1.

3 Gervase Rosser, *The Art of Solidarity in the Middle Ages: Guilds in England 1250–1550*, Oxford, 2015; Catherine Vincent, *Les Confréries médiévales dans le royaume de France, XIIIe–Xve siècle*, Paris, 1994. On the role of a confraternity in the life of a judge from Brescia, see James M. Powell, *Albertanus of Brescia: The Pursuit of Happiness in the Early Thirteenth Century*, Philadelphia, 1992, chapter 5.

4 Brunetto Latini, *The Book of the Treasure*, pp. 351–2:

une qui sont en France & as autres païs, qui sont sommis a la seignorie des rois & des autres princes perpetuel qui vendent les provestés & les baillent a ciaus qui plus les chacent (poi gradent ne sa bonté ne le profit de ces borgiois) … L'autre est en Ytalie, que li citain et li borgois & les chomunités de villes exlissent lor poesté & lor seignor tel come il cuident qu'il soit meillor & plus profitable au comun pro de la ville & de tos ses subjés.

Brunetto Latini, *Li Livres dou Tresor*, c. 73, pp. 363–4.

5 T. H. Lloyd, *The English Wool Trade in the Middle Ages*, Cambridge, 1977, pp. 45–56. On the status of foreign merchants, see Keechang Kim, *Aliens in Medieval Law: The Origins of Medieval Citizenship*, Cambridge, 2000, pp. 9–13. On royal involvement in the regulation of trade, see James Davis, *Medieval Market Morality: Life, Law and Ethics in the English Marketplace, 1200–1500*, Cambridge, 2012, pp. 141–4.

6 'quod consuetudinem quadraginta dierum ad commorandum in civitate penitus ignorabant', *Liber custumarum*, ed. Henry Thomas Riley, London, 1860, Kraus reprint 1967, p. 71.

7 Kim, *Aliens in Medieval Law*, pp. 37–41. On 'merchant strangers', see Ormrod, Lambert, and Mackman, *Immigrant England, 1300–1550*, pp. 143–6.

8 Jan Dumolyn and Milan Pajic, 'Enemies of the Count and of the City: The Collective Exile of Rebels in Fourteenth-Century Flanders', *The Legal History Review* 84 (2016), 461–501; Bart Lambert and Milan Pajic, 'Drapery in Exile: Edward III, Colchester and the Flemings', *History: The Journal of the Historical Association* 99(2014), 733–53.

9 Lambert and Ormrod, 'Friendly Foreigners', 1–24; and Ormrod, Lambert, and Mackman, *Immigrant England, 1300–1550*, pp. 18–29. On the banishment from Flanders, see Dumolyn and Pajic, 'Enemies of the Count and of the City'; Claudine Billot, 'L'Assimilation des étrangers dans le royaume de France aux XIVe et XVe siècle', *Revue historique* 107 (1983), 273–96, and Milan Pajic, *Flemish Textile Workers in England, 1331–1400: Immigration, Integration and Economic Development*, Cambridge, 2020, chapter 1.

10 W. Mark Ormrod and Jonathan Mackman, 'Resident Aliens in Later Medieval England: Sources, Contexts, and Debates', in *Resident Aliens in Later Medieval England*, ed. W. Mark Ormrod, Nicola McDonald, and Craig Taylor, Turnhout, 2017, pp. 3–31. Readers may consult such letters at www.englandsimmigrants.com/

11 Maria del Carmen Carlé, 'Mercaderes en Castilla (1252–1512)', *Cuadernos de Historia de España* 21–2 (1954), 146–328; at 231.

12 James M. Murray, *Bruges, Cradle of Capitalism, 1280–1390*, Cambridge, 2005, pp. 223–6.

13 For central Europe, see Szende, '*Iure Theutonico?*', 1–20.

14 Sofia Gustafsson, 'German Influence in Swedish Medieval Towns: Reflections upon the Time-Bound Historiography of the Twentieth Century', in *Guilds, Towns and Cultural Transmission in the North, 1300–1500*, ed. Lars Bisgaard, Lars Boje Mortensen, and Tom Pettitt, Odense, 2013, pp. 109–29; at pp. 110–11.

15 Benedykt Zientara, 'Foreigners in Poland in the 10th–15th Centuries: Their Role in the Opinion of the Polish Medieval Community', *Acta Poloniae Historica* 29 (1974), 5–27.

16 Szende, *Trust, Authority, and the Written Word*, pp. 27–33.

17 Martyn Rady, 'The Government of Medieval Buda', in *Medieval Buda in Context*, ed. Balázs Nagy, Martyn Rady, Katalin Szende, and András Vadas, Leiden, 2016, pp. 301–21; at pp. 312–13. On language use, see Szende, *Trust, Authority, and the Written Word*, pp. 209–17.

18 Katalin Szende, 'Power and Identity: Royal Privileges to the Towns of Medieval Hungary in the Thirteenth Century', *Urban Liberties and Civic Participation from the Middle Ages to Modern Times*, ed. Michel Pauly and Alexander Lee, Trier, 2015, pp. 27–67; at pp. 56–9. See also Szende, *Trust, Authority, and the Written Word*, pp. 135–6.

19 Andrzej Janaczek, 'Ethnicity, Religious Disparity and the Formation of the Multicultural Society of Red Ruthenia in the Late Middle Ages', in *On the Frontier of Latin Europe: Integration and Segregation in Red Ruthenia, 1350–1600*, ed. Andrzej Janaczek and Thomas Wünsch, Warsaw, 2004, pp. 15–45; esp. 15–21.

20 Kozubska-Andrusiv, ' *"Propter disparitatem linguae"* ', pp. 51–66; at pp. 51–3. See also her 'Comparable Aspects in Urban Development: Kievan Rus and the European Middle Ages', in *Medieval East Central Europe in a Comparative Perspective: From Frontier Zones to Lands in Focus*, ed. Gerhard Jaritz and Katalin Szende, Abingdon, 2016, pp. 139–56.

21 Robin Frame, *Colonial Ireland 1169–1389*, Dublin, 2012, chapter 1, and pp. 102–3. See the location www.ria.ie/irish-historic-towns-atlas-online-kilkenny

22 Matthew Frank Stevens, *Urban assimilation in Post-Conquest Wales: Ethnicity, Gender and Economy in Ruthin, 1282–1348*, Cardiff, 2010, pp. 7–20.

23 Ibid., pp. 39–40.

24 Joëlle Rollo-Koster, '*Mercator Florentinensis* and Others: Immigration in Papal Avignon', in *Urban and Rural Communities in Medieval France: Provence and Languedoc, 1000–1500*, ed. Kathryn Reyerson and John Drendel, Leiden, 1998, pp. 73–100, with helpful tables.

25 Anna Esposito, 'Forestiere e straniere a Roma tra '400 e primo '500', http://romatrepress.uniroma3.it/ojs/index.php/forestieri/article/view/1585

26 This volume develops the concept: Gherardo Ortalli, Oliver Jens Schmitt, and Ermanno Orlando (eds.), *Il Commonwealth Veneziano tra 1204 e la fine della repubblica: Identità e peculiarità*, Venice, 2015. Even more modest empires, such as that of the Plantagenets, produced diversity: see Ormrod, Lambert, and Mackman, *Immigrant England, 1300–1550*, pp. 14–18.

27 Ersie C. Burke, *The Greeks of Venice: Immigration, Settlement, and Integration*, Turnhout, 2016.

28 Fabian Kümmeler, 'The World in a Village: Foreigners and Newcomers on Late Medieval Korčula', in *Towns and Cities of the Croatian Middle Ages: The City and the Newcomers*, ed. Irena Benyovski Latin and Zrinka Pešorda Vardić, Zagreb, 2019, forthcoming.

29 For a discussion of the identities that co-existed in the polities created by Europeans in Syria/Palestine, see James G. Schryver, 'Identities in the Crusader East', in *Mediterranean Identities in the Premodern Era: Entrepôts, Islands, Empires*, ed. John Watkins and Kathryn L. Reyerson, Farnham, 2014, pp. 173–89.

30 De Clercq et al., 'Ballasting the Hanse', 710–36.

31 This affair has been much illuminated thanks to the findings presented in Sebastian Sobecki, '"The writyng of this tretys": Margery Kempe's Son and the Authorship of Her Book', *Studies in the Age of Chaucer* 37 (2015), 257–83; see the document at 269. On Hanseatic culture, see Müller, 'Network of the Centres', pp. 145–87.

32 Gabriella Piccinni and Lucia Travaini, *Il Libro de Pellegrino (Siena 1382–1446): Affari, uomini, monete nell'Ospedale di Santa Maria della Scala*, Naples, 2003. A whole volume of statutes regarding pilgrims was created by the commune of Siena, *Statuti senesi scritti in volgare ne' secoli XIII e XIV*, vol. III, ed. Luciano Banchi, Bologna, 1877. On the integration of pilgrims into urban life, see the essays in Giampaolo Cagnin, *Pellegrini e vie del pellegrinaggio a Treviso nel medioevo (secoli XII–XV)*, Verona, 2000. See also Heers, *La Ville au Moyen Âge*, pp. 160–2.

33 Cagnin, *Pellegrini e vie del pellegrinaggio*, pp. 157–78.

34 Federico Botana, *The Works of Mercy in Italian Art (c. 1050–c. 1400)*, Turnhout, 2011, pp. 28–48, as the inscription 'open the door to pilgrims' ('peregrinis hostiam pandas') explains; see also figures 8, 9, and 16.

35 J. M. Fletcher, 'The Organisation of the Supply of Food and Drink to the Medieval Oxford Colleges', in *Università in Europa: Le istituzioni universitarie dal Medio Evo ai nostri giorni; strutture, organizzazione, funzionamento. Atti del Convegno Internazionale di Studi, Milazzo 28 Settembre – 2 Ottobre 1993*, ed. Andrea Romano, Soveria Mannelli, 1995, pp. 199–211.

36 Hilde De Ridder-Symoens, 'Mobility', in *A History of the University in Europe*, vol. I: *Universities in the Middle Ages*, ed. Hilde De Ridder-Symoens, Cambridge, 1992, pp. 280–304; Ian Wei, 'Scholars and Travel in the Twelfth and Thirteenth Centuries', in *Freedom of Movement in the Middle Ages: Proceedings of the 2003 Harlaxton Symposium*, ed. Peregrine Horden, Donnington, 2007, pp. 73–85.

37 On students in nations, Jacques Verger, 'Le nazioni studentesche a Parigi nel Medio Evo: Qualche osservazione', in *Comunità forestiere e 'nationes' nell'Europa dei secoli XIII–XVI*, ed. Giovanna Petti Balbi, Naples, 2001, pp. 3–10. On the social life of the nations of the University of Paris, see William J. Courtenay, *Rituals for the Dead: Religion and Community in the Medieval University of Paris*, South Bend, IN, 2019, esp. chapter 3.

38 'Maryners se lowent a lour mestre, et ja ascunes de eux senissent hors sauntz coinge, et senyueront, et fount conteks, et ascunes de ex sont Nafretz; le mestre nest pas tenuz a lour faire garir, ne les pourveyer de rien, mes il les pust bien mettre hors, et lower vn aultre en Noun de lui ... Mes si le mestre lem voie en ascune seruise ... Il doit estre garry et sauuetz sur les coustez de la Nieff', *The Oak Book of Southampton of c. A.D. 1300*, vol. II, ed. P. Studer, Southampton, 1911, c. 6, p. 62. See Erik Spindler, 'Between Sea and City: Portable Communities in Late Medieval London and Bruges', in *London and Beyond: Essays in Honour of Derek Keene*, ed. Matthew Davies and James A. Galloway, London, 2012, pp. 181–99, and Maryanne Kowaleski, '"Alien" Encounters in the Maritime World of Medieval England', *Medieval Encounters* 13 (2007), 96–121.

39 *Statuti Bonacolsiani*, ed. Ettore Dezza, Anna Maria Lorenzoni, and Mario Vaini, Mantua, 2002, c. 42, pp. 340–1.

40 'gli statuti ... sono naturalmente le prime fonti con le quali confrontarsi per tratteggiare il regime cui è sottoposto lo straniero nelle nostre città', M. Ascheri, 'Lo straniero nella legislazione e nella letteratura giuridica del Tre-Quattrocento: Un primo approccio', in *Forestieri e stranieri nella città basso-medievali*, Florence, 1987, pp. 7–18.

41 *The Charters of the Borough of Cambridge*, Frederic William Maitland and Mary Bateson, Cambridge, 1901, p. ix. Similarly, on statutes and urban autonomy, see Giorgio Chittolini, 'Statuti e autonomie urbane: Introduzione', in *Statuti, città, territori in Italia e Germania tra Medioevo ed età moderna*, ed. Giorgio Chittolini and Dietmar Willoweit, Bologna, 1991, pp. 7–45; esp. pp. 7–21.

42 Mario Ascheri, 'Statutory Law of Italian Cities from Middle Ages to Early Modern', in *Von der Ordnung zur Norm: Statuten in Mittelalter und Früher Neuzeit*, ed. Gisela Drossbach, Paderborn, 2010, pp. 201–16, supplies excellent references to sources and discussion of urban statutes. For a discussion of the customs underlying the 1277 statutes of Ragusa/Dubrovnik, see Nella Lonza, 'The Statute of Dubrovnik of 1272: Between Legal Code and Political Symbol', in *The Statute of Dubrovnik 1271 = Liber statutorum civitatis Ragusii compositus anno MCCLXXII*, trans. Vesna Rimać and ed. Nella Lonza, Dubrovnik, 2012, pp. 7–25.

43 Chris Wickham, *Courts and Conflict in Twelfth-Century Tuscany*, Oxford, 2003, pp. 116–18.

44 See, for example, the works of Boncampagno of Signa: Daniela Goldin Folena, 'Il punto su Boncampagno da Signa', in *Il Pensiero e l'opera di Boncampagno da Signa*, ed. Massimo Baldini, Florence, 2002, pp. 9–22; or the annotated statutes of Toulouse, written a

decade after their promulgation: Henri Gilles, *Les Coutumes de Toulouse (1286) et leur premier commentaire (1296)*, ed. Henri Gilles, Toulouse, 1969.

45 Mario Sbriccoli, *L'interpretazione dello statuto: Contributo allo studio della funzione dei giuristi nell'età comunale*, Milan, 1969. There was a rush of *consilia*, legal opinions on statutes and on matters of citizenship, in the fourteenth century: Diego Quaglioni, 'The Legal Definition of Citizenship in the Late Middle Ages', in *City States in Classical Antiquity and Medieval Italy*, ed. Anthony Molho, Kurt Raaflaub, and Julia Emlen, Stuttgart, 1991, pp. 155–67. On *consilia* in general, see Ingrid Baumgärtner (ed.), *Consilia im späten Mittelalter: Zum historischen Aussagwert einer Quellengattung*, Sigmaringen, 1995.

46 Chittolini, 'Statuti e autonomie', p. 15.

47 As suggested recently in Etienne Anheim, Philippe Bernardi, Maëlle Ramage, and Valérie Theis, 'La Notion de *libri statutorum*: "Tribut philologique" ou réalité documentaire? Les statuts communaux du Moyen Âge conservés pour l'actuel département de Vaucluse', *Mélanges de l'École française de Rome. Moyen Âge* 126/2 (2014), 447–60.

48 Duccio Balestracci, 'La Valdelsa e i suoi statuti: Alcune riflessioni', *Miscellanea storica della Valdelsa* 15 (1999), 99–110; Alessandro Dani, *Gli statuti dei comuni della repubblica di Siena (secoli XIII–XV): Profilo di una cultura communitaria*, Monteriggioni, 2015; Philippe Bernardi and Didier Boisseuil, 'Les Statuts de 1380 de Méthamis (Vaucluse)', *Histoire et sociétés rurales* 26 (2006), 95–127. On the right to make statutes, see Claudia Storti Storchi, 'Appunti in tema di "potestas condendi statuta"', in *Statuti città territori in Italia e Germania tra medioevo e età moderna*, ed. Giorgio Chittolini and Dietmar Willoweit, Bologna, 1991, pp. 319–43. On civic aspects of rural life, see Reynolds, *Kingdoms and Communities*, pp. 138–54.

49 On Siena, see Valeria Capelli and Andrea Giorgi, 'Gli statuti del Comune di Siena fino allo "Statuto del Buongoverno" (secoli XIII–XIV)', *Mélanges de l'École francçise de Rome. Moyen Âge* 126/2 (2014), 1–22.

50 Ulrich Simon, 'Das Lübecker Niederstadtbuch: Seine Charakterisierung über das Jahr 1400 hinaus', in *Gelebte Normen im urbanen Raum? Zur sozial- und kulturgeschichtlichen Analyse rechtlicher Quellen in Städten des Hanseraums (13. bis 16. Jahrhundert)*, ed. Hanno Brand, Sven Rabeler, and Harm von Seggern, Hilversum, 2014, pp. 63–82; p. 65.

51 See Anheim et al., 'La Notion', 453.

52 *I frammenti epigrafici degli statuti di Ferrara del 1173 venuti in luce nella cattedrale*, ed. Adriano Franceschini, Ferrara, 1969, pp. 11–12.

53 The city of Perugia laid out a procedure for consultation leading to 'reformationes', and, regarding their publication, see *Statuto del Comune di Perugia del 1279*, vol. I, ed. Severino Caprioli, Perugia, 1996, c. 27, p. 29.

54 'lecto et audito ipso capitulo magna divisio orta est in ipso populo', Anonymous Ghibelline of Piacenza, 'Chronicon de rebus in Italia gestis', in *Chronicon Placentium et Chronicon de rebus in Italia gestis*, ed. J. L. A. Huillard-Breholles, Paris, 1856, pp. 107–390; at p. 224. I am grateful to Lorenzo Caravaggi, who pointed this instance out to me. On the technologies for the dissemination of princely law for the cities of Hainaut, see Jean-Marie Cauchies, *La Législation princière pour le comté de Hainaut (ducs de Bourgogne et premiers Habsbourg, 1427–1506)*, Brussels, 1982, pp. 212–38. The ordinances of London

were proclaimed periodically, probably when each mayor assumed office, as on 11 November 1354, *Calendar of Letter-Books Preserved among the Archives of the Corporation of the City of London at the Guildhall: Letter-Book G,* ed. Reginald R. Sharpe, London, 1905, p. 33.

55 'Quante volte, del tempo che rimembre,/ legge, moneta, officio e costume/ hai tu mutato e rinovato membre!' https://digitaldante.columbia.edu/dante/divine-comedy/purgatorio/purgatorio-6/

56 *Statuti notarili di Bergamo (secolo XIII),* ed. Giuseppe Scarazzini, Rome, 1977. Notaries brought their personal experience of citizens to bear upon the work of authenticating documents: Étienne Hubert, 'Qui est qui? L'individu inconnu dans la cite médiévale', *Archivio storico italiano* 175 (2017), 483–515; esp. 489–91.

57 'Ut pauperes persone et alie persone, gramaticam nescientes et alii qui voluerint possint ipsum videre et copiam exinde sumere', Mario Ascheri, 'Il Costituto di Siena: Sintesi di una cultura giuridico-politica e fondamento del "Buongoverno"', in *Il costituto del Comune di Siena,* vol. II, pp. 24–57, at p. 24. On the development of statutes in the vernacular, see Federigo Bambi, 'Alle origini del volgare del diritto: La lingua degli statuti di Toscana tra XII e XIV secolo', *Mélanges de l'École française de Rome. Moyen Âge* 126 (2014), 1–8; Duccio Balestracci, *Il potere e la parola: Guida al Costituto volgarizzato di Siena (1309–1310),* Siena, 2011, pp. 79–81. See, on the use of Occitan in statutes from eastern Languedoc, Nicolas Leroy, '*Carta, consuetudines, statuta...* Langue et conservation des statuts municipaux en Languedoc', *Mélanges de l'École française de Rome* 126/2 (2014), 567–80.

58 'Sono stati letti e publicati li soprascritti statuti per me Parisio Beto notaro di Porlezza, de mandato e impositione del signor Iacomazzo Ferraro de Vigevano, podestà della detta pieve di Porlezza, sopra la piazza del commune', *Statuti dei Laghi di Como e di Lugano dei secoli XIII e XIV,* vol. II, ed. Emilio Anderloni and A. Lazzati, Milan, 1915, c. 160, p. 359.

59 See, for example, *Das älteste Rostocker Stadtbuch (etwa 1254–1275),* ed. Hildegard Thierfelder, Göttingen, 1967; also *Das zweite Wismarsche Stadtbuch 1272–1297,* ed. Lotte Knabe, Weimar, 2 vols., 1966, and *Das älteste Greifswalder Stadtbuch (1291–1332),* ed. Dietrick W. Poeck, Cologne, 2000, with a very good introduction to the genre on pp. xxiv–lxxiii.

60 On trends in the illumination of urban statutes, see Robert Gibbs, 'The 13th- and 14th-Century Illuminated Statutes of Bologna in Their Social-Political Context', in *Von der Ordnung zur Norm: Statuten in Mittelalter und Früher Neuzeit,* ed. Gisela Drossbach, Paderborn, 2010, pp. 183–200.

61 For a summary of their provisions, see Dante Cecchi, 'Disposizioni statuarie sugli stranieri e sui forestieri', in *Stranieri e forestieri nella Marca dei secc. XIV–XVI: Atti del 30 convegno di studi maceratesi, Macerata, 19–20 novembre 1994,* Macerata, 1996, pp. 29–91; at pp. 36–9.

62 Lonza, 'The Statute of Dubrovnik of 1272'. This was true in other regions: after the Norman Conquest, the Laws of Breteuil offered the model for English towns, see Lilley, *City and Cosmos,* pp. 146–9; later, Bristol and London provided the model for English and Irish towns.

63 Katalin Szende, '*Iure Theutonico?*', 14–18.

64 Szende, *Trust, Authority and the Written Word*, pp. 35–6. For a discussion of the applicabil-
ity of the term 'statute' to the town laws of German cities, see Felicitas Schmieder,
'Stadtstatuten deutscher Städte? Einige Überlegungen im europäischen Vergleich', in
Von der Ordnung zur Norm: Statuten in Mittelalter und Früher Neuzeit, ed. Gisela Drossbach,
Paderborn, 2010, pp. 217–23; see also comment by Hans-Georg Hermann, pp. 225–8.

65 *Statuta comunis et populi civitatis Camerini (1424)*, ed. Fabrizio Ciapparoni, Naples, 1977,
Lib. III, rubrica 81, p. 10. On the sale of salt, see also *The Statute of Dubrovnik*, Lib. VI,
c. xvi, p. 234.

66 *Calendar of Ancient Records of Dublin in the Possession of the Municipal Corporation of that City*,
vol. I, ed. John T. Gilbert, Dublin, 1889, document IV, c. 1 4, p. 4. For a royal inquisition
in Oxford, related to a marketplace for strangers, see *Munimenta Civitatis Oxonie*, ed.
H. E. Salter, Devizes, 1920, no. 34, pp. 31–4.

67 The rubric is: 'De pena merchatoris forensic ementis vel vendentis (merchationes) cum
aliquot mercatore forense mercationem latam de foris', *Statuti di Bologna dell'anno 1288*,
vol. I, ed. Gina Fasoli and Pietro Sella, Vatican City, 1937, Book IV, rubric 72, p. 231.

68 'non exbannire vel exbanniri facere aliquam personam castri et curtis Sancti Geminiani
pro aliquo vel aliquibus forensibus pro avere vel pecunia vel aliquo debito', *Lo statuto di
San Gimignano del 1255*, ed. Silvia Diacciatti and Lorenzo Tanzini, Florence, 2016, II. 34,
p. 82. Similar provisions to protect locals from business or bodily harm by foreigners
were made by the commune of Valréas in 1297, Archives du département de Vaucluse.
Statuts de la commune de Valréas 1231, Serie A A 6 des A C Grillon, fols. 2v–3r. I am
grateful to Étienne Anheim and Valérie Theis for sharing with me a digital version of
these statutes.

69 *Statuto di Forlì*, ed. Evelina Rinaldi, Milan, 1913, c. 67, pp. 98–9.

70 On the choices of town leaders in the face of the growing diversity of urban populations,
see the introduction by Donatella Calabi and Paola Lanaro to their *La città italiana*,
pp. xi–xiii.

71 *Statuti pistoiesi del secolo XIII, Studi e testi*, vol. II, ed. Renzo Nelli and Giuliano Pinto,
Pistoia, 2002, Lib. 2, no. 151, p. 119.

72 On the typology of drinking, eating, and lodging establishments, see Peter Clark, *The
English Alehouse: A Social History, 1200–1830*, Harlow, 1983, esp. chapters 1–3. On
medieval inns, see Julian Munby, 'Zacharias's: A 14th-Century Oxford New Inn and
the Origins of the Medieval Urban Inn', *Oxoniensia* 57 (1992), 245–309; and, with
attention to gender, see Barbara A. Hanawalt, 'The Host, the Law, and the Ambiguous
Space of Medieval London Taverns', in *'Of Good and Ill Repute': Gender and Social Control
in Medieval England*, New York, 1998, pp. 104–23. See also Hans Conrad Peyer, *Von der
Gastfreundschaft zum Gasthaus: Studien zur Gastlichkeit im Mittelalter*, Hanover, 1987.

73 'Item, si è deliberato et ordinato che niuna persona della detta Valle debba tenere, nè
recettare, nè dar casa ad alcun forastiero, se non darà bon conto et sigurtà qualche
persona che sii della detta Valle, la qual sigurtà deve essere almeno di lire venticinque
della nostra moneta', *Statuti dei Laghi di Como e di Lugano*, c. 52, p. 274. See also the
statutes of Malamocco (1351–60), *Statuti della Laguna Veneta dei secoli XIV–XVI*, ed.

Gherardo Ortalli, Monica Pasqualetto, and Alessandra Rizzi, Rome, 1989, c. 28, p. 92. The Fuero of Úbeda, granted by the kings of Castile between 1200 and 1225, laid even more responsibilities on the shoulders of those offering hospitality in taverns or homes: *Fuero de Úbeda*, ed. Juan Guttiérrez Cuadrado, and with studies by Mariano Peset and Juan Guttiérrez Cuadrado, Valencia, 1979, title 69, pp. 391–2.

74 Foreigners in London were meant to stay no longer than a night; if the stay was longer, the host was 'bound' in surety for the foreigner and was fined. See *Munimenta Gildhallæ Londoniensis: Liber albus, Liber custumarum, et Liber Horn*, vol. III, ed. Henry Thomas Riley, London, 1859, p. 86. Yet people in transit found useful employment in port taverns: see William Chester Jordan, *From England to France: Felony and Exile in the High Middle Ages*, Princeton, NJ, 2015, pp. 91–3.

75 *Die Statuten der Reichsstadt Muelhausen in Thüringen*, ed. Wolfgang Weber and Gerhard Lingelbach, Cologne, 2005, no. 38, p. 14.

76 'quod nulla persona civitatis Pistorii vel districtus vendat, obliget, pignoret, locet vel aliquot modo alienet terras sive possessiones vel aliquas res immobiles alicui persone vel loco, qui non sit de civitate Pistorii vel districtu', in *Statuti pistoiesi del secolo XIII*, c. 30, p. 114.

77 'Keÿn purger In ofner stadt schol seyn gut einem fremden verkauffen', *Das Ofner Stadtrecht: Eine deutschsprachige Rechtssammlung des 15. Jahrhunderts aus Ungarn*, ed. Karl Mollay, Budapest, 1959, Book 3, c. 200, p. 128.

78 'E le bestie minute de'detti forestieri, le quali pasturasseno ne la cerbaja del decto Commune, per ciascheduna e ciascheduno capo il signore or guardian di qualle sia condapnato in denari dodici; e per ciaschuna bestia grossa in soldi due', *Statuti del Comune di Cecina nel 1409*, ed. Pietro Fanfani, Florence, 1857, c. CX, p. 42.

79 'nullus forensis qui non sit habitator terre Montis Boni audeat nec presumat pastorizare cum bestiis tam grossis quam minutis infra confines dicte terre', *Lo Statuto di Montebuono in Sabina del 1437*, with contributions by Mario Ascheri, Tersilio Leggio, and Sandro Notari, and ed. Alda Spotti, Rome, 2011, c. 85, p. 99.

80 Denis Menjot, 'Introduction: Les gens venus d'ailleurs dans les villes médiévales: Quelques acquis de la recherche', in *'Arriver' en ville: Les migrants en milieu urbain au Moyen Âge*, ed. Cédric Quertier, Roxane Chilà, and Nicolas Pluchot, Paris, 2013, pp. 15–29; at p. 19. On modes of identification of non-citizens, see Hubert, 'Qui est qui?'. For the distribution of taxed aliens in English counties, see Ormrod, Lambert, and Mackman, *Immigrant England, 1300–1550*, table 2, p. 62.

81 Étienne Hubert, *'Una et eadem persona sive aliae personae.* Certifier l'identité dans une société mobile (à propos de l'Italie communale)', in *'Arriver' en ville: Les migrants en milieu urbain au Moyen Âge*, ed. Cédric Quertier, Roxane Chilà, and Nicolas Pluchot, Paris, 2013, pp. 51–64; esp. 52–5. On signs for identification, see Valentin Groebner, *Who Are You? Identification, Deception and Surveillance in Early Modern Europe*, New York, 2007, pp. 39–48.

82 Denis Menjot, 'L'Immigration à Murcie, et dans son territoire, sous les premiers Trastamares (1370–1420 environ)', *Revue d'histoire économique et sociale* 53 (1975), 216–65; esp. 219–22.

83 Julius Kirshner, 'Women Married Elsewhere: Gender and Citizenship in Italy', in *Time, Space, and Women's Lives in Early Modern Europe*, ed. Anne Jacobson Schutte, Thomas Kuehn, and Silvana Seidel Menchi, Kirksville, MI, 2001, pp. 117–49.

84 'multi homines et femine habentes dominos et etiam alii non habentes dominos ... quidam cum rebus suis, quidam etiam sine rebus, quia non habebant ... predicta civitas Tolose et suburbium et universitas multum meliorabatur et augebatur et recipiebat inde cotidie incrementum', *La Commune de Toulouse et les sources de son histoire (1120–1249): Étude historique et critique suivie de l'édition du Cartulaire du Consulat*, ed. Roger Limouzin-Lamothe, Toulouse, 1932, p. 454.

85 *Les Coutumes de Toulouse, 1286, et leur premier commentaire, 1296*, Toulouse, pp. 147–8. Local sources allow the study of migrants' names from the later twelfth century, and this shows that most came from the Toulousain, with some from as far as Quercy: see Charles Higounet, 'Le Peuplement de Toulouse au XIIe siècle', *Annales de Midi* 55 (1943), 489–98, esp. map at 497.

86 *The Costuma d'Agen: A Thirteenth-Century Customary Compilation in Old Occitan. Transcribed from the Livre Juratoire*, trans. F. R. P. Akehurst, Turnhout, 2010, pp. 54–5. On the dating, see pp. xiii–xvii.

87 'deu primerament forsjurar, toquats los sants evangelis, hyretges, e sabatats, e tota manera e tota error de hyretgia'; 'estara a dreghs e esgart del senhor e del cosselh, a tots sos rancurants, e que dints un an e un mes comprara a Agen maio, o terra, o vinha ... E deu ester quitis e francs aquel an e aquel mes d'ost, e de gacha', ibid., p. 54 (translation from p. 55). Similarly, the statutes of Carcassone (c. 1205) freed a foreigner marrying a local woman from military and guard service for a year and a day: *Layettes du trésor des chartes*, vol. I, ed. Alexandre Teulet, Paris, 1863, pp. 272–81, at c. 67, p. 278: 'Extraneus homo qui in villam Carcassona ducat [corr. duxerit] uxorem et ibi remanebit, liber sit per annum et diem de cavalgada et ost et gaita.' I am grateful to John Arnold for pointing this out to me.

88 'Quicumque de nostro comitatu aut districtu steterit in ciuitate uel burgis Perusii cum sua familia per decem annos continuos, et non fecerit aliquod seruitium per hominiciam, et querimonia de ipso non fuit uel erit intra dictum tempus decem annorum, sit liber et absolutus cum omnibus suis rebus', *Statuto del commune di Perugia del 1279*, vol. I, c. 389, pp. 363–4; at p. 363, lines 3–7.

89 On the saying, see Reynolds, *Kingdoms and Communities*, p. liii and n. 138.

90 'tutti e ciascuni de la città di Siena, e' quali divennero cittadini di Siena, o vero per inanzi diveneranno, sieno tenuti e debiano abitare ne la città di Siena con tutta la famellia sua, continuamente, ne la casa propia o vero che tenga a pigione, secondo che abitano et fanno li altri cittadini di Siena, assidui, senza fraude, excetti li tempi de le metiture et de le vendemmie', *Il costituto del Comune di Siena*, vol. II, Dist. IV, c. LI, p. 186.

91 'inter ipsos potestatem et antianos ad fabas albas et nigras, ita quod person capitaney vel potestatis vel eius vicarii computetur pro duodecim vocibus', *Statuto di Forlì*, c. 64, p. 97, lines 16–19.

92 Reinhold C. Mueller, '"Veneti facti privilegio": Stranieri naturalizzati a Venezia tra XIV e XVI secolo', in *La città italiana e i luoghi degli stranieri (XIV–XVIII secolo)*, ed. Donatella Calabi and Paola Lanaro, Bari, 1998, pp. 41–51; at p. 44.

93 'Item, che se algun forester vegnirà a Venetia e vorrà questa arte lavorar, sia tegnù debbia zurar l'arte e pagar soldi cinque de grossi, delli quali la terza parte vegna alla camera della Giustitia, e le do parte alla scola', 'Capitolare dei cristallai', *I capitolari delle arti veneziani: Sottoposte alla giustizia e poi alla giustizia vecchia dalle origini al 1330*, vol. III, ed. Giovanni Monticolo and Enrico Besta, Rome, 1914, pp. 123–52; c. 23, p. 143.

94 Cédric Quertier, 'La Stigmatisation des migrants à l'épreuve des faits: Le règlement de la faillite Aiutamicristo da Pisa devant la *Mercanzia* florentine (1390)', in *'Arriver' en ville: Les migrants en milieu urbain au Moyen Âge*, ed. Cédric Quertier, Roxane Chilà, and Nicolas Pluchot, Paris, 2013, pp. 243–59; at pp. 249–51.

95 Emilia Saracco Previdi, 'L'Inserimento dei forestieri nel complesso urbanistico delle città marchigiane e nel paesaggio medievale', in *Stranieri e forestieri nella Marca dei secc. XIV–XVI: Atti del 30 convegno di studi maceratesi, Macerata, 19–20 novembre 1994*, Macerata, 1996, pp. 1–28; pp. 12–13; Cecchi, 'Disposizioni statuarie', p. 33.

96 Cecchi, 'Disposizioni statuarie', pp. 76–7.

97 *Statuta, capitula, sive ordinamenta communis Carij*, c. LXXVI: www.cairomontenotte.com/biblioteca/scorzoni/b-1.html

98 Lonza, *The Statute of Dubrovnik of 1272*, Lib. VI, c. xvi, p. 234 and c. xxiv, p. 238.

99 Cities also kept lists of their own banished citizens, as in the *Statuti di Verona del 1327*, vol. II, ed. Silvana Anna Bianchi and Rosalba Granuzzo, Rome, 1992, c. 71, p. 475.

100 Raccagni, *The Lombard League 1164–1225*, p. 58. I am grateful to Gianluca Raccagni for interesting conversations on the League. See also articles in Laurence Buchholzer and Olivier Richard (eds.), *Ligues urbaines et espace à la fin du Moyen Âge*, Strasburg, 2012.

101 On these categories of settlement in the towns, see Heath Dillard, *Daughters of the Reconquest: Women in Castilian Town Society 1100–1300*, Cambridge, 1984, pp. 17–23.

102 Cagnin, *Cittadini e forestieri*, pp. 89–90.

103 *Statuti pistoiesi del secolo XII*, ed. Natale Rauty, Pistoia, 1996, B.5, p. 136. On family networks in the city, see Christiane Klapisch-Zuber, 'Kin, Friends, and Neighbors: The Urban Territory of a Merchant', in her *Work, Family, and Ritual in Renaissance Italy*, trans. Lydia Cochrane, Chicago, 1985, pp. 68–93.

104 'Si qua mulier alicui forensi vel non substinenti onera dicti comunis se maritaverit aut in uxorem dederit et de suis bonis contractum seu donationem fecerit ipsi forensi, non valeat ullo modo, ymo ipsa bona semper remaneant et sint dicti comunis oneribus obligata', *Lo statuto comunale di Sassoferrato*, ed. Ugo Paoli, Sassoferrato, 1993, Lib. 2, c. 58, p. 118. In the Thuringian city of Mühlhausen, a foreigner who married the daughter of a citizen was obliged to pay all dues expected of citizens, *Die Statuten der Reichsstadt Muehlhausen*, no. 132, p. 46.

105 *Codice degli statute della repubblica di Sassari*, ed. Pasquale Tola, Cagliari, 1850, c. 45, p. 46.

106 See the detailed provision made for the people of Agen, in *The Costuma d'Agen*, c. 34, pp. 56–9. See also Hubert, 'Qui est qui', 491–2.

107 'vi siano presenti sette testimonii e tre secondi notari e che delli testimonii ve ne siano tre, conoschino il testatore overo si provi la buona fama delli sette testimonii', *Statuti dei Laghi di Como e di Lugano*, c. 156, p. 358. The *fuero* of Cuenca (1177) combines the discussion of marriage and wills in a single section (IX), *The Code of Cuenca, Municipal*

Law and the Twelfth-Century Castilian Frontier, trans. and intro. James F. Powers, Philadelphia, 2000, c. 9, pp. 64–6.

108 Andrée Courtemanche, 'Women, Family, and Immigration in Fifteenth-Century Manosque: The Case of the Dodi Family of Barcelonnette', in *Urban and Rural Communities in Medieval France: Provence and Languedoc, 1000–1500*, ed. Kathryn Reyerson and John Drendel, Leiden, 1998, pp. 101–27.

109 'debet sibi domum emere in villa nostra, et in eadem ipse cum familia sua et uxore sua debet personalem facere mansionem, quam si non faciet, domus ab eo emta debet ville remanere, et deinceps non est burgensis', *Recueil diplomatique du Canton de Fribourg*, vol. I, ed. Romain Werro, Jean Berchtold, and Jean Gremaud, Fribourg, 1839, no. 44, p. 131.

110 The process is described on two sheets of parchment, in Bowsky, 'Medieval Citizenship', 193–243; at 206–8.

111 Previdi, 'L'Inserimento dei forestieri', pp. 21–2.

112 On the presence of Lombards in Tuscan towns, see Duccio Balestracci, 'L'Immigrazione di manodopera nella Siena medievale', in *Forestieri e stranieri nella città basso-medievali*, Florence, 1988, pp. 163–80; at pp. 164–5.

113 On house-building materials, see Piekalski, *Prague, Wrocław and Kraków*, chapter 5. On the control of the use of wood for housing in Dalmatia, see Danko Zelić, 'Wooden Houses in the Statutes and Urban Landscapes of Medieval Dalmatian Communes', in *Splitski statut iz 1312. godine – povijest i pravo [The Statute of Split – the History and the Law]*, ed. Željko Radić, Marko Trogrlić, Massimo Meccarelli, and Ludwig Steindorff, Split, 2015, pp. 489–507.

114 While the town of Camerino was careful about receiving new citizens, it allowed 'scolares venientes ad studendum' to stay freely in the town: *Statuta comunis et populi civitatis Camerini*, book 1, c. 104, p. 36.

115 Previdi, 'L'Inserimento', pp. 12–14. An average house in York c. 1280 was more spacious than these starter homes, at 3 x 10.2 square meters: Sarah Rees Jones 'Building Domesticity in the City: English Urban Housing before the Black Death', in *Medieval Domesticity: Home, Housing and Household in Medieval England*, ed. Maryanne Kowaleski and P. J. P. Goldberg, Cambridge, 2008, pp. 66–91; at p. 68.

116 'nullus amodo posit habere aliquod officium terre in palacio, nisi prius steterit per viginti annos et plures Clugie habitator; et hoc intelligendum est de officio consiliariorum Minoris Consilii et tocius Maioris concilii et cancellarie', *Statuti e capitolari di Chioggia del 1272–1279 con le aggiunte fino al 1327*, ed. Gianni Penzo Doria and Sergio Perini, Venice, 1993, c. 83, p. 107.

117 'avere li uficj del Comune', *Statuti del Comune di Cecina nel 1409*, c. 22, p. 13.

118 Albini, '"Civitas tunc quiescit et fulget"', p. 100, n. 17.

119 Dino Compagni, *Cronica*, ed. Davide Cappi, Rome, 2000, Lib. I, cs. 4–6, pp. 4–6.

120 Catherine Keen, *Dante and the City*, Stroud, 2003, pp. 30–6.

121 See the discussion in Jean-Claude Maire-Vigueur, *Cavaliers et citoyens: Guerre, conflits et société dans l'Italie communale, XIIe–XIIIe siècles*, Paris, 2003, and, on Bologna, Sarah Rubin Blanshei, *Politics and Justice in Late Medieval Bologna*, Leiden, 2010. On conflict

within cities, see again Lantschner, *The Logic of Political Conflict in Medieval Cities*. On the entry of aristocrats into citizenship in German towns, see Dorothea A. Christ, 'Hochadelige Eidgenossen: Grafen und Herren im Burgrecht eidgenössischer Orte', in *Neubürger im späten Mittelalter: Migration und Austausch in der Städtelandschaft des alten Reiches (1250–1550)*, ed. Rainer Christoph Schwinges, Berlin, 2002, pp. 99–123.

122 Enrico Artifoni, 'I podestà professionali e la fondazione retorica della politica comunale', *Quaderni storici* 21 (1986), 687–709.

123 *Statuti di Spoleto del 1296*, ed. Giovanni Antonelli, Florence, 1962, c. LIIII, p. 52; the constitution required that a foreign notary serve as *viarius*, the supervisor of roads, c. 1, p. 63. Notaries were early to organise in professional associations, like that at Piacenza, whose activities were regulated by statute, *Statuti notarili piacentini del XIV secolo*, ed. Corrado Pecorella, Milan, 1971.

124 Such participation of religious in the workings of Italian towns is explored in the collection by Frances Andrews (ed.), with Agata Pincelli, *Churchmen and Urban Government in Late Medieval Italy, c. 1200–c.1450*, New York, 2013. The resulting reports, the *biccherne*, were bound with painted boards, where scenes of such religious oversights were sometimes captured: see Alessandro Tomei (ed.), *Le Biccherne di Siena: Arte e finanza all'alba dell'economia moderna*, Rome, 2002; see examples at pp. 108–11, 122–7, 130–3, 138–41, 146–9, 154–5.

125 *Statuti pistoiesi del secolo XIII*, vol. II, Lib. 2, c. 152, p. 120.

126 'Item statuimus quod aliquis clericus vel frater ecclesie, qui habeat sive non habeat prebendam seu beneficium, non possit habere aliquod officium in comuni Verone', *Statuti di Verona del 1327*, vol. I, c .151, p. 207.

127 Martha C. Howell, 'Citizen-clerics in Late Medieval Douai', in *Statuts individuels, statuts corporatifs et statuts judiciaires dans les villes européennes (Moyen Âge et temps modernes)*, ed. Marc Boone and Maarten Prak, Leuven and Apeldoorn, 1996, pp. 11–22. See the provision in the statutes of Rouen, when jurisdiction was disputed by knights and clerics: *Les Établissements de Rouen: Études sur l'histoire des institutions municipales de Rouen, Falaise, etc.*, vol. I, ed. A. Giry, 1883, c. 21, p. 28. On the clergy as a category of stranger, see Hans-Jörg Gilomen, 'Städtliche Sondergruppen im Bürgerrecht', in *Neubürger im späten Mittelalter: Migration und Austausch in der Städtelandschaft des alten Reiches (1250–1550)*, ed. Rainer Christoph Schwinges, Berlin, 2002, pp. 125–67; at pp. 159–65.

128 On the migration of highly skilled workers, artisans, and service providers, see Bruno Koch, '*Quare magnus artificus est*: Migrierende Berufsleute als Innovationsträger im späten Mittelalter', in *Neubürger im späten Mittelalter: Migration und Austausch in der Städtelandschaft des alten Reiches (1250–1550)*, ed. Rainer Christoph Schwinges, Berlin, 2002, pp. 409–43.

129 Viviana Bonazzoli, *Il prestito ebraico nelle economie cittadine delle Marche fra '200 e '400*, Ancona, 1990, pp. 15, 44–5; on the need for credit in Italian communes, see Claudia Becker, '"Sub gravioribus usuris": Darlehensverträge der Kommunen Chiavenna im 12. und 13. Jahrhundert', in *Bene vivere in communitate: Beiträge zum italienischen und deutschen Mittelalter. Hagen Keller zum 60. Geburtstag überreicht von seinen Schülerinnen und Schülern*, ed. Thomas Scharff and Thomas Behrmann, Münster, 1997, pp. 25–48.

130 Bonazzoli, *Il prestito*, p. 171.

131 'civis Astensis apud Friburgum Oechtlandie commorans', Giulia Scarcia, '"Comburgenses et cohabitatores": Aspetti e problemi della presenza dei "Lombardi" tra Savoia e Svizzera', in *Comunità forestiere e 'nationes' nell'Europa dei secoli XIII–XVI*, ed. Giovanna Petti Balbi, Naples, 2001, pp. 113–33; p. 113. In 1303 the city of Fribourg freed two merchants of Asti, settled in the city, from the citizenship fee, since they had provided a loan of 100 pounds to the city, *Recueil diplomatique du Canton de Fribourg*, vol. I, no. 73, pp. 22–3.

132 See below, Chapter 4, p. 77.

133 On the popularization of such ideas, see Jacques Le Goff, *Money and the Middle Ages: An Essay in Historical Anthropology*, trans. Jean Birrell, Cambridge, 2012, pp. 61–73; Giacomo Todeschini, *Franciscan Wealth: From Voluntary Poverty to Market Society*, trans. Donatella Melucci, New York, 2009, and Davis, *Medieval Market Morality*, pp. 65–8, 213–15.

134 Joel Kaye, *A History of Balance, 1250–1375: The Emergence of a New Model of Equilibrium and Its Impact on Thought*, Cambridge, 2014, pp. 20–75; esp. pp. 28–30.

135 For a subtle analysis of the change in attitude to moneylenders, see Rowan W. Dorin, '"Once the Jews Have Been Expelled": Intent and Interpretation in Late Medieval Canon Law', *Law and History Review* 34 (2016), 335–62.

136 Miriam Davide, *Lombardi in Friuli: Per la storia delle migrazioni interne nell'Italia del Trecento*, Trieste, 2008, pp. 23–8.

137 Mueller, '"Veneti facti privilegio"'.

138 *Chronicles of London*, ed. Charles Lethbridge Kingsford, Oxford, 1905, p. 15. For an analysis of the full context of the event, see Erik Spindler, 'Flemings in the Peasants' Revolt, 1381', in *Contact and Exchange in Later Medieval Europe: Essays in Honour of Malcolm Vale*, ed. Hannah Skoda, Patrick Lantschner, and R. L. J. Shaw, Woodbridge, 2012, pp. 59–78; Ormrod, Lambert, and Mackman, *Immigrant England, 1300–1550*, p. 242.

139 For an interesting discussion of identity associated with the region of Salento, see Linda Safran, *The Medieval Salento: Art and Identity in Southern Italy*, Philadelphia, 2014, esp. chapter 8.

140 Campbell, *The Great Transition*. For Genoa and Venice, see Benjamin Z. Kedar, *Merchants in Crisis: Genoese and Venetian Men of Affairs and the Fourteenth-Century Depression*, New Haven, CN, 1976, *passim*, and figure 1, p. 18. On regional variation in the spread and effects of the Black Death, see Ole J. Benedictow, *The Black Death 1346–1353: The Complete History*, Woodbridge, 2004. The Alpine regions saw growth through migration after the Black Death, by which they were little touched: Pier Paolo Viazzo, *Upland Communities: Environment, Population and Social Structure in the Alps since the Sixteenth Century*, Cambridge, 1989, pp. 128–30.

141 On the impact of decline on urban landscape, see Keith D. Lilley, 'Decline or Decay? Urban Landscapes in Late-Medieval England', in *Towns in Decline: AD 100–1600*. ed. T. R. Slater, Aldershot, 2000, pp. 235–65. On the effects on the Low Countries, see W. P. Blockmans, 'The Social and Economic Effects of Plague in the Low Countries: 1349–1500', *Revue belge de philologie et d'historie* 58 (1980), 833–63.

142 Gian Savino Pene Vidari, 'Statuti signorili', in *Signori, regimi signorili e statuti nel tardo medioevo*, ed. Rolando Dondarini, Maria Varanini, and Maria Venticelli, Bologna, 2003, pp. 51–62. On some characteristics of sovereignty in this period, see Serena Ferente, 'Popolo and Law', in *Popular Sovereignty in Historical Perspective*, ed. Richard Bourke and Quentin Skinner, Cambridge 2016, pp. 96–114; pp. 113–14.

143 Albini, '"Civitas tunc quiescit et fulget"', pp. 103–11.

144 Andrew Brown, 'Medieval Citizenship: Bruges in the Later Middle Ages', in *The Citizen Past and Present*, ed. Andrew Brown and John Griffiths, Auckland, 2017, pp. 93–117; at pp. 98–100.

145 P. Camp, *Histoire d'Auxonne au Moyen Âge*, Dijon, 1960, p. 81.

146 Alessandro Barbero, 'Una rivolta antinobiliare nel Piemonte del Trecento: Il Tuchinaggio del Canavese', in *Rivolte urbane e rivolte contadine nell'Europa del Trecento: Un confronto*, ed. Monique Bourin, Giovanni Cherubini, and Giuliano Pinto, Florence, 2008, pp. 153–96; pp. 170–1.

147 Marc Boone, 'Les Gens de métiers à l'époque corporative à Gand et les litiges professionnels (1350–1450)', in *Statuts individuels, statuts corporatifs et statuts judiciaires dans les villes européennes (Moyen Âge et temps modernes)*, ed. Marc Boone and Maarten Prak, Leuven, 1996, pp. 23–47; esp. pp. 23, 30–2.

148 Marc Boone, 'State Power and Illicit Sexuality: The Persecution of Sodomy in Late Medieval Bruges', *Journal of Medieval History* 22 (1996), 135–53.

149 On restriction of entry to guilds, see P. J. P. Goldberg, *Women, Work, and Life Cycle in a Medieval Economy: Women in York and Yorkshire c. 1300–1520*, Oxford, 1992, pp. 299–300.

150 Winfried Schich, *Wirtschaft und Kulturlandschaft: Gesammelte Beiträge 1977 bis 1999 zur Geschichte der Zisterzienser und der 'Germania Slavica'*, Berlin, 2007, pp. 407–26; esp. pp. 419–20.

151 Anti Selart, 'Non-German Literacy in Medieval Livonia', in *Uses of the Written Word in Medieval Towns: Medieval Urban Literacy*, vol. II, ed. Marco Mostert and Anna Adamska, Turnhout, 2014, pp. 37–63; pp. 48–9.

152 Debra Blumenthal, *Enemies and Familiars: Slavery and Mastery in Fifteenth-Century Valencia*, Ithaca, NY, 2009, pp. 118–19.

153 *The People of Curial Avignon*, pp. 13–14.

154 In some communities there are signs of such activity already in the earlier fourteenth century: see Pierre Monnet, 'Les Révoltes urbaines en Allemagne au XIVe siècle: Un état de la question', in *Rivolte urbane e rivolte contadine nell'Europa del Trecento*, Monique Bourin, Giovanni Cherubini, and Giuliano Pinto, Florence, 2008, pp. 105–53; pp. 136–7.

155 Such a programme was laid out clearly in the 1403 statutes for his territory of Duke Amadeus VIII of Savoy: Neithard Bulst, 'La Législation somptuaire d'Amédée VIII', in *Amédée VIII – Félix V: Premier duc de Savoie et pape (1383 – 1451)*, ed. Bernard Andenmatten and Agostino Paravicini Bagliani, Lausanne, 1992, pp. 191–20; esp. pp. 192–6.

156 Eugene Smelyansky, 'Urban Order and Urban Other: Anti-Waldensian Inquisition in Augsburg, 1393', *German History* 34 (2016), 1–20.

157 Sabine von Heusinger, *Johannes Mulberg OP (+1414): Ein Leben im Spannungsfeld von Dominikanerobservanz und Beginenstreit*, Berlin, 2000, pp. 47–66.

158 J. L. Bolton, 'London and the Anti-Alien Legislation of 1439–40', in *Resident Aliens in Later Medieval England*, ed. W. Mark Ormrod, Nicola McDonald, and Craig Taylor, Turnhout, 2017, pp. 33–47.

159 Sarah Rees Jones, 'Scots in the North of England: The First Alien Subsidy, 1440–43', in *Resident Aliens in Later Medieval England*, ed. W. Mark Ormrod, Nicola McDonald, and Craig Taylor, Turnhout, 2017, pp. 51–75.

3 JEWS: FAMILIAR STRANGERS

1 Yehuda Amichai, *A Life in Poetry, 1948–1994*, trans. Benjamin and Barbara Harshav, New York, 1994, at p. 81.

2 *The Dialogue of Andreas Meinhardi: A Utopian Description of Wittenberg and Its University, 1508*, ed. and trans. Edgar C. Reinke, Ann Arbor, MI, 1976, p. 308; 'Rein. Quod nomen vico per quem citus irruit? Mein. Iudaicus vicus a iudeis illius quondam, incolis nominatus. Rein. Nunc vero expulsis? Mein. Penitus', p. 177.

3 On the expulsions from cities of the Holy Roman Empire, see Markus J. Wenninger, *Man bedarf keiner Juden mehr: Ursachen und Hintergründe ihrer Vertreibung aus den deutschen Reichsstädten im 15. Jahrhundert*, Cologne, 1981, esp. chapter 4; Franz-Josef Ziwes, 'Territoriale Judenvertreibungen in Südwesten und Süden Deutschlands im 14. und 15. Jahrhundert,' in *Judenvertreibungen in Mittelalter und früher Neuzeit*, ed. Friedhelm Burgard, Alfred Haverkamp, and Gerd Mentgen, Hanover, 1999, pp. 165–87; and, in the same volume, Rotraud Ries, '"De joden to verwisen" – Judenvertreibungen in Nordwestdeutschland im 15. und 16. Jahrhundert', pp. 189–224. On the expulsion from Wiener Neustadt, see Martha Keil, 'Der Liber Judeorum von Wr. Neustadt (1453–1500) – Edition', in *Studien zur Geschichte der Juden in Österreich*, ed. Martha Keil and Klaus Lohrmann, Vienna and Cologne, 1994, pp. 41–99. On the remains of the Jewish presence after expulsions, see also William Chester Jordan, 'The Jewish Cemeteries of France after the Expulsion of 1306', in *Studies in Medieval Jewish Intellectual and Social History: Festschrift in Honor of Robert Chazan*, ed. David Engel, Lawrence H. Schiffman, and Elliot R. Wolfson, Leiden, 2012, pp. 227–44.

4 See, for example, deeds attesting transactions conveying agricultural land and vineyards between Catalan Jews in *Hebrew Deeds of Catalan Jews/Documents hebraics de la Catalunya medieval: 1117–1316*, ed. Elka Klein, Barcelona and Girona, 2004.

5 On settlement in the Holy Roman Empire, see Michael Toch, *Die Juden im mittelalterlichen Reich*, 2nd edn, Munich, 2010, pp. 5–13. See also Peter Johanek, 'Die Frühzeit jüdischer Präsenz in Westfalen', in *Historisches Handbuch der jüdischen Gemeinschaften in Westfalen und Lippe: Grundlagen – Erträge – Perspektiven*, Susanne Freund, Münster, 2013, pp. 21–58.

6 He describes the itinerary in the preface to *The Itinerary of Benjamin of Tudela*, ed. Marcus Nathan Adler, London, 1907, pp. 2–9.

7 Martin Allen, *Mints and Money in Medieval England*, Cambridge, 2012; on Jewish minting in the kingdom of Hungary, see Csaba Tóth, 'Minting, Financial Administration and Coin Circulation in Hungary in the Árpádian and Angevin Periods (1000–1387),' in *The*

Economy of Medieval Hungary, ed. József Laszlovszky, Balázs Nagy, Péter Szabó, and András Vadas, Leiden, 2018, pp. 279–94; at pp. 288–9.

8 Anna Sapir Abulafia, *Christian–Jewish Relations 1000–1300: Jews in the Service of Medieval Christendom*, Harlow, 2011, pp. 88–97.

9 Robin Mundill, *England's Jewish Solution: Experiment and Expulsion, 1262–1290*, Cambridge, 1998, chapter 6; see also Ormrod, Lambert, and Mackman, *Immigrant England, 1300–1550*, pp. 183–7.

10 Abulafia, *Christian-Jewish Relations, 1000–1300*, part 2. David Abulafia, '"Nam iudei servi regis sunt, et semper fisco regio deputati": The Jews in the Municipal Fuero of Teruel (1176–7)', in *Jews, Muslims and Christians in and around the Crown of Aragon: Essays in Honour of Professor Elena Lourie*, ed. Harvey J. Hames, Leiden, 2003, pp. 97–123.

11 Jews were not serfs, but 'like' serfs: Gavin I. Langmuir, '"Tanquam servi": The Change in Jewish Status in French Law about 1200', in *Toward a Definition of Antisemitism*, Berkeley, CA, 1990, pp. 167–94.

12 See, on cases between Jews and Christians, *The Code of Cuenca*, c. 29, pp. 160–5.

13 'Qual los jodios sieruos son del sennor Rey et sienpre a la real bolsa son co[n]tados', *El Fuero de Teruel*, vol. I, ed. Max Gorosch, Stockholm, 1950, no. 568, p. 320.

14 Abulafia, '"Nam iudei servi regis sunt"', pp. 104–6; Langmuir '"Tanquam servi"'.

15 Keiko Nowacka, 'Prosecution, Margnalization, or Tolerance: Prostitutes in Thirteenth-Century Parisian Society', in *Difference and Identity in Francia and Medieval France*, ed. Meredith Cohen and Justine Finnhaber-Baker, Farnham, 2020, pp. 175–96; Marie Dejoux, 'Gouvernement et pénitence: Les enquêtes de réparation des usures juives de Louis IX (1247–1270)', *Annales: Histoire, Sciences Sociales* 69 (2014), 849–74; *The Trial of the Talmud, Paris, 1240*, trans. John Friedman and Jean Connell Hoff, with an essay by Robert Chazan, Toronto, 2012.

16 William Chester Jordan, *The Apple of his Eye: Converts from Islam in the Reign of Louis IX*, Princeton, NJ, 2019.

17 Hussein Fancy, *The Mercenary Mediterranean: Sovereignty, Religion, and Violence in the Medieval Crown of Aragon*, Chicago, 2016, esp. chapter 3.

18 Chapin, *Les Villes de foires de Champagne*, no. 6, pp. 288–91; at p. 289.

19 Brigit Wiedl, 'Jews and the City: Parameters of Jewish Urban Life in Late Medieval Austria', in *Urban Space in the Middle Ages and the Early Modern Age*, ed. Albrecht Classen, Berlin and New York, 2009, pp. 273–308. This *Judenprivileg* in turn formed the basis for King Bela IV's charter of 1251: Nora Berend, *At the Gate of Christendom: Jews, Muslims and 'Pagans' in Medieval Hungary, c. 1000–c. 1300*, Cambridge, 2001, pp. 74–84; there was no such privilege for the Muslim population, pp. 84–7.

20 Eva Haverkamp, 'Jewish Images on Christian Coins: Economy and Symbolism in Medieval Germany', in *Jews and Christians in Medieval Europe: The Historiographical Legacy of Bernhard Blumenkranz*, ed. Philippe Buc, Martha Keil, and John Tolan, Turnhout, 2015, pp. 189–226. On the advice given by a Jew on the interpretation of the bible, see Avraham (Rami) Reiner, 'Bible and Politics: A Correspondence between Rabbenu Tam and the Authorities of Champagne', in *Entangled Histories: Knowledge, Authority,*

and Jewish Culture in the Thirteenth Century, ed. Elisaheva Baumgarten, Ruth Mazo Karras, and Katelyn Mesler, Philadelphia, 2016, pp. 59–72.

21 For an illuminating discussion, see Rowan Dorin, 'Les Maîtres parisiens et les juifs (fin XIIIe siècle): Perspectives nouvelles sur un dossier d'avis concernant le *regimen judaeorum*', *Journal des savants* (2016), 241–82.

22 For some discussions of the ethics of business at the University of Paris, see Wei, *Intellectual Culture in Medieval Paris,* chapter 6.

23 In 1324 and 1360 respectively: 'Christiani sive iudei'; 'de Austria seu Bohemia vel de aliis quibuscumque partibus extraneis', Katalin Szende, 'Integration through Language: The Multilingual Character of Late Medieval Hungarian Towns', in *Segregation – Integration – Assimilation: Religious and Ethnic Groups in the Medieval Towns of Central and Eastern Europe,* ed. Derek Keene, Balázs Nagy, and Katalin Szende, Farnham, 2009, pp. 205–33; at p. 208.

24 'Item si aliquis [de quacunque vil]la in civitatem Posoniensem [causa] commorandi venire voluerint, dominus [i]p[siu]s ville seu poss[essionis] ipsum impedire non presumat, sed [cum] omnibus bonis suis libere habere permittat. Iutso tamen et consueto terragio [domi]no terre persoluto. [Item Iudei, in] ip[sa] civitate [consti]tuti, habe [ant] eandem libertatem quam et ipsi [ci]ves, salvo [iure] archyepiscopi Strigoniensis et prepositi Posoniensis remanente', *Výsady Miest a Mestečiek na Slovensku (1238–1350),* Bratislava, 1984, no. 77, pp. 74–6; at p. 76.

25 'alle Kawerzin wuocher und Juden unser und des Richs kamer diener', in Felicitas Schmieder, 'Various Ethnic and Religious Groups in Medieval German Towns? Some Evidence and Reflections', in *Segregation – Integration – Assimilation: Religious and Ethnic Groups in Medieval Towns of Central and Eastern Europe,* ed. Derek Keene, Balázs Nagy, and Katalin Szende, Farnham, 2009, pp. 15–31; at p. 30. On the term, see Gilomen, 'Städtliche Sondergruppen im Bürgerrecht', pp. 125–67; at pp. 154–9.

26 For a collection of articles on Jewish–Christian disputations, see Anna Sapir Abulafia, *Christians and Jews in Dispute: Disputational Literature and the Rise of Anti-Judaism in the West (c. 1000–1150),* Aldershot, 1998. See also Robert Chazan, *Barcelona and Beyond: The Disputation of 1263 and Its Aftermath,* Berkeley, CA, 1992.

27 See the introduction to *Die Disputationen zu Ceuta (1179) und Mallorca (1286): Zwei antijüdische Schriften aus dem mittelalterlichen Genua,* ed. Ora Limor, Munich, 1994, esp. pp. 12–30 on the commercial setting for the Mallorca disputation.

28 For all these cases, see Miri Rubin, *Gentile Tales: The Narrative Assault on Late Medieval Jews,* London and New Haven, CN, 1999.

29 Samuel K. Cohn, Jr, 'The Black Death and the Burning of Jews', *Past and Present* 196 (2007), 3–36.

30 *Pirkei Avot,* Perek 3, Mishna 2: www.sefaria.org/Pirkei_Avot.3?lang=bi

31 On Jewish attitudes to conversion, in its many forms, see Simha Goldin, *Apostasy and Jewish Identity in High Middle Ages Northern Europe: 'Are you still my brother?',* trans. Jonathan Chipman, Manchester, 2014. See also Ira Katznelson and Miri Rubin (eds.), *Religious Conversion: History, Experience and Meaning,* Farnham, 2014.

32 See above, pp. 44–45.

33 Archives Départementales Tarn-et-Garonne A 297, fol. 1159. I am extremely grateful to Mr François Arbelet for introducing me to this document.

34 Ibid.: 'Et may que elhi juziou ou juzieves questario a Gordo ou la Bastida menavo mercadarias que daquelleas mercadarias paguesso et redesso lo peatge ainsi cum fan autre mercadier.'

35 Ibid.: lines 54–9: 'Et may quesi causa era quant li juzieu auzario a Gordo estar ung an ou dos ans et no lor plazia l'estagha de Gorfo ou de la Bastida et s'en vol anar, nos permeten lor que nos pagat nostre ces que nos devrio et tot lorz *denies* que devrio en la villa que nos lor guidasen et lotz assolassessen una jornada fors de Gordo et de la Bastida et si estavo vas qual que s'en volguisse anar a lor cost messio.'

36 See, for example, canon 69 the Fourth Lateran Council, against Jews holding public offices, in *Decrees of the Ecumenical Councils*, vol. I, ed. Norman P. Tanner, London, 1990, c. 69, pp. 266–7.

37 See a case from thirteenth-century Siena, Archivio di Stato di Siena, Diplomatico Riformagioni (26 August 1230).

38 Ferdinando Treggiari, 'Bartolo e gli ebrei', in *Bartolo da Sassoferrato nella cultura europea tra Medioevo e Rinascimento*, ed. Victor Crescenzi and Giovanni Rossi, Sassoferrato, 2015, pp. 155–206; esp. pp. 192–206.

39 Gilomen, 'Städtliche Sondergruppen im Bürgerrecht'. See, in a later period, the struggle over linguistic categories for Black citizenship: Kantrowitcz, *More than Freedom*, pp. 28–43, like the category 'coloured citizens', pp. 33–40.

40 Alfred Haverkamp, '"Concivilitas" von Christen und Juden in Aschkenas im Mittelalter', in *Jüdische Gemeinden und Organisationsformen von der Antike bis zur Gegenwart*, ed. Robert Jütte and Abraham P. Kustermann, Cologne, 1996, pp. 103–36. The word *concivis* sometimes just meant other citizens: see Giuliano Milani, *L'esclusione dal Comune: Conflitti e bandi politici a Bologna e in altre città italiane tra XII e XIV secolo*, Rome, 2003, p. 27.

41 Gilomen, 'Städtliche Sondergruppen im Bürgerrecht', figure 1, p. 128.

42 Katalin Szende, 'Laws, Loans, Literates: Trust in Writing in the Context of Jewish–Christian Contacts in Medieval Hungary', in *Religious Cohabitation in Medieval Towns*, ed. Stephane Bosselier and John Tolan, Turnhout, 2014, pp. 243–71, p. 254.

43 Wiedl, 'Jews and the City', pp. 290–5.

44 Madeline H. Caviness and Charles G. Nelson, *Women and Jews in the Sachsenspiegel Picture-Books*, London, 2018, figures 5.15–5.17. For sealed documents composed in a variety of fashions to accommodate the use of Hebrew, French, and Latin among the contractors, see *Hebrew and Hebrew–Latin Documents from Medieval England: A Diplomatic and Palaeographical Study*, ed. Judith Olszowy-Schlanger, 2 vols., Turnhout, 2015.

45 Caviness, *Women and Jews*, figure 5.20.

46 Ephraim Shoham Steiner, '"*And in most of their business transactions they rely on this*": Some Reflections on Jews and Oaths in the Commercial Arena in Medieval Europe", in *On the Word of a Jew: Religion, Reliability, and the Dynamics of Trust*, ed. Nina Caputo and Mitchell B. Hart, Bloomington, IN, 2019, pp. 36–61.

47 Osvaldo Cavallar and Julius Kirshner, 'Jews as Citizens in Late Medieval and Renaissance Italy: The Case of Isacco da Pisa', *Jewish History* 25 (2011), 269–318; 272.

48 Daniel Lord Smail, *Imaginary Cartographies: Possession and Identity in Late Medieval Marseille*, Ithaca, NY, 1999, p. 14. On Bondavin, see Joseph Shatzmiller, *Shylock Reconsidered: Jews, Moneylending, and Medieval Society*, Berkeley, CA, 1990, pp. 112–18.

49 María del Pilar Laguzzi, 'Ávila a comienzos del siglo XIV', *Cuadernos de Historia de España* 12 (1949), 145–80; at 159. I am most grateful to Dr Cecil Reid, from whose research I came to know of the Ávila survey.

50 'Sobresta casa cae el agua del tejado de Yuçef Davila e non debe y caer', ibid., 159.

51 David Nirenberg, *Communities of Violence: Persecution of Minorities in the Middle Ages*, updated edn, Philadelphia, 2015, esp. chapters 5 and 6.

52 Tom Nickson, 'The Sound of Conversion in Medieval Iberia', in *Resounding Images: Medieval Intersections of Art, Music, and Sound*, ed. Susan Boynton and Diane J. Reilly, Turnhout, 2015, pp. 91–107.

53 See the treatment of pawned household goods during the preparations for Passover offered by Yaakov ben Moshe Levi Moelin (1263–1427), the Maharil, *Minhagim*, Sabbioneta, 1556, p. 5v.

54 For a subtle analysis of such matters, see William Chester Jordan, *Women and Credit in Pre-Industrial and Developing Societies*, Philadelphia, 1993, pp. 13–49.

55 Carsten Wilke, 'Jewish Erotic Encounters with Christians and Muslims in Late Medieval Iberia: Testing Ibn Verga's Hypothesis', in *Intricate Interfaith Networks in the Middle Ages: Quotidian Jewish–Christian Contacts*, ed. Ephraim Shoham-Steiner, Turnhout, 2016, pp. 193–230.

56 'Fermosa gentil judia/ antier quando vos vi/ tanta Gloria senti/ que desir non se podria ... Yo, sennora, confio/en la mesura de vos/ sy por my,/ sy no por Dios,/ que vos me dareys lo mio.// Fyn./ Sy no tornarme judio,/ pues no me debo tornar/ por vos server y loar/ todas penas desafio', cited and discussed ibid., p. 213.

57 Nirenberg, *Communities of Violence*, pp. 138–41.

58 Patricia MacCaughan, *La Justice à Manosque au XIIIe siècle: Évolution et représentation*, Paris, 2005, p. 80.

59 For insights into the collaboration between Jews and Christians in the making of works of art, see Marc Michael Epstein, *The Medieval Haggadah: Art, Narrative, and Religious Imagination*, New Haven, CN, 2011, esp. chapter 1; and Sarit Shalev-Eyni, *Jews among Christians: Hebrew Book Illumination from Lake Constance*, Turnhout, 2010, esp. chapters 4–6; Susan Einbinder, *Beautiful Death: Jewish Martyrdom and Poetry in Medieval France*, Princeton, NJ, 2002.

60 'cum venenis et potionibus pestiferis et sortilegiis', *Études historiques et documents inédits sur l'albigeois, le castrais et l'ancien diocèse de Lavaur*, ed. Claude Compayré, Albi, 1841, no. 71, pp. 255–7; at p. 257.

61 Nirenberg, *Communities of Violence*, pp. 43–5, 69–80.

62 For reflection on the causes of urban unrest in this period, see Cohn, Jr, *Lust for Liberty*, chapters 9 and 10.

63 Cohn, Jr, 'The Black Death and the Burning of Jews'. See, for two small towns of the Hainaut, Blockmans, 'The Social and Economic Effects of Plague in the Low Countries', 833–63, at 837–8; and elsewhere in the Low Countries, Christoph Cluse, *Studien zur Geschichte der Juden in den mittelalterlichen Niederlanden*, Hanover, 2000, pp. 214–21.

64 'diabolico spiritu incitati, manu armata et mente deliberata ad callum ipsius aljame hostiliter accesserunt et ausibus indebitis violenter ostias ipsius callis tamen securibus et aliis [sic] armorum generibus fregerunt et etiam destruxerunt ipsumque callum intrarunt unanimiter et potenter clamosis vocibus emittentes "Muyren los traydors"', in Anna Colet, Josep Xavier Muntané I Santiveri, Jordi Ruíz Ventura, Oriol Saula, M. Eulàlia Subirà de Galdàcano, and Clara Jáuregui, 'The Black Death and Its Consequences for the Jewish Community in Tàrrega: Lessons from History and Archaeology', in *Pandemic Disease in the Medieval World: Rethinking the Black Death*, ed. Monica H. Green, Kalamazoo, MI, 2015, pp. 63–96; at pp. 71–2.

65 'Iudeos ipsos et alias nationes plurimas, que cohabitationem Iudeorum eorundem non noverant, pestis hec ubique fere communis afflixit, occulto Dei iudicio, et affligit, et proinde verisimilitudo non recipit, quod Iudei predicti occasionem tanto flagicio presisterint', *The Apostolic See and the Jews*, vol. I: *Documents 492–1404*, ed. Shlomo Simonsohn, Toronto, 1988, no. 373, pp. 397–8. See also Joëlle Rollo-Koster, *Avignon and Its Papacy, 1309–1417: Popes, Institutions, and Society*, Lanham, MD, 2015, p. 83. Maryanne Kowaleski summarises interesting comparative evidence on Jewish mortality, albeit from the late thirteenth century, in 'Medieval People in Town and Country: New Perspectives from Demography and Bioarchaeology', *Speculum* 89 (2014), 573–600; 579–83.

66 *Urkunden der Stadt Strassburg*, vol. V, ed. Hans Witte and Georg Wolfram, Strasburg, 1895, no. 190, pp. 178–9: 'quod talis mortalitas per intoxicationes foncium et puteorum, quibus ipsi judei venenoses res debuissent inspersisse'; 'quem tamen in nostra civitate remover intendimus nostro posse'. I am grateful to Simone Brehmer, for a useful exchange on this letter.

67 See Carole Rawcliffe, *Urban Bodies: Communal Health in Late Medieval English Towns*, Woodbridge, 2013, esp. chapters 1–2.

68 For a discussion of the contents of reformist preaching in Florence, see Peter Howard, 'Making a City and Citizens: The "Fruits" of Preaching in Renaissance Florence', in *Medieval Urban Culture*, ed. Andrew Brown and Jan Dumolyn, Turnhout, 2017, pp. 59–73. See also his 'The Aural Space of the Sacred in Renaissance Florence', in *Renaissance Florence: A Social History*, ed. Roger J. Crum and John T. Paoletti, New York, 2006, pp. 376–93, and notes: pp. 584–96. Stephen J. Milner, 'Rhetorics of Transcendence: Conflict and Intercession in Communal Italy 1300–1500', in *Charisma and Religious Authority: Jewish, Christian, and Muslim Preaching, 1200–1500*, ed. Katherine L. Jansen and Miri Rubin, Turnhout, 2010, pp. 235–51.

69 'allain dy Juden hausseren dy habent chaynen chrautgarten nicht', Szende, *Trust, Authority, and the Written Word*, pp. 142–4, figure 30, and p. 267. On the evolution of cabbage patches around the town, see Katalin G. Szende, 'Some Aspects of Urban Landownership in Western Hungary', in *Power, Profit and Urban Land: Landownership in Medieval and Early Modern Northern European Towns*, ed. Finn-Einar Eliassen and Geir Atle Ersland, Aldershot, 1996, pp. 141–66; at p. 149.

70 Treggiari, 'Bartolo e gli ebrei', p. 169.

71 *The Apostolic See and the Jews*, vol. II: *Documents 1394–1464*, ed. Shlomo Simonsohn, Toronto, 1989, no. 591, pp. 669–71.

72 Martin John Cable, *"Cum essem in Constantie..."*: *Raffaele Fulgosio and the Council of Constance 1414–1415*, Leiden, 2015, p. 279.

73 Dorin, '"Once the Jews have been Expelled"', 335–62. For an interesting discussion of the place of Jews in discussions on business ethics, see Francesca Trivellato, *The Promise and Peril of Credit: What a Forgotten Legend about Jews and Finance Tells Us about the Making of European Commercial Society*, Princeton, NJ, 2019, esp. Introduction.

74 Schmieder, 'Various Ethnic and Religious Groups', pp. 30–1. On Lombards in German towns, see Gilomen, 'Städtliche Sondergruppen im Bürgerrecht', pp. 154–9. On ideas arising from reform preaching about belonging to the city, see Paolo Evangelisti, '"Misura la città, chi è la communità, chi è il suggetto, chi è nella città...": Bernardino da Siena, *Prediche volgari sul Campo di Siena*, CVII, 64)', in *Identità cittadina e comportamenti socio-economici tra Medioevo ed Età moderna*, ed. Paolo Prodi, Maria Giuseppina Muzzarelli, and Stefano Simonetta, Bologna, 2007, pp. 19–52.

75 See the interesting analysis offered in Christoph Cluse, *Darf ein Bischof Juden zulassen? Die Gutachten des Siffridus Piscator OP (gest. 1473) zur Auseinandersetzung um die Vertreibung der Juden aus Mainz*, Trier, 2013, esp. pp. 76–9.

76 Ibid., pp. 76–9.

77 On these expulsions, see Mundill, *England's Jewish Solution*, chapter 8, and Jordan, *The French Monarchy and the Jews: From Philip Augustus to the Last Capetians*, Philadelphia, 1989, pp. 155–76, 214–38; Wolfgang Bunte, *Juden und Judentum in der mittelniederländischen Literatur (1100–1600)*, Frankfurt, 1989, pp. 99–111.

78 Szende, *Trust, Authority, and the Written Word*, p. 216.

79 Giacomo Todeschini, *Richezza francescana: Dalla povertà volontaria alla società del mercato*, Bologna, 2004, pp. 167–72.

80 Marina Montesano, 'Aspetti e conseguenze della predicazione civica di Bernardino da Siena', in *Religion civique à l'époque médiévale et moderne: Chrétienté et islam*, ed. André Vauchez, Rome: École française de Rome, 1995, pp. 265–75.

81 Gábor Klaniczay, 'The "Bonfires of the Vanities" and the Mendicants', in *Emotions and Material Culture*, ed. Gerhard Jaritz, Vienna, 2003, pp. 31–59.

82 'le quali prediche duravano tre et quattro ore; et fece che si abbrugiò in circa a 116 tavoglieri et un sacco di carte, dadi et paltri di giuocare che furono similmente abbrugiati su la piaza di Modena il dì 5 Dicembre; et questo perchè fu tenuto per santo questo frate. Il dì 10 del detto mese fece abbruggiare da 2000 brevi d'ogni ragione e più d'un sacco di capelli da donna e belletti ... Addì 13 detto, detto frate Bernardino donò il Giesù grande messo a oro in campo azzuro in un quadretto di legno ad uso di madonna a la compagnia dell'Annunciata', in Teodosio Lombardi, *Presenza e culto di san Bernardino da Siena nel Ducato Estense*, Ferrara, 1981, p. 86.

83 Todeschini, *Franciscan Wealth*, p. 160.

84 Michele Cassandro, *Gli ebrei e il prestito ebreo nel Cinquecento*, Milan, 1979, p. 7.

85 'certi sani huomini amatori della fede di Xto et dellonore della gloriosa e beatissima virgine maria e del buono stato presente e dellonore del popolo e del commune di Siena, providero che nenno Judeo possa stare ne abitare in neuna casa overo palagio e quale confia col campo della citta di Siena ne in nouna casa overo palagio el quale

confini colla strada overo via per laquale si va dala punta di san Marcci a la croce altravaglio', Archivio di Stato di Siena Consiglio Generale 194, Reformationes; on this, see Duccio Balestracci and Gabriella Piccinni, *Siena nel Trecento: Assetto urbano e strutture edilizie*, Florence, 1977, pp. 61–2. See, on town halls and their surroundings, Gabriella Garzella, 'I palazzi pubblici a Pisa nel medioevo come specchio dell'evoluzione politico-istituzionale e delle vicende urbanistiche', in *Les Palais dans la ville: Espaces urbains et lieux de la puissance publique dans le Méditerranée médiévale*, ed. Patrick Boucheron and Jacques Chiffoleau, Lyons, 2004, pp. 109–22.

86 'Omnes et singuli Hebrei tam mares quam foeminae cujuscunque aetatis fuerint, qui sunt, essent, aut in futurum venient ... unum O magnu et amplum infrascripte rotunditatis panni crocei idest gialli', Archivio di Stato di Siena, 123. On the Jewish community in Siena, see Patrizia Turrini, *La comunità ebraica di Siena: I documenti dell'Archivio di Stato dal Medioevo alla Restaurazione*, Siena, 2008, pp. 1–21. Similar O signs were enforced in Ancona: see Cecchi, 'Disposizioni statuarie', pp. 29–91; at p. 39. On distinguishing marks for Jews with reference to French sources, see Danièle Sansy, 'Signes de judéité dans l'image', *Micrologus* 15 (2007), 87–105; and in the statutes of Buda c. 1403, *Das Ofner Stadtrecht*, Part III, c. 193, p. 126.

87 The decree was reissued in 1439 and 1444.

88 'Che dicti juderi debbano e di delle domeniche delle pasque delle feste di nostra dopna et di tucti gli appostoli abstenirse da ogni presto et trafico palese et tenere serrata la loro botiga ogni exceptione tolta via', Archivio di Stato di Siena, Consiglio generale 213, fol. 110v.

89 'Et si haec ad paucos reductio divitiarum periculosa est statui civitatis, multo gravius periculum imminet cum reducuntur et coadunantur hae divitiae et denarii in manibus iudaeorum; quia tunc naturalis civitatis calor, qui eius divitiae dici potest, non recurrit ad cor neque subvenit ei, sed per fluxum pestiferum currit ad apostema, cum omnes iudaei, et maxime faenerantes, sint capitales inimici omnium christianorum', Bernardino of Siena, 'Sermo XLIII. Quantum usura adversetur Deo et usurarium idolatrare facit', Bernardino of Siena, *Opera IV*, Florence, 1956, sermon 43, at p. 383, lines 31–6.

90 'Divitias spirituales, id est fidem et ecclesiasticorum praeceptorum obedientiam cum ceteris spiritualibus thesauris verorum christicolarum, suis blanditiis venenatis et amicitiis exquisitis et muneribus toxicatis et conversationibus simulantes et proditionibus excogitatis et libertatibus ac favoribus acquisitis rapere, dispergere, comsumere, devorare et disspiare non cessant, secum ad inferos christianorum insensatorum trahentes animas infelices', ibid., sermon 42, at p. 384, lines 16–21.

91 For a useful introduction, see Maria Giuseppina Muzzarrelli, *Il denaro e la salvezza: L'invenzione del Monte di Pietà*, Bologna, 2001; see also Todeschini, *Franciscan Wealth*, pp. 174–81.

92 Carol Bresnahan Menning, 'The Monte's "Monte": The Early Supporters of Florence's Monte di Pietà', *The Sixteenth Century Journal* 23 (1992), 661–76.

93 Dana E. Katz, *The Jew in the Art of the Italian Renaissance*, Philadelphia, 2008, chapter 1.

94 There was a decline in the Jewish share of lending in other regions, too, in the later fifteenth century: Szende, *Trust, Authority, and the Written Word*, pp. 269–71.

95 On Capistrano's preaching campaigns through the Empire, see Pawel Kras and James
D. Mixson (eds.), *The Grand Tour of John of Capistrano in Central and Eastern Europe
(1451–1456): The Transfer of Ideas and Strategies of Communication and the Transfer of Ideas
in the Late Middle Ages*, Lublin, 2018, and Ottó Sándor Gecser, 'Preaching and Public-
ness: St John of Capestrano and the Making of His Charisma North of the Alps', in
Charisma and Religious Authority: Jewish, Christian, and Muslim Preaching, 1200–1500, ed.
Katherine L. Jansen and Miri Rubin, Turnhout, 2010, pp. 145–59; Howard, 'Making a
City and Citizens'.

96 Klaniczay, 'The "Bonfires of the Vanities"'.

97 On the arrival of those who came to be known as gypsies or Bohemians, see Shulamith
Shahar, 'Religious Minorities, Vagabonds and Gypsies in Early Modern Europe', in *The
Roma – A Minority in Europe: Historical, Political and Social Perspectives*, ed. Roni Stauber
and Raphael Vago, Budapest, 2007, pp. 1–18.

98 'Han stablit e hordenat que neguna persona de qualque ley stament o condicio sia no
gos tirar pedres ala ma no ab baceja no ab mandro ne ab altre strument de lançar
pedres contra los dits juheus ni la juheria de la dita ciutat ni als murs de aquella ... ni
gos entrar en la dita juheria per fer mal', Christoph Cailleaux, 'Les Juifs et les musulmans en Catalogne à la fin du Moyen Âge: Des étrangers dans la ville', in *'Arriver' en
ville: Les migrants en milieu urbain au Moyen Âge*, ed. Cédric Quertier, Roxane Chilà, and
Nicolas Pluchot, Paris, 2013, pp. 193–210; at p. 207, n. 36.

99 David Nirenberg, 'Mass Conversion and Genealogical Mentalities: Jews and Christians
in Fifteenth-Century Spain', *Past and Present* 174 (2002), 3–41.

100 For an analysis of the logic of the 1391 violence, and a reconstruction of its unfolding
in Valencia, see David Nirenberg, 'Massacre or Miracle? Valencia, 1391', in *Neighboring
Faiths: Christianity, Islam, and Judaism in the Middle Ages and Today*, Chicago, 2014,
pp. 75–88.

101 Cailleaux, 'Les Juifs et les musulmans en Catalogne', pp. 202–3.

102 Olivia Remie Constable, 'From Hygiene to Heresy: Changing Perceptions of Women
and Bathing in Medieval and Early Modern Iberia', *Religious Cohabitation in European
Towns (10th–15th Centuries)*, ed. Stéphane Boisselier and John Tolan, Turnhout, 2014,
pp. 185–206. See also James F. Powers, 'Frontier Municipal Baths and Social Interaction in Thirteenth-Century Spain', *American Historical Review* 84 (1979), 649–67.

103 Jan Stejskal, 'A Catholic City in the Hussite Era, 1400–1450s', in *The Transformation of
Confessional Cultures in a Central European City: Olomouc, 1400–1750*, ed. Antonin Kalous,
Rome, 2015, pp. 23–39; at pp. 35–9.

104 John Van Engen, 'A World Astir: Europe and Religion in the Early Fifteenth Century',
in *Europe after Wyclif*, ed. J. Patrick Hornbeck and Michael Van Dussen, New York, 2017,
pp. 11–45.

105 Dana E. Katz, *The Jewish Ghetto and the Visual Imagination of Early Modern Venice*,
Cambridge, 2017.

106 See, for example, Bolton, 'London and the Anti-Alien Legislation', pp. 33–47.

107 Diane Owen Hughes, 'Distinguishing Signs: Earrings, Jews, and Franciscan Rhetoric in
the Italian Renaissance City', *Past and Present* 112 (1986), 3–59.

108 Previdi, 'L'Inserimento dei forestieri', 1–28; at 22–4.

109 Hubert Damisch, *The Origins of Perspective*, trans. John Goodman, Cambridge, MA, 1984, chapter 11; Arthur Groos, 'The City as Community and Space: Nuremberg *Stadtlob*, 1447–1530', in *Spatial Practices: Medieval/Modern*, ed. Markus Stock and Nicola Vöhringer, Göttingen, 2014, pp. 187–206, at pp. 192–3. On attempts to control the appearance of the city in this period, see Marco Folin, 'Il governo degli spazi urbani negli statuti cittadini di area estense', in *Signori, regimi signorili e statuti nel tardo medioevo*, ed. Rolando Dondarini, Rolando Varanini, and Maria Venticelli, Bologna, pp. 337–66; at pp. 357–8.

4 WOMEN: SOMETIMES STRANGERS IN THEIR CITIES

1 Gloria Anzaldúa, *Borderlands. La Frontera. The New Mestiza*, San Francisco, CA, 1987, p. 77.

2 For a leading legal scholar's discussion of women's status, by means of a discussion of husbands' rights, see Paolo Mari, 'Bartolo e la condizione femminile: Brevi punti dalle *lecturae* bartoliane', in *Bartolo da Sassoferrato nella cultura europea tra Medioevo e Rinascimento*, ed. Victor Crescenzi and Giovanni Rossi, Sassoferrato, 2015, pp. 239–52. And for the transmission of ideas about women and home in the learned vernacular, see Claire Richter Sherman, 'Representations of Maternal and Familial Roles in French Translations of the Pseudo-Aristotelian "Economics" Book I', in *Tributes to Lucy Freeman Sandler: Studies in Illuminated Manuscripts*, ed. Kathryn A. Smith and Carol H. Krinsky, London, 2007, pp. 287–98.

3 This was stated influentially in the essays collected in Joan Wallach Scott, *Gender and the Politics of History*, New York, 1988.

4 On the visual representation of women's capacity at law, see Madeline H. Caviness and Charles G. Nelson, 'Silent Witnesses, Absent Women, and the Law Courts in Medieval Germany', in *Fama: The Politics of Talk and Reputation in Medieval Europe*, ed. Thelma Fenster and Daniel Lord Smail, Ithaca, NY, 2003, pp. 47–72.

5 'Tres haulte et honoree dame ... encore me dites, s'il vous agree la verité pourquoy ce est que les femmes ne tiennent plaidoirie en cours de justice ne cognoiscent des causes, ne font jugements', Christine de Pizan, *Livre de la cité des dames [La città delle dame]*, ed. Patrizia Caraffi and Earl Jeffrey Richards, Milan, 1998, Lib. I, xi, p. 92; translation in Christine de Pizan, *The Book of the City of Ladies*, trans. and ed. Rosalind Brown-Grant, London, 1999, p. 29.

6 Carol Lansing, 'Concubines, Lovers, Prostitutes: Infamy and Female Identity in Medieval Bologna', in *Beyond Florence: The Contours of Medieval and Early Modern Italy*, ed. Paula Findlen, Michelle M. Fontaine, and Duane J. Osheim, Stanford, CA, 2003, pp. 85–100.

7 Cordelia Beattie, *Medieval Single Women: The Politics of Social Classification in Late Medieval England*, Oxford, 2007; and Judith M. Bennett and Amy M. Froide (eds.), *Singlewomen in the European Past, 1250–1800*, Philadlephia, 1998. In German towns of the fourteenth century, up to 20 per cent of women lived in female households: see Barbara Studer, 'Frauen im Bürgerschaft: Überlegungen zur rechtlichen und sozialen Stellung der Frau

in spätmittelalterlichen Städten', in *Neubürger im späten Mittelalter: Migration und Austausch in der Städtelandschaft des alten Reiches (1250–1550)*, ed. Rainer Christoph Schwinges, Berlin, 2002, pp. 169–200; at p. 180.

8 Goldberg, *Women, Work, and Life Cycle in a Medieval Economy*, pp. 294–304.

9 'Et sachiez que communement telles femmes d'estrange pays ont esté blasmees d'aucun vice en leur pays; car c'est la cause qui les amaine a servir hors de leur lieu', *Le Mesnagier de Paris*, ed. Georgina E. Brereton and Janet M. Ferrier, trans. Karin Ueltschi, Paris, 1994, p. 438 (lines 115–18).

10 'Sachent tout cil qui sont et ki avenir sont que Jake de France et Liegars de Ghesnaing se compaignesse font leur devise ensanle', Ellen E. Kittell, 'The Construction of Women's Social Identity in Medieval Douai: Evidence from Identifying Epithets', *Journal of Medieval History* 25 (1999), 215–27; 220–1, cited at 220, n. 20.

11 On sex ratios, see Kowaleski, 'Medieval People in Town and Country', 573–600; esp. 577–83; and P. J. P. Goldberg, 'Urban Identity and the Poll Taxes of 1377, 1379 and 1381', *Economic History Review* 2nd series, 43 (1990), 194–216.

12 I am grateful to Richard Smith for instructive conversations on issues in medieval demography over many years. See, on the demography of later medieval northern Europe, Tine de Moor and Jan Luiten van Zanden, 'Girl Power: The European Marriage Pattern and Labour Markets in the North Sea Region in the Late Medieval and Early Modern Period', *Economic History Review* new series 63 (2010), 1–33. On slavery, see Susan Mosher Stuard, '"To Town to Serve": Urban Domestic Slavery in Medieval Ragusa', in *Women and Work in Pre-industrial Europe*, ed. Barbara Hanawalt, Bloomington, IN, 1987, pp. 39–55.

13 Theofilo F. Ruiz, 'Expansion et changement: La conquête de Séville et la société castillane (1248–1350)', *Annales: Histoire, Sciences Sociales* 34 (1979), 548–65, at 550–3.

14 Viazzo, *Upland Communities*, pp. 108–12.

15 See, again, Boucheron, *The Power of Images*.

16 Urban statutes often dealt with the need to keep dogs tied, as in *Lo statuto comunale di Sassoferrato*, Lib. V, c. 5, p. 252.

17 Visitors to Florence in the sixteenth century remarked on the absence of women from the streets: Natalie Tomas, 'Did Women Have a Space?', in *Renaissance Florence: A Social History*, ed. Roger J. Crum and John T. Paoletti, Cambridge, 2006, pp. 311–28; at p. 314.

18 Thelma Fenster and Daniel Lord Smail (eds.), *Fama: The Politics of Talk and Reputation in Medieval Europe*, Ithaca, NY, 2003.

19 *Il costituto del Comune di Siena volgarizzato nel MCCCIX–MCCCX*, vol. I, ed. Alessandro Lisini, Siena, 1903, Dist. 2, c. 39, p. 400. See the Sassoferrato statutes, issued in 1457 and largely based on the statutes of 1370: *Lo statuto communale di Sassoferrato*, c. 53, p. 118. See also, above, Chapter 2, pp. 34–5.

20 Michael Prestwich, *York Civic Ordinances, 1301*, York, 1976, p. 7.

21 On women and the sale of ale, see Judith M. Bennett, *Ale, Beer, and Brewsters in England: Women's Work in a Changing World 1300–1600*, New York and Oxford, 1996, esp. chapter 7.

22 'Item statuimus quod si quis habens uxorem et, ipsa vivente, cum alia de facto contraxerit matrimonium, puniatur in c libris ... Idem observetur de mulieribus predicata

commitentibus', *Statuti di Verona del 1327*, vol. II, c. 59, p. 468. On bigamy, see Anna Esposito, 'Adulterio, concubinato, bigamia: Testimonianze dalla normativa statutaria dello Stato pontificio (secoli XIII–XVI)', in *Trasgressioni: Seduzione, concubinato, adulterio, bigamia (XIV–XVIII secolo)*, ed. Silvana Seidel Menchi and Diego Quaglioni, Bologna, 2004, pp. 21–42; at pp. 40–1.

23 See *Les langues de l'Italie medieval: Textes d'histoire et de littérature, Xe–XIVe siècle*, Odile Redon, Lucia Battaglia Ricci, Pietro G. Beltrami, Jacqueline Brunet, and Allen J. Grieco, Brepols, 2002, pp. 192–4, and, in English translation, Margherita Datini, *Letters to Francesco Datini*, ed. Carolyn James and Antonio Pagliaro, Toronto, 2012, pp. 65–6.

24 See a letter by Francesco of 6 February 1394 in which he responds to points raised by Margherita in hers, *Lettere di Francesco Datini alla moglie Margherita (1385–1410)*, ed. Elena Cecchi, Prato, 1990, no. 18, pp. 60–1.

25 Daniel Lord Smail, *Legal Plunder: Households and Debt Collection in Late Medieval Europe*, Cambridge, MA, 2016, esp. pp. 92–113.

26 Studer, 'Frauen im Bürgerschaft' – see table 1, p. 170, for the forty or so towns that received women to citizenship; and on the terms offered, see pp. 172–8.

27 Ibid., pp. 172–3, 175, n. 11.

28 Marc Boone and Peter Stabel, 'New Burghers in the Late Medieval Towns of Flanders and Brabant: Conditions of Entry, Rules and Reality', in *Neubürger im späten Mittelalter: Migration und Austausch in der Städtelandschaft des alten Reiches (1250-1550)*, ed. Rainer Christoph Schwinges, Berlin, 2002, pp. 317–32.

29 *Liber primus Kilkenniensis*, ed. Charles McNeill, Dublin, 1931, p. 39. Mabina was listed as a burgess in a list of 1383/4, p. 70.

30 Davis, *Medieval Market Morality*, pp. 211–13; Martha C. Howell, *Commerce before Capitalism in Europe, 1300–1600*, Cambridge, 2010, pp. 108–10.

31 On this complex issue, see Julius Kirshner, '*Mulier alibi nupta*', in Baumgärtner (ed.), *Consilia im später Mittelalter: Zum historischen Aussagwert einer Quellengattung*, pp. 147–75.

32 On the categories of women's work, see Cordelia Beattie, 'The Problem of Women's Work: Identities in Post Black Death England', in *The Problem of Labour in Fourteenth-Century England*, ed. James Bothwell, P. J. P. Goldberg, and W. M. Ormrod, Woodbridge, 2000, pp. 1–19.

33 'Item, se algun maistro de quest'Arte morise e lasase fio o fioli mascoli de menor etade de anni. xvii., se la moièr vorà tegnir l'Arte per lo fio o fioli, posa tor maistro .i. in la soa staçone a lavorar ad insegnar a li fenti la dita arte in fina che algun d'esi serà ad etade de anni .xvii. e saverà l'arte lavorare per maistro', 'Capitolare dei bottai', in *I capitolari delle arti veneziani: Sottoposte alla giustizia e poi alla giustizia vecchia dalle origini al 1330*, vol. II, ed. Giovanni Monticolo, Rome, 1905, pp. 397–454, at c. 86, p. 454.

34 'extunc magistri sint obligati ad dandum eidem maccellum et famulum unum secundum considerationem ipsorum magistrorum, qui eidem fideliter serviat et artem carnificature in persona sua exerceat', Péter Kis and Iván Petrik, 'Mittelalterliche Urkunden der deutschen Fleischerzunft zu Ofen (1235/70–1519)', in *Zunftbuch und Privilegien der Fleischer zum Ofen aus dem Mittelalter*, ed. István Kenyeres, Budapest, 2008, pp. 329–39; article 8, p. 360.

35 'tutte le muggier di maestri della ditta arte li quali sia in station, debbia esser in la scola como sè li huomini, et debiase mover la crose e il penello, e debbia li maestri accompagnar lo corpo quando alcuna serà passada di questa vita', 'Capitolare dei Fabbri di Stoviglie', in *I capitolari delle arti veneziani: Sottoposte alla giustizia e poi alla giustizia vecchia dalle origini al 1330*, vol. III, ed. Giovanni Monticolo and Enrico Besta, Rome, 1914, pp. 208–14; c. 27, p. 213.

36 For an analysis of the participation of women in the London Brewers' guild, see Bennett, *Ale, Beer, and Brewsters*, chapter 4.

37 'Capitolare dei Bottai', c. 8, p. 360.

38 Jane Laughton, 'Mapping the Migrants: Welsh, Manx and Irish Settlers in Fifteenth-Century Chester', in *Mapping the Medieval City: Space, Place and Identity in Chester c. 1200–1600*, ed. Catherine A. M. Clarke, Cardiff, 2011, pp. 169–83; at pp. 176–7.

39 *Das Wiener Handwerksordnungsbuch (1364–1555): Edition und Kommentar*, ed. Markus Gneiß, Cologne, 2017, pp. 148–51.

40 *Poll Taxes*, vol. III, ed. Caroline C. Fenwick, Oxford, 2005, pp. 110–18.

41 Kowaleski, *Local Markets and Regional Trade*, p. 153.

42 Boone, 'Les Gens de métiers', pp. 23–47, at p. 45.

43 On Boileau's survey, see Farmer, *The Silk Industries of Medieval Paris*, pp. 7, 76.

44 Paula Clarke, 'Le "mercantesse" di Venezia nei secoli XIV e XV', *Archivio Veneto* 6th series 3 (2012), 67–84; esp. 74–6.

45 Ibid., 78–82.

46 For an historiographical overview, see Kevin Mummey and Kathryn Reyerson, 'Whose City is This? Hucksters, Domestic Servants, Wet-Nurses, Prostitutes, and Slaves in Late Medieval Western Mediterranean Urban Society', *History Compass* 9 (2011), 910–22.

47 'En la rue au Roy-de-Sezille/ Entrai, tantost trouvai Sedile:/ En la rue Renaut-le-Fevre/ Maint ou el vent et pois et feves', *Le Dit des rues de Paris (1300) par Guillot (de Paris)*, ed. Edgar Mareuse, Paris, 1875, republished with a translation by Catherine Nicolas, Paris, 2012, lines 478–81, p. 102. For some interesting reflections on women in city streets, see Christiane Klapisch-Zuber, 'Les Femmes dans les espaces publics de la ville italienne (XIVe–XVe)', in *Anthropologie de la ville médiévale*, ed. Mychal Tymowski, Warsaw, 1999, pp. 83–90.

48 Stevens, *Urban Assimilation*, pp. 178–84. On forestalling in Colchester, see R. H. Britnell, *Growth and Decline in Colchester, 1300–1525*, Cambridge, 1986, pp. 40–1; in some small towns enforcement was less consistent, see Davis, *Medieval Market Morality*, pp. 323–31.

49 Stevens, *Urban Assimilation*, table 5.1, p. 181.

50 Boone, 'Les Gens de métiers', p. 44.

51 'ex odii fomite diffamauit, asserendo et publice predicando de eadem quod dicta Agnes crimen annone defraudate [incurrit], uidelicet ut ipsa ad mercatum annonarum publicum in dicta uilla Oxonie accedens cum uenditoribus granorum societatem coiens at colludens multum plus iusto precio pro granis eorum emendis sepius palam et fraudulenter optulisset', *Munimenta Civitatis Oxonie*, no. 193, pp. 188–90; at p. 189.

52 'Nec aliqua mulier possit vel debeat extra domum sequi corpus defuncti vel interesse modo aliquot vel ingenio sepulture; liceat tamen ipsis mulieribus ire et esse ad domum

defuncti et intra domum stare et plangere ad suam voluntatem', *Statuti Bonacolsiani*, c. 44, pp. 152–3, at p. 152.

53 'nulla mulier intret vel exeat per portam Sancti Iohannis plebis Sancti Giminiani quando aliquis mortuus portabitur ad ecclesiam seu ad sepolturam ad sepelliendum … Item non levetur plantus nisi viderint venire catalectum ad domum defunti, et tunc elevetur plantus solum per mulieres et non per homines, set per homines et etiam mulieres elevetur plantus in ecclesia, si voluerint, quando ibi corpus defunti de sua domo fuerit deportatum ad ecclesiam', *Lo Statuto di San Gimignano del 1255*, III.54, pp. 104–6; at pp. 104–5.

54 Susan L'Engle, 'Justice in the Margins: Punishment in Medieval Toulouse', *Viator* 33 (2002), 133–65. And, for an overview, John H. Arnold, 'Sexualité et déshonneur dans le Midi (XIIIe–XIVe siècles): Les péchés de la chair et l'opinion collective', in *L'Église et la chair (XIIe–XVe siècle)*, ed. Michèle Fournié, Daniel Le Blévec, and Julien Théry, Toulouse, 2019, pp. 305–39.

55 Gourdon, Hotel de Ville, Archives municipales de Gourdon, FF11, fol. 9r.

56 Daniel Lord Smail, 'Démanteler le patrimoine: Les femmes et les biens dans la Marseille médiévale', *Annales* 52 (1997), 343–68; at 358.

57 Daniel Lord Smail, *The Consumption of Justice: Emotions, Publicity, and Legal Culture in Marseille, 1264–1423*, Ithaca, NY, 2003, pp. 56–7.

58 Stevens, *Urban Assimilation*, pp. 119–38.

59 Emma Cavell, 'The Measure of Her Actions: A Quantitative Assessment of Anglo-Jewish Women's Litigation at the Exchequer of the Jews, 1219–1281', *Law and History* (2020), forthcoming.

60 As has been shown and discussed in Bronach Kane, *Popular Memory and Gender in Medieval England: Men, Women, and Testimony in the Church Courts, c. 1200–1500*, Woodbridge, 2019.

61 *Codice degli statuti della repubblica di Sassari*, c. 8, p. 243.

62 'Jst sÿe aber eÿne fragnerin, sÿ sol auf dem rothaus sweren vnnd sÿ mag auch deß aides nicht verfelen', *Das Ofner Stadtrecht*, Book 3, no. 315, p. 164.

63 'et talis mulier possit secum ducere unum hominem quando esset ad testifationem predictam', *Lo Statuto di Montebuono in Sabina del 1437*, c. 90, p. 100.

64 Maria Teresa Brolis, 'Ceci in pentola e desiderio di Dio: Religiosità femminile in testamenti bergamaschi (secoli xiii–xiv)', in *Margini di libertà: Testamenti femminili nel medioevo*, ed. Maria Clara Rossi, Verona 2010, pp. 333–53; at pp. 333–4.

65 Farmer, *The Silk Industries of Medieval Paris*, esp. pp. 143–8. For a seminal insight into women as lenders, see Jordan, *Women and Credit*.

66 Hannah Meyer, 'Female Moneylending and Wet-Nursing in Jewish–Christian Relations in Thirteenth-Century England', unpublished PhD thesis, University of Cambridge, 2009, Part I: 'Analysis of Female Moneylending in Thirteenth-Century England'.

67 Jacqueline Murray, 'On the Origins and Role of "Wise Women" in Causes for Annulment on the Grounds of Male Impotence', *Journal of Medieval History* 16 (1990), 235–49. On the tensions between physicians and female practitioners over their knowledge, see Monica H. Green, *Making Women's Medicine Masculine: The Rise of Male Authority in Pre-*

Modern Gynaecology, Oxford, 2008, esp. pp. 291–301. For an interesting case that involved Jewish and Christian midwives as witnesses, see Monica H. Green and Daniel Lord Smail, 'The Trial of Floreta d'Ays (1403): Jews, Christians, and Obstetrics in Later Medieval Marseille', *Journal of Medieval History* 34 (2008), 185–211.

68 Debra Blumenthal, '"With My Daughter's Milk": Wet Nurses and the Rhetoric of Lactation in Valencian Court Records', in *Medieval and Renaissance Lactations: Images, Rhetorics, Practices*, ed. Jutta Gisela Sperling, Farnham, 2013, pp. 101–14.

69 Cagnin, *Cittadini e forestieri*, pp. 21–2.

70 The classic study of this process is Lester K. Little, *Religious Poverty and the Profit Economy in Medieval Europe*, London, 1978.

71 David L. d'Avray, *The Preaching of the Friars: Sermons Diffused from Paris before 1300*, Oxford, 1985.

72 On Francis's early life and chocies, see André Vauchez, *Francis of Assisi: The Life and Afterlife of a Medieval Saint*, trans. Michael F. Casuto, New Haven, CN, 2012, pp. 3–29.

73 For an interesting case from Rome, see *Visions of Sainthood in Medieval Rome: The Lives of Margherita Colonna by Giovanni Colonna and Stefania*, ed. and intro. Lezlie S. Knox and Sean L. Field, and trans. Larry L. Field, South Bend, IN, 2017.

74 Ella Kilgallon, 'Creating a Space of Penance: Women of the Franciscan Third Order in the Cities of Central Italy', unpublished doctoral thesis, Queen Mary University of London, 2018, pp. 88–132.

75 André Vauchez, *Catherine of Siena: A Life of Passion and Purpose*, Mahwah, NJ, 2018.

76 Walter Simons, *Cities of Ladies: Beguine Communities in the Medieval Low Countries, 1200–1565*, Philadelphia, pp. 104–9.

77 Ibid., pp. 85–7; for a register of established houses, see pp. 256–9.

78 Thérèse de Hemptinne, 'Reading, Writing, and Devotional Practices: Lay and Religious Women and the Written Word in the Low Countries (1350–1550)', in *The Voice of Silence: Women's Literacy in a Men's Church*, ed. Thérèse de Hemptinne and María Eugenia Góngora, Turnhout, 2004, pp. 111–26; Thérèse de Hemptinne, 'Des Femmes copistes dans les Pays-Bas au bas Moyen Âge (14e–15e siècle): Approche d'une activité feminine malconnue', in *Secretum scriptorum: Liber alumnorum Walter Prevenier*, ed. Willem Pieter Blockmans, Marc Boone, and Thérèse de Hemptinne, Leuven, 1999, pp. 129–43; at pp. 133–4.

79 Walter Simons, 'In Praise of Faithful Women: Count Robert of Flanders' Defense of Beguines against the Clementine Decree *Cum de quibusdam mulieribus* (c. 1318–1320)', in *Christianity and Culture in the Middle Ages: Essays in Honor of John Van Engen's 35th Anniversary of Teaching at Notre Dame*, ed. David Mengel and Lisa Wolverton, South Bend, IN, 2014, pp. 331–57.

80 On signs, see Michael Camille, 'Signs of the City: Place, Power, and Public Fantasy in Medieval Paris', in *Medieval Practices of Space*, ed. Barbara A. Hanawalt and Michal Kobialka, Minneapolis, 2000, pp. 1–36.

81 For some interesting reflections on women and walking in cities, see Lauren Elkin, *Flâneuse: Women Walk the City in Paris, New York, Tokyo, Venice and London*, London, 2016.

82 'Item, sy aucsu'un [connoist] charnellement une femme outre son gré et volonté, sy lad. femme en fait plainte et que led. crime soit prouvé, celuy quy aura fait le crime payera à

lad. femme pour l'amende trante sols toulouzains . . . Toutes fois sy lad. femme estoit noble, de bonne extraction et de bonnes mœurs, l'amende luy en sera faicte selon sa qualitté à la connoissance de la cour', *Chartes de franchises du Lauragais*, ed. Jean Ramière de Fortanier, Toul, 1939, no. 44, pp. 130–5; c. 13, p. 133.

83 'Une dame vi sus .i. seil,/ Qui moult se portoit noblement./ Je la saluai simplement,/ Et elle moi, par Saint Loÿs', *Le Dit des rues de Paris*, p. 84, lines 364–7. I cite for this the translation in Emma Dillon, *The Sense of Sound: Musical Meaning in France, 1260–1330*, Oxford, 2012, p. 64.

84 'Item establem que non porton vestidura neguna de ceda, mais cendat puescon portar en folraduras de lurs vestirs, et estiers non', Sarah-Grace Heller, 'Limiting Yardage and Changes of Clothes: Sumptuary Legislation in Thirteenth-Century France, Languedoc and Italy', in *Medieval Fabrications: Dress Textiles, Clothwork, and Other Cultural Imaginings*, ed. E. Jane Burns, New York, 2004, pp. 121–36; p. 127.

85 Hughes, 'Distinguishing Signs', pp. 3–59; esp. pp. 47–59.

86 'gitet una vet a la dicha juona ab una peira, la qual no ferit. E poichas gitet lhi autra vet ab una peira: Feir la sus la camba. E, quant la ac ferida, la dicha juona pres una peira e feit lo dig Peyre', Archives municipales de la Ville de Gourdon, FF 11, fol. 152v. On the archive, see François Arbelet, 'Histoire des archives de Gourdon', *Bulletin de la Société des Études du Lot* 137 (2016), 11–18.

87 'Mulier que aliquem hominem ferro petra vel baculo sive alia re percusserit, et sanguis inde exierit, si percussio fuerit in visu ita quod signum ibi remaneat, condempnetur per potestatem in libras x pro libero, et pro servo in soldos xx', *Codice degli statuti della repubblica di Sassari*, c. 7, p. 243.

88 'Si qua mulier ferro petra vel baculo sive alia re aliquam mulierem percusserit et sanguis inde exierit, si percussio fuerit in visu, ita quod signum ibi remaneat, condempnetur a potestate, pro libera in libras decem Ianue, et pro ancilla in libras iiii', 'De percussione membri', ibid., c. 6, p. 242.

89 'dont elle ay eu et ay des empôles au visaige', Roger Kohn, *Les Juifs de la France du Nord dans la seconde moitié du XIVe siècle*, Leuven, 1988, p. 178; some of the councilmen who judged her complained she had transgressed against the local custom by which Jews lived in Dijon.

90 Pajic, *Flemish Textile Workers in England*, pp. 200–5.

91 Archives municipales de Gourdon, FF11, 71r.

92 'auzit plorar lefan dela dicha R. e ela intert lains ela maio dela dicha R', Archives municipales de Gourdon, FF11, 16v. Similarly, for the theft of malt in Ruthin in 1314, see Stevens, *Urban Assimilation*, p. 122, n. 10.

93 Walter Benjamin captures well this type of neighbouring intimacy in his 'Naples', in *One-Way Street and Other Writings*, trans. Edmund Jephcott and Kingsley Shorter, London, 1979, pp. 167–76, esp. at pp. 174–5.

94 On the gendered aspects of the migration of fifteenth-century Scots, see Judith M. Bennett, 'Women (and Men) on the Move: Scots in the English North c. 1440', *Journal of British Studies* 57 (2018), 1–28.

95 *The Book of Margery Kempe*, trans. and ed. Lynn Staley, New York, 2001, p. 172. On the linguistic challenges and possibilities of travel, as arising from Margery's *Book*, see

Jonathan Hsy, *Trading Tongues: Merchants, Multilingualism, and Medieval Literature*, Columbus, OH, 2013, chapter 4.

96 'והאישה שהולכת בדרך ושמעה שפוגעין בה גוים ויראה פן ישכבו עמה יכולה ללבוש את עצמה בבגדי כומרת כדי שיהיו
סבורים שהיא כומרת ולא ישכבו עמה. ואם היא שמעה שפריצי ישראל יפגעו בה כמו כן מותרת ללבוש מלבוש נכרית ולומר
שהיא גויה'. *Das Buch der Frommen*, c. 261. p.85.

97 Maryse Guénette, 'Errance et solitude féminines à Manosque (1314–1358)', in *Vie privée et ordre publique à la fin du Moyen Âge: Études sur Manosque, la Provence et le Piémont (1250–1450)*, ed. Michel Hébert, Aix-en-Provence, 1987, pp. 23–43; esp. pp. 23–6.

98 Stevens, *Urban Assimilation*, pp. 213–19, esp. figure 5.4, p. 218; see pp. 208–9.

99 Pajic, *Flemish Textile Workers in England*, p. 55.

100 Kate J. P. Lowe, 'Introduction', in *Black Africans in Renaissance Europe*, ed. T. F. Earle and K. J. P. Lowe, Cambridge, 2005, pp. 1–14.

101 Sergio Tognetti, 'The Trade in Black African Slaves in Fifteenth-Century Florence', in *Black Africans in Renaissance Europe*, ed. T. F. Earle and K. J. P. Lowe, Cambridge, 2005, pp. 213–24; at p. 214.

102 Debra Blumenthal, 'Black African Solidarity in Late Medieval Valencia', in *Black Africans in Renaissance Europe*, ed. T. F. Earle and K. J. P. Lowe, Cambridge, 2005, pp. 225–46; at pp. 230–2.

103 On England, see Ormrod, Lambert, and Mackman, *Immigrant England, 1300–1550*, pp. 187–92.

104 Ruth Mazo Karras, *Common Women: Prostitution and Sexuality in Medieval England*, Oxford, 1996, esp. chapters 1 and 2.

105 See, for example, one from 1261: 'Encara, fem fur nou que negú qui haurà sarrahina no la tingue per putana sabuda', *Furs de València*, vol. II, ed. Germà Colon and Arcadi Garcia, Barcelona, 1974, Book II, rubric 3, p. 85.

106 Rossella Rinaldi, '"Mulieres publicae": Testimonianze e note sulla prostituzione tra pieno e tardo medioevo', in *Donne e lavoro nell'Italia medievale*, ed. Maria Giuseppina Muzzarelli, Paola Galetti, and Bruno Andreolli, Turin, 1991, pp. 105–25; at pp. 110–11.

107 'a d'intorno al fosso infino a' luogo de' frati Servi Sancte Marie', *Il costituto del Comune di Siena*, vol. II, Dist. III, c. LV, p. 35. The *brachium* is an arm's length. On the regulation of prostitution in Pisa in the 1286 statutes, see *Statuti inediti della città di Pisa dal XII al XIV secolo*, vol. II, ed. Francesco Bonaini, Florence, 1854, c. 33, pp. 395–8.

108 *Memorials of London and London Life in the XIIIth, XIVth, and XVth Centuries*, ed. Henry Thomas Riley, London, 1868, p. 458.

109 'sullen eÿn gelbs fechil zum mÿnsten oÿner handt prait tragen auf iren haŭp tuchern', *Das Ofner Stadtrecht*, Book 3, no. 186, pp. 124–5.

110 Prestwich, *York Civic Ordinances, 1301*, pp. 16–17; The National Archives 13/26 mm.75–6.

111 'quod nulla publica meretrix stet nec stare debeat nec habitare in civitate seu intra muros civitatis Pergami, sub pena ad arbitrium vicarii. Et quod nullus intra muros civitatis debeat ipsi meretricibus vel alicui earum locare vel gratis concedere aliquam domum ad standum vel habitandum in ea, sub pena soldorum centum imperialium pro quolibet et qualibet vice', *Lo statuto di Bergamo del 1331*, ed. Claudia Storti Storchi, Milan, 1986, Collatio VIII, c. 70, p. 157.

112 'Enprés est rue de l'Escole:/ La demeure Dame Nicole./ En celle rue ce me samble/ Vent on et fain et fuerre ensamble', *Le Dit des rues de Paris*, p. 50, lines 145–8.

113 David C. Mengel, 'From Venice to Jerusalem and Beyond: Milíč of Kroměříž and the Topography of Prostitution in Fourteenth-Century Prague', *Speculum* 79 (2004), 407–42; see also his David Mengel, 'Emperor Charles IV (1346–1378) as the Architect of Local Religion in Prague', *Austrian History Yearbook* 41 (2010), 15–29, esp. 24–5.

114 Fear that poor women without a dowry might fall into prostitution inspired much charitable work in this area: see Julius Kirshner, *Pursuing Honor while Avoiding Sin: The Monte dell doti of Florence*, Milan, 1978. See also Anna Esposito, '*Ad dotandum puellas virgines, pauperes et honestas*: Social Needs and Confraternal Charity in Rome in the Fifteenth and Sixteenth Centuries', *Renaissance and Reformation* 18 (1994), 5–18.

115 Dennis Romano, 'Gender and the Urban Geography of Renaissance Venice', *Journal of Social History* 23 (1989), 339–53; esp. 345.

116 'et possit quilibet eam offendere sine pena et banpno [dampno]', *Statuta comunis et populi civitatis Camerini (1424)*, lib. III, rub. 125, p. 251.

117 Valérie Toureille, *Vol et brigandage au Moyen Âge*, Paris, 2006, pp. 94–106.

118 David Cressy, *Gypsies: An English Story*, Oxford, 2018, pp. 1–10.

CONCLUSION

1 Elizabeth Bishop, *Poems, Prose, and Letters*, New York, 2008, p. 75.

2 Bennett, 'Women (and Men) on the Move'. A collection that combines attention to major demographic shifts as well as to regional trends is found in Cavaciocchi (ed.), *Le migrazioni in Europa secc. XIII–XVIII*. For several early modern studies, see the special issue of *Quaderni Storici* 36 (2001) entitled 'Migrazioni', edited by Angiolina Arru, Josef Ehmer, and Franco Ramella.

3 On the biblical phrase and its interpretation in late medieval and early modern England, see Naomi Tadmor, *The Social Universe of the English Bible: Scripture, Society, and Culture in Early Modern England*, Cambridge, 2010, pp. 20–1, 23–49.

4 'Siamo tutti stranieri. Ma solo alcuni ne sono consapevoli', Heleni Porfyriou, 'Gli stranieri e la città', in *Lo spazio narrabile: Scritti di storia della città in onore di Donatella Calabi*, ed. Rosa Tamborrino and Guido Zacconi, Macerata, 2014, pp. 83–92; p. 91.

5 'En être réduit à recourir à moi, c'est cela l'apatridie ou l'étrangeté du prochain. Elle m'incombe', Emmanuel Levinas, *Autrement qu'être ou au-delà de l'essence*, The Hague, 1974, pp. 15–16. The English translation is from Emmanuel Lévinas, *Otherwise Than Being or beyond Essence*, trans. Alphonso Lingis, Dordrecht and Boston, MA, 1978, p. 91.

6 For several studies of new intersections of religion, trade, and travel in this period, see Francesca Trivellato, Leor Halevi, and Cátia Antunes (eds.), *Religion and Trade: Cross-Cultural Exchanges in World History, 1000–1900*, Oxford, 2014.

7 Mark Greengrass, *Christendom Destroyed: Europe 1517–1648*, London, 2014. On the new discussions of toleration in sixteenth-century Europe, see Ole Peter Grell and Bob Scribner (eds.), *Tolerance and Intolerance in the European Reformation*, Cambridge, 1996.

8 'Observations des ordres mendicants de la ville d'Ypres sur le règlement de la bienfaisance', in J. Nolf, *La Réforme de la bienfaisance publique à Ypres au XVIe siècle*, Ghent, 1915,
pp. 40–76, at p. 64.

9 See Annabel S. Brett, *Changes of State: Nature and the Limits of the City in Early Modern
Natural Law*, Princeton, NJ, 2011, pp. 18–19.

10 Ibid., pp. 15–20.

11 London British Library Harley ms 7368. And on the riots, see Ian. W. Archer, *The Pursuit
of Stability: Social Relations in Elizabethan London*, Cambridge, 1991, pp. 131–40. I am
enormously grateful to Shannon McSheffrey for sharing with me a most interesting
lecture she has written, based on her research into the May Day riots, which is as yet
unpublished.

Bibliography

PRIMARY SOURCES CITED

Albertanus of Brescia, *Liber de doctrina dicendi et tacendi: La parola del cittadino nell'Italia del Duecento*, ed. Paola Navone, Florence: Galluzzo, 1998.

Das älteste Greifswalder Stadtbuch (1291–1332), ed. Dietrick W. Poeck, Cologne: Böhlau, 2000.

Das älteste Rostocker Stadtbuch (etwa 1254–1275), ed. Hildegard Thierfelder, Göttingen: Vandenhoeck & Ruprecht, 1967.

Amichai, Yehuda, *A Life in Poetry, 1948–1994*, trans. Benjamin and Barbara Harshav, New York: HarperCollins, 1994.

Anzaldúa, Gloria, *Borderlands. La Frontera. The New Mestiza*, San Francisco: Aunt Lute Book Company, 1987.

The Apostolic See and the Jews, vol. I: *Documents 492–1404*, ed. Shlomo Simonsohn, Toronto: Pontifical Institute of Medieval Studies, 1988.

The Apostolic See and the Jews, vol. II: *Documents 1394–1464*, ed. Shlomo Simonsohn, Toronto: Pontifical Institute of Medieval Studies, 1989.

Auden, W. H., *The Shield of Achilles*, London: Faber and Faber, 1955.

Bernardino of Siena, *Opera IV*, Florence: College of St Bonaventure's Press, 1956.

Bishop, Elizabeth, *Poems, Prose, and Letters*, New York: Literary Classics of the United States, 2008.

The Book of Margery Kempe, trans. and ed. Lynn Staley, New York: W. W. Norton, 2001.

Brunetto Latini, *Li livre dou Tresor*, ed. Spurgeon Baldwin and Paul Barrette, Medieval and Renaissance Texts and Studies 257, Tempe, AZ: Arizona Center for Medieval and Renaissance Studies, 2003 [*The Book of Treasure (Li Livres dou Tresor)*, trans. Paul Barrette and Spurgeon Baldwin, New York: Garland, 1993].

Das Buch der Frommen, ed. Jehuda Wistinetzki, Frankfurt: M. A. Wahrmann, 1924, repr. Jerusalem: Sifre Vahrman, 1969.

Buoncampagno da Signa, *Il pensiero e l'opera di Boncampagno da Signa*, ed. Massimo Baldini, Signa (Florence): Grevigiana, 2002.

Calendar of Ancient Records of Dublin in the Possession of the Municipal Corporation of the City I, ed. John T. Gilbert, Dublin: Joseph Dollard, 1889.

Calendar of Letter-Books Preserved among the Archives of the Corporation of the City of London at the Guildhall: Letter-Book G, ed. Reginald R. Sharpe, London: City of London Corporation, 1905.

Cancionero de Gallardo, ed. José María Azaceta, Madrid: CSIC, 1962.

'Capitolare dei Bottai', in *I capitolari delle arti veneziani: Sottoposte alla giustizia e poi alla giustizia vecchia dalle origini al 1330*, vol. II, ed. Giovanni Monticolo, Rome: Istituto storico italiano, 1905, pp. 397–454.

'Capitolare dei Cristallai', in *I capitolari delle arti veneziani: Sottoposte alla giustizia e poi alla giustizia vecchia dalle origini al 1330*, vol. III, ed. Giovanni Monticolo and Enrico Besta, Rome: Istituto storico italiano, 1914, pp. 123–52.

'Capitolare dei Fabbri di Stoviglie', in *I capitolari delle arti veneziani: Sottoposte alla giustizia e poi alla giustizia vecchia dalle origini al 1330*, vol. III, ed. Giovanni Monticolo and Enrico Besta, Rome: Istituto storico italiano, 1914, pp. 208–14.

The Charters of the Borough of Cambridge, ed. Frederic William Maitland and Mary Bateson, Cambridge University Press, 1901.

Chartes de franchises du Lauragais, ed. Jean Ramière de Fortanier, Toul: Imprimerie Toulouse, 1939.

Christine de Pizan, *Livre de la cité des dames [La città delle dame]*, ed. Patrizia Caraffi and Earl Jeffrey Richards, Milan: Luni, 1998 [Christine de Pizan, *The Book of the City of Ladies*, trans. and ed. Rosalind Brown-Grant, London: Penguin, 1999].

Chronicles of London, ed. Charles Lethbridge Kingsford, Oxford: Clarendon, 1905.

Chronicon Placentium et Chronicon de rebus in Italia gestis, ed. J. L. A. Huillard-Breholles, Paris: Henri Plon, 1856, pp. 107–390.

The Code of Cuenca, Municipal Law and the Twelfth-Century Castilian Frontier, trans. and intro. James F. Powers, Philadelphia: University of Pennsylvania Press, 2000.

Codice degli statuti della repubblica di Sassari, ed. Pasquale Tola, Cagliari: A. Timon, 1850.

La Commune de Toulouse et les sources de son histoire (1120–1249): Étude historique et critique suivie de l'édition du Cartulaire du Consulat, ed. Roger Limouzin-Lamothe, Toulouse: E. Privat, 1932.

Il costituto del Comune di Siena, volgarizzato nel MCCCIX–MCCCX, vol. I, ed. Alessandro Lisini, Siena: Archivio di stato di Siena, 1903.

Il costituto del Comune di Siena, volgarizzato nel MCCCIX–MCCCX, vol. II, ed. Mahmoud Salem Elsheik, Siena: Fondazione Monte dei Paschi, 2002.

The Costuma d'Agen: A Thirteenth-Century Customary Compilation in Old Occitan.
Transcribed from the Livre Juratoire, trans. F. R. P. Akehurst, Turnhout: Brepols,
2010.

Les Coutumes de Toulouse, 1286, et leur premier commentaire, 1296, ed. Henri Gilles,
Toulouse: M. Espic, 1969.

Decrees of the Ecumenical Councils, vol. I, ed. Norman P. Tanner, London: Sheed &
Ward Ltd, 1990.

The Dialogue of Andreas Meinhardi: A Utopian Description of Wittenberg and Its University, 1508, ed. and trans. Edgar C. Reinke, Ann Arbor, MI: University Microfilms International, 1976.

Dino Compagni, *Cronica,* ed. Davide Cappi, Rome: Istituto Palazzo Borromini,
2000 [*Dino Compagni's Chronicle of Florence,* trans. with introduction, Daniel
E. Bornstein, Philadelphia: University of Pennsylvania Press, 1986].

*Die Disputationen zu Ceuta (1179) und Mallorca (1286): Zwei antijüdische Schriften aus
dem mittelalterlichen Genua,* ed. Ora Limor, Monumenta Germaniae Historica,
Quellen zur Geistesgeschichte des Mittelalters 15, Munich: Monumenta
Germaniae Historica, 1994.

Le Dit des rues de Paris (1300) par Guillot (de Paris), ed. Edgar Mareuse, Paris:
Librairie Générale, 1875, republished with a translation by Catherine Nicolas, Paris: Éditions de Paris Max Chaleil, 2012.

*Les Établissements de Rouen: Études sur l'histoire des institutions municipales de
Rouen, Falaise, etc., vol. I,* ed. A. Giry, Paris: École Pratique des Hautes Études,
1883.

*Études historiques et documents inédits sur l'albigeois, le castrais et l'ancien diocèse de
Lavaur,* ed. Claude Compayré, Albi: Maurice Papailhiau, 1841.

I frammenti epigrafici degli statuti di Ferrara del 1173 venuti in luce nella cattedrale, ed.
Adriano Franceschini, Ferrara: Ferrariae decus and Deputazione provinciale
ferrarese di storia patria, 1969.

El Fuero de Teruel, vol. I, ed. Max Gorosch, Stockholm: Almquist & Wiksell, 1950.

Fuero de Úbeda, ed. Juan Guttiérrez Cuadrado, and with studies by Mariano Peset
and Juan Guttiérrez Cuadrado, Publications of the University of Valencia,
1979.

Furs de València, vol. II, ed. Germà Colon and Arcadi Garcia, Barcelona: Barcino,
1974.

Hartmann Schedel, *Chronicle of the World: The Complete and Annotated Nuremberg
Chronicle of 1493,* intro. Stephan Füssel, Cologne: Taschen, 2001.

Hebrew Deeds of Catalan Jews/Documents hebraics de la Catalunya medieval: 1117–1316,
Girona Judaica 1, ed. Elka Klein, Barcelona and Girona: Societat catalana
d'estudis hebraics, 2004.

Hebrew and Hebrew–Latin Documents from Medieval England: A Diplomatic and Palaeographical Study, ed. Judith Olszowy-Schlanger, 2 vols., Turnhout: Brepols, 2015.

Isidore of Seville, *Etimologiarum sive originum libri XX*, trans. W. M. Lindsay, Oxford: Clarendon, 1911 [*Etymologies*, vol. II, trans. Priscilla Throop, Charlotte, VT: Medieval Ms, 2005].

The Itinerary of Benjamin of Tudela, ed. Marcus Nathan Adler, London: Henry Frowde, 1907.

Layettes du trésor des chartes, vol. I, ed. Alexandre Teulet, Paris: H. Plon, 1863.

Les Langues de l'Italie médiévale: Textes d'histoire et de littérature, Xe–XIVe siècle, Odile Redon, Lucia Battaglia Ricci, Pietro G. Beltrami, Jacqueline Brunet, and Allen J. Grieco, Brepols: Turnhout, 2002.

Lettere di Francesco Datini alla moglie Margherita (1385–1410), ed. Elena Cecchi, Prato: Società pratese di storia patria, 1990.

Liber custumarum, ed. Henry Thomas Riley, Rerum Britannicarum Medii Aevi Scriptores 12, Munimenta Gildhallae Londonienses 12, I, London: HMSO, 1860, Kraus reprint 1967.

Liber primus Kilkenniensis, ed. Charles McNeill, Dublin: Stationery Office, 1931.

Libro della comunità dei mercanti lucchesi in Bruges, ed. Eugenio Lazzareschi with a preface by Armando Sapori, Milan: Rodolfo Malfasi, 1947.

Das Liegnitzer Stadtrechtsbuch des Nikolaus Wurm: Hintergrund, Überlieferung und Edition eines schlesischen Rechtsdenkmals, ed. Hans-Jörg Leuchte, Quellen und Darstellungen zur schlesischen Geschichte 25, Sigmaringen: Jan Thorbecke, 1990.

Maharil (Yaakov ben Moshe Levi Moelin), *Minhagim*, Sabyonetah: Vicenzo Conti, 1556.

Marco Polo, *Milione, Le divisament dou monde: Il milione nelle redazioni toscana e franco-italiana*, ed. Cesare Segre, Milan: Mondadori, 1982 [*Il milione*, ed. Ruggero M. Ruggieri, Florence: Leo S. Olschki, 1986].

Margherita Datini, *Letters to Francesco Datini*, ed. Carolyn James and Antonio Pagliaro, Toronto: Center for Reformation and Renaissance Studies, 2012.

Memorials of London and London Life in the XIIIth, XIVth, and XVth Centuries, ed. Henry Thomas Riley, London: Longmans, Green, and Co., 1868.

Le Mesnagier de Paris, ed. Georgina E. Brereton and Janet M. Ferrier, trans. Karin Ueltschi, Paris: Livre de Poche, 1994.

Munimenta Civitatis Oxonie, ed. H. E. Salter, Oxford Historical Society 71 (1917), Devizes: George Simpson and Co., 1920.

The Oak Book of Southampton of c. A.D. 1300, vol. II, ed. P. Studer, Publications of the Southampton Record Society, Southampton: Cox and Sharland, 1911.

Das Ofner Stadtrecht: Eine deutschsprachige Rechtssammlung des 15. Jahrhunderts aus Ungarn, ed. Karl Mollay, Budapest: Akadémiai Kiadó, 1959.

The People of Curial Avignon: A Critical Edition of the Liber Divisionis and the Matriculae of Notre Dame la Majour, ed. Joëlle Rollo-Koster, Lewiston, NY: Edwin Mellen, 2009.

Plato, *Laws*, ed. Michael Schofield and trans. Tom Griffith, Cambridge University Press, 2016.

Poll Taxes, vol. III, ed. Caroline C. Fenwick, Oxford: Oxford University Press and the British Academy, 2005.

Pommersches Urkundenbuch, vol. I, ed. Klaus Conrad, Veröffentlichungen der Historischen Kommission für Pommern 2, Cologne: Böhlau, 1970.

Recueil diplomatique du Canton de Fribourg, vol. I, ed. Romain Werro, Jean Berchtold, and Jean Gremaud, Fribourg: Jospeh-Louis Pillier, 1839.

Statuta, capitula, sive ordinamenta communis Carij, www.cairomontenotte.com/biblioteca/scorzoni/b-1.html

Statuta comunis et populi civitatis Camerini (1424), ed. Fabrizio Ciapparoni, Naples: Jovene, 1977.

The Statute of Dubrovnik 1271 = Liber statutorum civitatis Ragusii compositus anno MCCLXXII, trans. Vesna Rimać and ed. Nella Lonza, Dubrovnik: Državni arhiv u Dubrovniku, 2012.

Die Statuten der Reichsstadt Mühlhausen, ed. Wolfgang Weber and Gerhard Lingelbach, Cologne: Böhlau, 2005.

Statuti Bonacolsiani, ed. Ettore Dezza, Anna Maria Lorenzoni, and Mario Vaini, Mantua: Gianluigi Arcari, 2002.

Statuti dei Laghi di Como e di Lugano dei secoli XIII e XIV, vol. II, ed. Emilio Anderloni and A. Lazzati, Milan: Ulrich Hoepli, 1915.

Statuti del Comune di Cecina nel 1409, ed. Pietro Fanfani, Florence: M. Cellini, 1857.

Statuti della Laguna Veneta dei secoli XIV–XVI, ed. Gherardo Ortalli, Monica Pasqualetto, and Alessandra Rizzi, Rome: Jouvence, 1989.

Statuti di Bologna dell'anno 1288, ed. Gina Fasoli and Pietro Sella, 2 vols., Vatican City: Biblioteca apostolica vaticana, 1937–9.

Statuti di Spoleto del 1296, ed. Giovanni Antonelli, Florence: Leo S. Olschki, 1962.

Statuti di Verona del 1327, vols. I–II, ed. Silvana Anna Bianchi and Rosalba Granuzzo, Rome: Jouvence, 1992.

Statuti e capitolari di Chioggia del 1272–1279 con le aggiunte fino al 1327, ed. Gianni Penzo Doria and Sergio Perini, Venice: Il Cardo, 1993.

Statuti inediti della città di Pisa dal XII al XIV secolo, vol. II, ed. Francesco Bonaini, Florence: G. P. Vieusseux, 1854.

Statuti notarili di Bergamo (secolo XIII), ed. Giuseppe Scarazzini, Rome: Consiglio nazionale del notariato, 1977.

Statuti notarili piacentini del XIV secolo, ed. Corrado Pecorella, Milan: A. Giuffrè, 1971.

Statuti pistoiesi del secolo XII, ed. Natale Rauty, Pistoia: Società pistoiese di storia patria, 1996.

Statuti pistoiesi del secolo XIII, Studi e testi, vols. II–III, ed. Renzo Nelli and Giuliano Pinto, Pistoia: Società pistoiese di storia patria, 2002.

Statuti senesi scritti in volgare ne' secoli XIII e XIV, vol. III, ed. Luciano Banchi, Bologna: G. Romagnoli, 1877.

Lo statuto comunale di Sassoferrato, ed. Ugo Paoli, Sassoferrato: Istituto internazionale di studi piceni, 1993.

Statuto del Comune di Perugia del 1279, vol. I, ed. Severino Caprioli, Perugia: Deputazione di storia patria per l'Umbria, 1996.

Lo statuto di Bergamo del 1331, ed. Claudia Storti Storchi, Milan: Giuffrè, 1986.

Statuto di Forlì, ed. Evelina Rinaldi, Milan: U. Hoepli, 1913.

Lo statuto di Montebuono in Sabina del 1437, with contributions by Mario Ascheri, Tersilio Leggio, and Sandro Notari, and ed. Alda Spotti, Rome: Viella, 2011.

Lo statuto di San Gimignano del 1255, ed. Silvia Diacciati and Lorenzo Tanzini, Florence: Leo S. Olschki, 2016.

Les Statuts municipaux de Marseille, ed. Régine Pernoud, Monaco and Paris: Picard, 1949.

The Trial of the Talmud, Paris, 1240, trans. John Friedman and Jean Connell Hoff, with an essay by Robert Chazan, Toronto: Pontifical Institute of Mediaeval Studies, 2012.

Urkunden der Stadt Strassburg, vol. V, ed. Hans Witte and Georg Wolfram, Strasburg: Karl J. Trübner, 1895.

Visions of Sainthood in Medieval Rome: The Lives of Margherita Colonna by Giovanni Colonna and Stefania, ed. and intro. Lezlie S. Knox and Sean L. Field, and trans. Larry L. Field, South Bend, IN: Notre Dame University Press, 2017.

Výsady Miest a Mestečiek na Slovensku (1238–1350), Bratislava: VEDA Publishing House of the Slovak Academy of Sciences, no. 77, 1984.

Das Wiener Handwerksordnungsbuch (1364–1555): Edition und Kommentar, ed. Markus Gneiß, Cologne: Böhlau, 2017.

Yaakov ben Moshe Levi Moelin (Maharil), *Minhagim,* Sabbioneta: Tobias Foa, 1556.

Zunftbuch und Privilegien der Fleischer zu Ofen aus dem Mittelalter, ed. István Kenyeres, Budapest Historical Museum, 2008.

Das zweite Wismarsche Stadtbuch 1272–1297, ed. Lotte Knabe, Weimar: Böhlau, 2 vols., 1966.

SECONDARY LITERATURE

Abulafia, Anna Sapir, *Christian–Jewish Relations 1000–1300: Jews in the Service of Medieval Christendom*, Harlow: Pearson Education, 2011.

Christians and Jews in Dispute: Disputational Literature and the Rise of Anti-Judaism in the West (c. 1000–1150), Aldershot: Variorum, 1998.

Abulafia, David, '"Nam iudei servi regis sunt, et semper fisco regio deputati": The Jews in the Municipal Fuero of Teruel (1176–7)', in *Jews, Muslims and Christians in and around the Crown of Aragon: Essays in Honour of Professor Elena Lourie*, ed. Harvey J. Hames, Leiden: Brill, 2003, pp. 97–123.

Albini, Giuliana, '"Civitas tunc quiescit et fulget cum pollentium numero decoratur": Le concessioni di cittadinanza tra età viscontea tra pratiche e linguaggi politici', in *The Languages of Political Society: Western Europe, 14th–17th Centuries*, ed. Andrea Gamberini, Jean-Philippe Genet, and Andrea Zorzi, Rome: Viella, 2011, pp. 97–120.

Allen, Martin, *Mints and Money in Medieval England*, Cambridge University Press, 2012.

Andersson, Hans, *Urbanisierte Ortschaften und lateinische Terminologie: Studien zur Geschichte des nordeuropäischen Städtewesens vor 1350*, Gothenburg: Kungl. Vetenskaps- och Vitterhets-Samhället, 1971.

Andrews, Frances with Maria Agata Pincelli (eds.), *Churchmen and Urban Government in Late Medieval Italy, c. 1200–c. 1450*, New York: Cambridge University Press, 2013.

Anheim, Etienne, Philippe Bernardi, Maëlle Ramage, and Valérie Theis, 'La Notion de *libri statutorum*: "Tribut philologique" ou réalité documentaire? Les statuts communaux du Moyen Âge conservés pour l'actuel département de Vaucluse', *Mélanges de l'École française de Rome. Moyen Âge* 126/2 (2014), 447–60.

Arbelet, François, 'Histoire des archives de Gourdon', *Bulletin de la Société des Études du Lot* 137 (2016), 11–18.

Archer, Ian W., *The Pursuit of Stability: Social Relations in Elizabethan London*, Cambridge University Press, 1991.

Arnade, Peter, Martha Howell, and Walter Simons, 'Fertile Spaces: The Productivity of Urban Space in Northern Europe', *Journal of Interdisciplinary History* 32 (2002), 515–48.

Arnold, John H., 'Sexualité et déshonneur dans le Midi (XIIIe–XIVe siècles): Les péchés de la chair et l'opinion collective', in *L'Eglise et la chair (XIIe–XVe siècle)*, ed. Michèle Fournié, Daniel Le Blévec, and Julien Théry, Cahiers de Fanjeaux 52, Toulouse: E. Privat, 2019, pp. 305–39.

Arru, Angiolina, Josef Ehmer, and Franco Ramella (eds.), 'Migrazioni', Special Edition, *Quaderni Storici* 36 (2001).

Artifoni, Enrico, 'I podestà professionali e la fondazione retorica della politica comunale', *Quaderni storici* 21 (1986), 687–709.

Ascheri, Mario, 'Lo straniero nella legislazione e nella letteratura giuridica del Tre–Quattrocento: Un primo approccio', in *Forestieri e stranieri nella città basso-medievali*, Florence: Salimbeni, 1987, pp. 7–18.

'Statutory Law of Italian Cities from Middle Ages to Early Modern', in *Von der Ordnung zur Norm: Statuten in Mittelalter und Früher Neuzeit*, ed. Gisela Drossbach, Paderborn: Ferdinand Schöningh, 2010, pp. 201–16.

Balestracci, Duccio, *Il potere e la parola: Guida al Costituto volgarizzato di Siena (1309–1310)*, Siena: Protagon Editori Toscani, 2011.

'La Valdelsa e i suoi statuti: Alcune riflessioni', *Miscellanea storica della Valdelsa* 15 (1999), 99–110.

'L'Immigrazione di manodopera nella Siena medievale', in *Forestieri e stranieri nella città basso-medievali*, Florence: Salimbeni, 1987, pp. 163–80.

Balestracci, Duccio and Gabriella Piccinni, *Siena nel Trecento: Assetto urbano e strutture edilizie*, Florence: Clusf, 1977.

Balestracci, Duccio, Laura Vigni, and Armando Costantini, *Memoria dell'acqua: I bottini di Siena*, Siena: Protagon Editori Toscani, 2006.

Bambi, Federigo, 'Alle origini del volgare del diritto: La lingua degli statuti di Toscana tra XII e XIV secolo', *Mélanges de l'École française de Rome. Moyen Âge* 126/2 (2014), 1–8.

Barbero, Alessandro, 'Una rivolta antinobiliare nel Piemonte del Trecento: Il Tuchinaggio del Canavese', in *Rivolte urbane e rivolte contadine nell'Europa del Trecento: Un confronto*, ed. Monique Bourin, Giovanni Cherubini, and Giuliano Pinto, Florence University Press, 2008, pp. 153–96.

Bartlett, Robert, *The Making of Europe: Conquest, Colonization and Cultural Change, 950–1350*, London: Allen Lane, 1993.

Barton, Thomas W., *Contested Treasure: Jews and Authority in the Crown of Aragon*, University Park, PA: Penn State Press, 2015.

Baumgärtner, Ingrid (ed.), *Consilia im späten Mittelalter: Zum historischen Aussagwert einer Quellengattung*, Sigmaringen: Jan Thorbecke, 1995.

Beattie, Cordelia, *Medieval Single Women: The Politics of Social Classification in Late Medieval England*, Oxford University Press, 2007.

'The Problem of Women's Work: Identities in Post Black Death England', in *The Problem of Labour in Fourteenth-Century England*, ed. James Bothwell, P. J. P. Goldberg, and W. M. Ormrod, Woodbridge: Boydell, 2000, pp. 1–19.

Becker, Claudia, '"Sub gravioribus usuris": Darlehensverträge der Kommunen Chiavenna im 12. und 13. Jahrhundert', in *Bene vivere in communitate: Beiträge zum italienischen und deutschen Mittelalter. Hagen Keller zum 60. Geburtstag, überreicht von seinen Schülerinnen und Schülern*, ed. Thomas Scharff and Thomas Behrmann, Münster: Waxmann, 1997, pp. 25–48.

Benedictow, Ole J., *The Black Death 1346–1353: The Complete History*, Woodbridge: Boydell Press, 2004.

Benjamin, Walter, 'Naples', in *One-Way Street and Other Writings*, trans. Edmund Jephcott and Kingsley Shorter, London: NLB, 1979, pp. 167–76.

Bennett, Judith M., *Ale, Beer, and Brewsters in England: Women's Work in a Changing World 1300–1600*, Oxford University Press, 1996.

'Women (and Men) on the Move: Scots in the English North c. 1440', *Journal of British Studies* 57 (2018), 1–28.

Bennett, Judith M. and Amy M. Froide (eds.), *Singlewomen in the European Past, 1250–1800*, Philadelphia: University of Pennsylvania Press, 1998.

Berend, Nora, *At the Gate of Christendom: Jews, Muslims and 'Pagans' in Medieval Hungary, c. 1000–c. 1300*, Cambridge University Press, 2001.

Berengo, Marino, *L'Europa delle città: Il volto della società urbana europea tra medioevo ed età moderna*, Turin: Einaudi, 1999.

Bernardi, Philippe and Didier Boisseuil, 'Les Statuts de 1380 de Méthamis (Vaucluse)', *Histoire et sociétés rurales* 26 (2006), 95–127.

Bertoni, Laura, *Pavia alla fine del duecento: Una società urbana fra crescita e crisi*, Bologna: CLUEB, 2013.

Biller, Peter, *The Measure of Multitude: Population in Medieval Thought*, Oxford University Press, 2000.

Billot, Claudine, 'L'Assimilation des étrangers dans le royaume de France aux XIVe et XVe siècles', *Revue historique* 107 (1983), 273–96.

Blanshei, Sarah, *Politics and Justice in Late Medieval Bologna*, Leiden: Brill, 2010.

Blockmans, W. P., 'The Social and Economic Effects of Plague in the Low Countries: 1349–1500', *Revue belge de philologie et d'histoire* 58 (1980), 833–63.

'L'Unification européenne par les circuits portuaires', in *La Ville médiévale en débat*, ed. Amélia Aguiar Andrade and Adelaide Millàn da Costa, Lisbon: Instituto de Estudos Medievais, 2013, pp. 133–44.

Blumenthal, Debra, 'Black African Solidarity in Late Medieval Valencia', in *Black Africans in Renaissance Europe*, ed. T. F. Earle and K. J. P. Lowe, Cambridge University Press, 2005, pp. 225–46.

Enemies and Familiars: Slavery and Mastery in Fifteenth-Century Valencia, Ithaca, NY: Cornell University Press, 2009.

'"With My Daughter's Milk": Wet Nurses and the Rhetoric of Lactation in Valencian Court Records', in *Medieval and Renaissance Lactations: Images, Rhetorics, Practices*, ed. Jutta Gisela Sperling, Farnham: Ashgate, 2013, pp. 101–14.

Bolton, J. L., 'London and the Anti-Alien Legislation of 1439–40', in *Resident Aliens in Later Medieval England*, ed. W. Mark Ormrod, Nicola McDonald, and Craig Taylor, Turnhout: Brepols, 2017, pp. 33–47.

Bombi, Barbara, 'The 'Babylonian Captivity' of Petracco di ser Parenzo dell'Incisa, Father of Francesco Petrarca', *Historical Research* 83 (2010), 431–43.

Bonazzoli, Viviana, *Il prestito ebraico nelle economie cittadine delle Marche fra '200 e '400*, Ancona: Proposte e ricerche, 1990.

Boone, Marc, 'Cities in Late Medieval Europe: The Promise and Curse of Modernity', *Urban History* 39 (2012), 329–49.

'Les Gens de métiers à l'époque corporative à Gand et les litiges professionnels (1350–1450)', in *Statuts individuels, statuts corporatifs et statuts judiciaires dans les villes européennes (Moyen Âge et temps modernes): Actes du colloque tenu à Gand les 12–14 octobre 1995*, ed. Marc Boone and Maarten Prak, Leuven: Garant, 1996, pp. 23–47.

'Medieval Europe', in *The Oxford Handbook of Cities in World History*, ed. Peter Clark, Oxford University Press, 2013, pp. 221–39.

'State Power and Illicit Sexuality: The Persecution of Sodomy in Late Medieval Bruges', *Journal of Medieval History* 22 (1996), 135–53.

Boone, Marc and Jelle Haemers, 'The "Common Good": Governance, Discipline, and Political Culture', in *City and Society in the Low Countries (1100–1600)*, ed. Bruno Blondé, Marc Boone, and Anne-Laure Van Bruane, Cambridge University Press, 2018, pp. 93–127.

Boone, Marc and Peter Stabel, 'New Burghers in the Late Medieval Towns of Flanders and Brabant: Conditions of Entry, Rules and Reality', in *Neubürger im späten Mittelater: Migration und Austausch in der Städtelandschaft des alten Reiches (1250–1550)*, ed. Rainer Christoph Schwinges, Berlin: Taschenbuch, 2002, pp. 317–32.

Botana, Federico, *The Works of Mercy in Italian Art (c. 1050–c. 1400)*, Turnhout: Brepols, 2011.

Bottin, Jacques and Donatella Calabi (eds.), *Les Étrangers dans la ville: Minorités et espace urbain du bas Moyen Âge à l'époque moderne*, Paris: Maison des sciences de l'homme, 1999.

Boucheron, Patrick, *Le Pouvoir de bâtir: Urbanisme et politique édilitaire à Milan (XIVe–XVe siècles)*, Rome: École française de Rome, 1998.

The Power of Images: Siena, 1338, trans. Andrew Brown, Cambridge: Polity, 2018.

Bousquet-Labouérie, Christine, 'L'Image de la ville dans les *Grandes Chroniques de France*: Miroir du prince ou du pouvoir urbain?', in *La Ville au Moyen Âge, vol. II: Sociétés et pouvoirs dans la ville*, ed. Noël Coulet and Olivier Guyotjeannin, Paris: CTHS, 1998, pp. 247–60.

Bowsky, William M., 'Medieval Citizenship: The Individual and the State in the Commune of Siena, 1287–1355', *Studies in Medieval and Renaissance History* 4 (1967), 193–243.

Brett, Annabel S., *Changes of State: Nature and the Limits of the City in Early Modern Natural Law*, Princeton University Press, 2011.

Britnell, R. H., *Growth and Decline in Colchester, 1300–1525*, Cambridge University Press, 1986.

Brodt, Bärbel, *Städte ohne Mauern: Stadtentwicklung in East Anglia im 14. Jahrhundert*, Paderborn: F. Schöningh, 1997.

Brogi, Andrea and Francesca Bianciardi, *Nella Siena ritrovata di Ambrogio Lorenzetti*, Siena: NIE, 2005.

Brolis, Maria Teresa, 'Ceci in pentola e desiderio di Dio: Religiosità femminile in testamenti bergamaschi (secoli xiii–xiv)', in *Margini di libertà: Testamenti femminili nel medioevo*, ed. Maria Clara Rossi, Verona: Cierre, 2010, pp. 333–53.

Brown, Andrew, 'Medieval Citizenship: Bruges in the Later Middle Ages', in *The Citizen Past and Present*, ed. Andrew Brown and John Griffiths, Auckland: Massey University Press, 2017, pp. 93–117.

Buchholzer, Laurence and Olivier Richard (eds.), *Ligues urbaines et espace à la fin du Moyen Âge*, Presses universitaires de Strasbourg, 2012.

Bulst, Neithard, 'La Législation somptuaire d'Amédée VIII', in *Amédée VIII – Félix V: Premier duc de Savoie et pape (1383–1451)*, ed. Bernard Andenmatten and Agostino Paravicini Bagliani, Lausanne: Fondation Humbert II et Marie José de Savoie, 1992, pp. 191–200.

Bunte, Wolfgang, *Juden und Judentum in der mittelniederländischen Literatur (1100–1600)*, Frankfurt: P. Lang, 1989.

Burgtorf, Jochen and Helen Nicholson (eds.), *International Mobility in the Military Orders (Twelfth to Fifteenth Centuries): Travelling on Christ's Business*, Cardiff: University of Wales Press, 2006.

Burke, Ersie C., *The Greeks of Venice: Immigration, Settlement, and Integration*, Turnhout: Brepols, 2016.

Cable, Martin John, *"Cum essem in Constantie...": Raffaele Fulgosio and the Council of Constance 1414–1415*, Leiden: Brill, 2015.

Cagnin, Giampaolo, *Cittadini e forestieri a Treviso nel Medioevo: Secoli XIII–XIV*, Verona: Cierre, 2004.

    Pellegrini e vie del pellegrinaggio a Treviso nel medioevo (secoli XII–XV), Verona: Cierre, 2000.

Cailleaux, Christoph, 'Les Juifs et les musulmans en Catalogne à la fin du Moyen Âge: Des étrangers dans la ville', in *'Arriver' en ville: Les migrants en milieu urbain au Moyen Âge*, ed. Cédric Quertier, Roxane Chilà, and Nicolas Pluchot, Paris: Publications de la Sorbonne, 2013, pp. 193–210.

Calabi, Donatella (ed.), and Paola Lanaro, *La città italiana e i luoghi degli stranieri XIV–XVIII secolo*, Rome: Laterza, 1998.

Calvino, Italo, *Le città invisibili*, Milan: Einaudi, 1972 [translated into English as *Invisible Cities*, trans. William Wever, London: Secker & Warburg, 1974].

Camille, Michael, 'Signs of the City: Place, Power, and Public Fantasy in Medieval Paris, in *Medieval Practices of Space*, ed. Barbara A. Hanawalt and Michal Kobialka, Minneapolis: University of Minnesota Press, 2000, pp. 1–36.

Camp, P., *Histoire d'Auxonne au Moyen-Age*, Dijon: Association bourguignonne des sociétés savantes, 1960.

Campbell, Bruce M. S., *The Great Transition: Climate, Disease and Society in the Late Medieval World*, Cambridge University Press, 2016.

Campbell, Bruce M. S., James A. Galloway, Derek Keene, and Margaret Murphy, *A Medieval Capital and Its Grain Supply: Agrarian Production and Distribution in the London Region c. 1300*, London: Institute of British Geographers, 1993.

Canning, Joseph, *The Political Thought of Baldus de Ubaldis*, Cambridge University Press, 1987.

Capelli, Valeria and Andrea Giorgi, 'Gli statuti del Comune di Siena fino allo "Statuto del Buongoverno" (secoli XIII–XIV)', *Mélanges de l'École française de Rome. Moyen Âge* 126/2 (2014), 1–22.

Carlé, Maria del Carmen, 'Mercaderes en Castilla (1252–1512)', *Cuadernos de Historia de España* 21–2 (1954), 146–328.

Cassandro, Michele, *Gli ebrei e il prestito ebreo nel Cinquecento*, Milan: Giuffré, 1979.

Castel, Robert, *La Montée des incertitudes: Travail, protections, statut de l'individu*, Paris: Seuil, 2009.

Cauchies, Jean-Marie, *La Législation princière pour le comté de Hainaut (ducs de Bourgogne et premiers Habsbourg, 1427–1506)*, Brussels: Publications des Facultés universitaires St. Louis, 1982.

Cavaciocchi, Simonetta (ed.), *Le migrazioni in Europa secc. XIII–XVIII: Atti della Venticinquesima Settimana di studi, 3–8 maggio 1993*, Florence: Le Monnier, 1994.

Cavallar, Osvaldo, 'Regulating Arms in Late Medieval and Renaissance Italian City-States', in *Privileges and Rights of Citizenship: Law and the Juridical Construction of Civil Society*, ed. Julius Kirshner and Laurent Mayali, Berkeley, CA: University of California Press, 2002, pp. 57–126.

Cavallar, Osvaldo and Julius Kirshner, 'Jews as Citizens in Late Medieval and Renaissance Italy: The Case of Isacco da Pisa', *Jewish History* 25 (2011), 269–318.

Cavell, Emma, 'The Measure of Her Actions: A Quantitative Assessment of Anglo-Jewish Women's Litigation at the Exchequer of the Jews, 1219–1281', *Law and History* (forthcoming).

Caviness, Madeline H. and Charles G. Nelson, 'Silent Witnesses, Absent Women, and the Law Courts in Medieval Germany', in *Fama: The Politics of Talk and*

Reputation in Medieval Europe, ed. Thelma Fenster and Daniel Lord Smail, Ithaca, NY: Cornell University Press, 2003, pp. 47–72.

Women and Jews in the Sachsenspiegel Picture-Books, London: Harvey Miller, 2018.

Cecchi, Dante, 'Disposizioni statuarie sugli stranieri e sui forestieri', in *Stranieri e forestieri nella Marca dei secc. XIV–XVI: Atti del 30 convegno di studi maceratesi, Macerata, 19–20 novembre 1994*, Macerata: Centro di studi storici maceratesi, 1996 pp. 29–91.

Cerutti, Simona, *Étrangers: Étude d'une condition d'incertitude dans une société d'Ancien Régime*, Montrouge: Bayard, 2012.

Chapin, Elizabeth, *Les Villes de foires de Champagne des origines au début du XIVe siècle*, Paris: Honoré Champion, 1937.

Chazan, Robert, *Barcelona and Beyond: The Disputation of 1263 and Its Aftermath*, Berkeley, CA: University of California Press, 1992.

Cherry, John, 'Seals of Cities and Towns: Concepts of Choice', in *Medieval Coins and Seals: Constructing Identity, Signifying Power*, ed. Susan Solway, Turnhout: Brepols, 2015, pp. 283–95.

Chittolini, Giorgio, 'Statuti e autonomie urbane: Introduzione', in *Statuti, città, territori in Italia e Germania tra Medioevo ed età moderna*, ed. Giorgio Chittolini and Dietmar Willoweit, Bologna: Il Mulino, 1991, pp. 7–45.

'Urban Populations, Urban Territories, Small Towns: Some Problems of the History of Urbanization in Northern and Southern Italy (Thirteenth–Sixteenth Centuries)', in *Power and Persuasion: Essays on the Art of State Building in Honour of W. P. Blockmans*, ed. Peter Hoppenbrouwers, Antheun Janse, and Robert Stein, Turnhout: Brepols, 2010, pp. 227–41.

Christ, Dorothea A., 'Hochadelige Eidgenossen: Grafen und Herren im Burgrecht eidgenössischer Orte', in *Neubürger im späten Mittelalter: Migration und Austausch in der Städtelandschaft des alten Reiches (1250–1550)*, ed. Rainer Christoph Schwinges, Berlin: Taschenbuch, 2002, pp. 99–123.

Clark, Peter, *The English Alehouse: A Social History, 1200–1830*, Harlow: Longman, 1983.

Clarke, Paula, 'Le "mercantesse" di Venezia nei secoli XIV e XV', *Archivio Veneto* 6th series, 3 (2012), 67–84.

Clauzel, Denis, Isabelle Clauzel-Delannoy, Laurent Coulon, Bertrand Haquette, and others, 'L'Activité legislative dans les villes du Nord à la fin du Moyen Âge', in *'Faire bans, édictz et status': Légiférer dans la ville médiévale*, ed. Jean-Marie Cauchies and Eric Bousmar, Brussels: Facultés universitaires Saint-Louis, 2001, pp. 295–329.

Cluse, Christoph, *Darf ein Bischof Juden zulassen? Die Gutachten des Siffridus Piscator OP (gest. 1473) zur Auseinandersetzung um die Vertreibung der Juden aus Mainz*, Trier: Kliomedia, 2013.

Studien zur Geschichte der Juden in den mittelalterlichen Niederlanden, Hanover: Hahn, 2000.

Cohn, Jr, Samuel K., *Lust for Liberty: The Politics of Social Revolt in Medieval Europe, 1200–1425: Italy, France, and Flanders*, Cambridge, MA: Harvard University Press, 2006.

'The Black Death and the Burning of Jews', *Past and Present* 196 (2007), 3–36.

Coleman, Janet, 'Negotiating the Medieval in the Modern: European Citizenship and Statecraft', *Transactions of the Royal Historical Society* 22 (2012), 75–93.

Colet, Anna, Josep Xavier Muntané Santiveri, Jordi Ruíz Ventura, Oriol Saula, M. Eulàlia Subirà de Galdàcano, and Clara Jáuregui, 'The Black Death and Its Consequences for the Jewish Community in Tàrrega: Lessons from History and Archaeology', in *Pandemic Disease in the Medieval World: Rethinking the Black Death*, ed. Monica Green, Kalamazoo, MI: ARC Medieval Press, 2015, pp. 63–96.

Constable, Olivia Remie, 'From Hygiene to Heresy: Changing Perceptions of Women and Bathing in Medieval and Early Modern Iberia', *Religious Cohabitation in European Towns (10th–15th Centuries)*, ed. Stéphane Boisselier and John Tolan, Turnhout: Brepols, 2014, pp. 185–206.

Housing the Stranger in the Mediterranean World: Lodging, Trade, and Travel in Late Antiquity and the Middle Ages, Cambridge University Press, 2003.

Cornish, Alison, '*Translatio Galliae*: Effects of Early Franco-Italian Literary Exchange', *Romanic Review* 97 (2006), 309–30.

Costantini, Valentina, 'Corporazioni cittadine e popolo di mercanti a Siena tra Due e Trecento: Appunti per la ricerca', *Bullettino Senese di Storia Patria* 120 (2013), 98–133.

'On a Red Line across Europe: Butchers and Rebellions in Fourteenth-Century Siena', *Social History* 41 (2016), 72–92.

Courtemanche, Andrée, 'Women, Family, and Immigration in Fifteenth-Century Manosque: The Case of the Dodi Family of Barcelonnette', in *Urban and Rural Communities in Medieval France: Provence and Languedoc, 1000–1500*, ed. Kathryn Reyerson and John Drendel, Leiden: Brill, 1998, pp. 101–27.

Courtenay, William J., *Rituals for the Dead: Religion and Community in the Medieval University of Paris*, South Bend, IN: Notre Dame University Press, 2019.

Cressy, David, *Gypsies: An English Story*, Oxford University Press, 2018.

Curveiller, Stéphane, 'Les Relations d'une ville du littoral flamand et de son hinterland: Dunkerque et Bergues au Moyen Âge', in *La Ville au Moyen Âge, vol. I: Ville et espace*, ed. Noël Coulet and Olivier Guyotjeannin, Paris: CTHS, 1998, pp. 213–31.

d'Alessandro, Vincenzo, 'Immigrazione e società urbana in Sicilia (secoli XII–XVI): Momenti e aspetti', in *Comunità forestiere e 'nationes' nell'Europa dei secoli XIII–XVI*, ed. Giovanna Petti Balbi, Naples: Liguori, 2001, pp. 165–90.

d'Alteroche, Bernard, 'L'Évolution de la notion et du status juridique de l'étranger à la fin du Moyen Âge (XIe–XVe siècle)', *Revue du Nord* (2002), 227–45.

Damisch, Hubert, *The Origins of Perspective*, trans. John Goodman, Cambridge, MA: MIT Press, 1984.

Dani, Alessandro, *Gli statuti dei comuni della repubblica di Siena (secoli XIII–XV): Profilo di una cultura communitaria*, Monteriggioni: Il Leccio, 2015.

Davide, Miriam, *Lombardi in Friuli: Per la storia delle migrazioni interne nell'Italia del Trecento*, Trieste: CERM, 2008.

Davies, R. R., *Domination and Conquest: The Experience of Ireland, Scotland and Wales, 1100–1300*, Cambridge University Press, 1990.

Davis, Adam J., *The Medieval Economy of Salvation: Charity, Commerce, and the Rise of the Hospital*, Ithaca, NY: Cornell University Press, 2019.

Davis, James, *Medieval Market Morality: Life, Law and Ethics in the English Marketplace, 1200–1500*, Cambridge University Press, 2012.

D'Avray, David L., *The Preaching of the Friars: Sermons Diffused from Paris before 1300*, Oxford University Press, 1985.

De Clerq, Wim, Roland Dreesen, Jan Dumolyn, Ward Leloup and Jan Trachet, 'Ballasting the Hanse: Baltoscandian Erratic Cobbles in the Later Medieval Port Landscape of Bruges', *European Journal of Archaeology* 20 (2017), 710–36.

De Ridder-Symoens, Hilde, 'Mobility', in *A History of the University in Europe, vol. I: Universities in the Middle Ages*, ed. Hilde De Ridder-Symoens, Cambridge University Press, 1992, pp. 280–304.

Dejoux, Marie, 'Gouvernement et pénitence: Les enquêtes de réparation des usures juives de Louis IX (1247–1270)', *Annales: Histoire, Sciences Sociales* 69 (2014), 849–74.

Deleuze, Gilles and Félix Guattari, *A Thousand Plateaus: Capitalism and Schizophrenia*, trans. Brian Massumi, London: Bloomsbury, 2013.

Dey, Hendrik, 'From "Street" to "Piazza": Urban Politics, Public Ceremony, and the Redefinition of *platea* in Communal Italy and Beyond', *Speculum* 91 (2016), 919–44.

Dillard, Heath, *Daughters of the Reconquest: Women in Castilian Town Society 1100–1300*, Cambridge University Press, 1984.

Dillon, Emma, *The Sense of Sound: Musical Meaning in France, 1260–1330*, Oxford University Press, 2012.

Dimmock, Spencer, 'Social Conflict in Welsh Towns c. 1280–1530', in *Urban Culture in Medieval Wales*, ed. Helen Fulton, Cardiff: University of Wales Press, 2012, pp. 117–35.

Dorin, Rowan W., 'Les Maîtres parisiens et les juifs (fin XIIIe siècle): Perspectives nouvelles sur un dossier d'avis concernant le *regimen judaeorum*', *Journal des savants* (2016), 241–82.

'"Once the Jews Have Been Expelled": Intent and Interpretation in Late Medieval Canon Law', *Law and History Review* 34 (2016), 335–62.

Dumolyn, Jan, 'Une Idéologie urbaine "bricolée" en Flandre médiévale: Les *Sept Portes de Bruges* dans le manuscrit Gruuthuse (début du XVe siècle)', *Revue belge de philologie et d'histoire* 88 (2010), 1039–84.

'Urban Ideologies in Later Medieval Flanders: Towards an Analytical Framework', in *The Languages of Political Society: Western Europe, 14th–17th Centuries*, ed. Andrea Gamberini, Jean-Philippe Genet, and Andrea Zorzi, Rome: Viella, 2011, pp. 69–96.

Dumolyn, Jan and Jelle Haemers, '*Takehan, Cokerulle*, and *Mutemaque*: Naming Collective Action in the Later Medieval Low Countries', in *The Routledge History Handbook of Medieval Revolt*, ed. Justine Firnhaber-Baker and Dirk Schoenaers, London: Routledge, 2016, pp. 39–54.

Dumolyn, Jan, and Milan Pajic, 'Enemies of the Count and of the City: The Collective Exile of Rebels in Fourteenth-Century Flanders', *The Legal History Review* 84 (2016), 461–501.

Dupâquier, Jacques, and others, *Historie de la population français, vol. I*, Paris: Presses universitaires de France, 1988.

Dutour, Thierry, 'Le Consensus des bonnes gens: La participation des habitants aux affaires communes dans quelques villes de la langue d'oïl (XIIIe–XVe siècle)', in *Le Pouvoir municipal: De la fin du Moyen Âge à 1789*, Presses universitaires de Rennes, 2010, pp. 187–208.

Sous L'Empire du bien: 'Bonnes gens' et pacte social (XIIIe–XVe siècle), Paris: Garnier, 2015.

Edwards, Catharine and Greg Woolf (eds.), *Rome the Cosmopolis*, Cambridge University Press, 2003.

Einbinder, Susan, *Beautiful Death: Jewish Martyrdom and Poetry in Medieval France*, Princeton University Press, 2002.

Elkin, Lauren, *Flâneuse: Women Walk the City in Paris, New York, Tokyo, Venice and London*, London: Chatto & Windus, 2016.

Ennen, Edith, *Die europäische Stadt*, Göttingen: Vandenhoeck & Ruprecht, 1972.

Epstein, Marc Michael, *The Medieval Haggadah: Art, Narrative, and Religious Imagination*, New Haven, CN: Yale University Press, 2011.

Epstein, Steven A., *An Economic and Social History of Later Medieval Europe, 1000–1500*, Cambridge University Press, 2009.

Esposito, Anna, '*Ad dotandum puellas virgines, pauperes et honestas*: Social Needs and Confraternal Charity in Rome in the Fifteenth and Sixteenth Centuries', *Renaissance and Reformation* 18 (1994), 5–18.

'Adulterio, concubinato, bigamia: Testimonianze dalla normativa statutaria dello Stato pontificio (secoli XIII–XVI)', in *Trasgressioni: Seduzione, concubinato, adulterio, bigamia (XIV–XVIII secolo)*, ed. Silvana Seidel Menchi and Diego Quaglioni, Bologna: Il Mulino, 2004, pp. 21–42.

'Forestiere e straniere a Roma tra '400 e primo '500', http://romatrepress .uniroma3.it/ojs/index.php/forestieri/article/view/1585

Evangelisti, Paolo, '"Misura la città, chi è la communità, chi è il suggetto, chi è nella città...": Bernardino da Siena, *Prediche volgari sul Campo di Siena*, CVII, 64)', in *Identità cittadina e comportamenti socio-economici tra Medioevo ed Età moderna*, ed. Paolo Prodi, Maria Giuseppina Muzzarelli, and Stefano Simonetta, Bologna: CLUEB, 2007, pp. 19–52.

Fancy, Hussein, *The Mercenary Mediterranean: Sovereignty, Religion, and Violence in the Medieval Crown of Aragon*, University of Chicago Press, 2016.

Farmer, Sharon, *The Silk Industries of Medieval Paris: Artisanal Migration, Technological Innovation, and Gendered Experience*, Philadelphia: University of Pennsylvania Press, 2016.

Fenster, Thelma and Daniel Lord Smail (eds.), *Fama: The Politics of Talk and Reputation in Medieval Europe*, Ithaca, NY: Cornell University Press, 2003.

Ferente, Serena, 'Popolo and Law', in *Popular Sovereignty in Historical Perspective*, ed. Richard Bourke and Quentin Skinner, Cambridge University Press, 2016, pp. 96–114.

'The Liberty of Italian City-States', in *Freedom and the Construction of Europe*, vol. I: *Religious Freedom and Civil Liberty*, ed. Quentin Skinner and Martin van Gelderen, Cambridge University Press, 2013, pp. 157–75.

Fletcher, J. M., 'The Organisation of the Supply of Food and Drink to the Medieval Oxford Colleges', in *Università in Europa: Le istituzioni universitarie dal Medio Evo ai nostri giorni; strutture, organizzazione, funzionamento. Atti del Convegno Internazionale di Studi, Milazzo 28 Settembre – 2 Ottobre 1993*, ed. Andrea Romano, Soveria Mannelli: Rubbettino, 1995, pp. 199–211.

Folena, Daniela Goldin, 'Il punto su Boncampagno da Signa', in *Il pensiero e l'opera di Boncampagno da Signa*, ed. Massimo Baldini, Florence: Signa, 2002, pp. 9–22.

Folin, Marco, 'Il governo degli spazi urbani negli statuti cittadini di area estense', in *Signori, regimi signorili e statuti nel tardo medioevo*, ed. Rolando Dondarini, Rolando Varanini, and Maria Venticelli, Bologna: Pàtron, pp. 337–66.

Fouquet, Gerhard, '"Kaufleute auf Reisen": Sprachliche Verständigung im Europa des 14. und 15. Jahrhunderts', in *Europa im späten Mittelalter: Politik – Gesellschaft – Kultur*, ed. Rainer C. Schwinges, Christoph Hesse, and Peter Moraw, Munich: Oldenbourg, 2006, pp. 465–87.

Frame, Robin, *Colonial Ireland 1169–1389*, Dublin: Four Court Press, 2012.

Fulton, Helen, 'The *encomium urbis* in Medieval Welsh Poetry', *Proceedings of the Harvard Celtic Colloquium* 26 (2006), 54–72.

Gans, Herbert J., *Urban Villages: Group and Class in the Life of Italian-Americans*, New York: Free Press, 1962.

Garzella, Gabriella, 'I palazzi pubblici a Pisa nel medioevo come specchio dell'evoluzione politico-istituzionale e delle vicende urbanistiche', in *Les Palais dans la ville: Espaces urbains et lieux de la puissance publique dans le Méditerranée médiévale*, ed. Patrick Boucheron and Jacques Chiffoleau, Presses universitaires de Lyon, 2004, pp. 109–22.

Gecser, Ottó Sándor, 'Preaching and Publicness: St John of Capestrano and the Making of His Charisma North of the Alps', in *Charisma and Religious Authority: Jewish, Christian, and Muslim Preaching, 1200–1500*, ed. Katherine L. Jansen and Miri Rubin, Brepols: Turnhout, 2010, pp. 145–59.

Gibbs, Robert, 'The 13th- and 14th-Century Illuminated Statutes of Bologna in Their Social-Political Context', in *Von der Ordnung zur Norm: Statuten in Mittelalter und Früher Neuzeit*, ed. Gisela Drossbach, Paderborn: Ferdinand Schöningh, 2010, pp. 183–200.

Gilchrist, Roberta, *Norwich Cathedral Close: The Evolution of the English Cathedral Landscape*, Woodbridge: Boydell, 2015.

Gilles, Henri, *Les Coutumes de Toulouse (1286) et leur premier commentaire (1296)*, Toulouse: Académie de législation, 1969.

Gilli, Patrick and Enrica Salvatori, 'Introduction: L'Autonomie et l'identité de la ville: Une question sociale?', in *Les Identités urbaines au Moyen Âge: Regards sur les villes du Midi français. Actes du colloque de Montpellier 8–9 décembre 2011*, Turnhout: Brepols, 2014, pp. 1–5.

Gilomen, Hans-Jörg, 'Städtliche Sondergruppen im Bürgerrecht', in *Neubürger im späten Mittelalter: Migration und Austausch in der Städtelandschaft des alten Reiches (1250–1550)*, ed. Rainer Christoph Schwinger, Berlin: Taschenbuch, 2002, pp. 169–200.

Gilsenan, Michael, *Imagined Cities of the East: An Inaugural Lecture Delivered before the University of Oxford on 27 May 1985*, Oxford: Clarendon, 1986.

Goldberg, P. J. P., 'Urban Identity and the Poll Taxes of 1377, 1379 and 1381', *Economic History Review* 2nd series, 43 (1990), 194–216.

——— *Women, Work, and Life Cycle in a Medieval Economy: Women in York and Yorkshire c. 1300–1520*, Oxford: Clarendon, 1992.

Goldin, Simha, *Apostasy and Jewish Identity in High Middle Ages Northern Europe: 'Are you still my brother?'*, trans. Jonathan Chipman, Manchester University Press, 2014.

Green, Monica H., *Making Women's Medicine Masculine: The Rise of Male Authority in Pre-Modern Gynaecology*, Oxford University Press, 2008.

Green, Monica H. and Daniel Lord Smail, 'The Trial of Floreta d'Ays (1403): Jews, Christians, and Obstetrics in Later Medieval Marseille', *Journal of Medieval History* 34 (2008), 185–211.

Greengrass, Mark, *Christendom Destroyed: Europe 1517–1648*, London: Allen Lane, 2014.

Grell, Ole Peter and Bob Scribner (eds.), *Tolerance and Intolerance in the European Reformation*, Cambridge University Press, 1996.

Groebner, Valentin, *Who Are You? Identification, Deception and Surveillance in Early Modern Europe*, New York: Zone, 2007.

Groos, Arthur, 'The City as Community and Space: Nuremberg *Stadtlob*, 1447–1530', in *Spatial Practices: Medieval/Modern*, ed. Markus Stock and Nicola Vöhringer, Göttingen: V&R unipress, 2014, pp. 187–206.

Guénette, Maryse, 'Errance et solitude féminines à Manosque (1314–1358)', in *Vie privée et ordre publique à la fin du Moyen-Âge: Études sur Manosque, la Provence et le Piémont (1250–1450)*, ed. Michel Hébert, Aix-en-Provence: Université de Provence, 1987, pp. 23–43.

Gustafsson, Sofia, 'German Influence in Swedish Medieval Towns: Reflections upon the Time-Bound Historiography of the Twentieth Century', in *Guilds, Towns and Cultural Transmission in the North, 1300–1500*, ed. Lars Bisgaard, Lars Boje Mortensen, and Tom Pettitt, Odense: University Press of Southern Denmark, 2013, pp. 109–30.

Hanawalt, Barbara A., 'The Host, the Law, and the Ambiguous Space of Medieval London Taverns', in *'Of Good and Ill Repute': Gender and Social Control in Medieval England*, New York: Oxford University Press, 1998, pp. 104–23.

Handlin, Oscar, *The Uprooted: The Epic Story of the Great Migrations That Made the American People*, New York: Grosset & Dunlap, 1951.

Haverkamp, Alfred, '"Concivilitas" von Christen und Juden in Aschkenas im Mittelalter', in *Jüdische Gemeinden und Organisationsformen von der Antike bis zur Gegenwart*, ed. Robert Jütte and Abraham P. Kustermann, Cologne: Böhlau, 1996, pp. 103–36.

Haverkamp, Eva, 'Jewish Images on Christian Coins: Economy and Symbolism in Medieval Germany', in *Jews and Christians in Medieval Europe: The Historiographical Legacy of Bernhard Blumenkranz*, ed. Philippe Buc, Martha Keil, and John Tolan, Brepols: Turnhout 2016, pp. 189–226.

Heers, Jacques, *La Ville au Moyen Âge en Occident: Paysages, pouvoirs et conflits*, Paris: Fayard, 1990.

Heller, Sarah-Grace, 'Limiting Yardage and Changes of Clothes: Sumptuary Legislation in Thirteenth-Century France, Languedoc and Italy', in *Medieval Fabrications: Dress Textiles, Clothwork, and Other Cultural Imaginings*, ed. E. Jane Burns, New York: St Martin's Press, 2004, pp. 121–36.

Hemptinne, Thérèse de, 'Des Femmes copistes dans les Pays-Bas au bas Moyen Âge (14e–15e siècle): Approche d'une activité feminine malconnue', in *Secretum scriptorum: Liber alumnorum Walter Prevenier*, ed. Willem Pieter

Blockmans, Marc Boone, and Thérèse de Hemptinne, Leuven: Garant, 1999, pp. 129–43.

'Reading, Writing, and Devotional Practices: Lay and Religious Women and the Written Word in the Low Countries (1350–1550)', in *The Voice of Silence: Women's Literacy in a Men's Church*, ed. Thérèse de Hemptinne and María Eugenia Góngora, Turnhout: Brepols, 2004, pp. 111–26.

Herrmann, Bernd, 'City and Nature and Nature in the City', in *Historians and Nature: Comparative Approaches to Environmental History*, ed. Ursula Lehmkuhl and Herrmann Wellenreuther, New York and Oxford: Berg, 2007, pp. 226–56.

Higounet, Charles, 'Le Peuplement de Toulouse au XIIe siècle', *Annales de Midi* 55 (1943), 489–98.

Hodges, Richard and Brian Hobley (eds.), *The Rebirth of Towns in the West AD 700–1050*, Council of British Archaeology Research Report 98, London: Council for British Archaeology, 1988.

Hoffmann, Richard C., 'Footprint Metaphor and Metabolic Realities: Environmental Impacts of Medieval European Cities', in *Natures Past: The Environment and Human History*, ed. Paolo Squatriti, Ann Arbor, MI, New York: University of Michigan Press, 2007, pp. 288–325.

Hosking, Geoffrey, *Trust: Money, Markets and Society*, London: Seagull, 2010.

Howard, Peter, 'Making a City and Citizens: The "Fruits" of Preaching in Renaissance Florence', in *Medieval Urban Culture*, ed. Andrew Brown and Jan Dumolyn, Turnhout: Brepols, 2017, pp. 59–73.

'The Aural Space of the Sacred in Renaissance Florence', in *Renaissance Florence: A Social History*, ed. Roger J. Crum and John T. Paoletti, New York: Cambridge University Press, 2006, pp. 376–93.

Howell, Martha C., 'Citizen-Clerics in Late Medieval Douai', in *Statuts individuels, statuts corporatifs et statuts judiciaires dans les villes européennes (moyen âge et temps modernes)*, ed. Marc Boone and Maarten Prak, Leuven and Apeldoorn: Garant, 1996, pp. 11–22.

Commerce before Capitalism in Europe, 1300–1600, Cambridge University Press, 2010.

Hsy, Jonathan, *Trading Tongues: Merchants, Multilingualism, and Medieval Literature*, Columbus, OH: Ohio State University Press, 2013.

Hubert, Étienne, 'Qui est qui? L'Individu inconnu dans la cite médiévale', *Archivio storico italiano* 175 (2017), 483–515.

'*Una et eadem persona sive aliae personae.* Certifier l'identité dans une société mobile (à propos de l'Italie communale)', in *'Arriver' en ville: Les migrants en milieu urbain au Moyen Âge*, ed. Cédric Quertier, Roxane Chilà, and Nicolas Pluchot, Paris: Publications de la Sorbonne, 2013, pp. 51–64.

Hughes, Diane Owen, 'Distinguishing Signs: Earrings, Jews, and Franciscan Rhetoric in the Italian Renaissance City', *Past and Present* 112 (1986), 3–59.

Isenmann, Eberhard, *Die deutsche Stadt im Spätmittelalter, 1250–1500: Stadtgestalt, Recht, Stadtregiment, Kirche, Gesellschaft, Wirtschaft*, Stuttgart: Ulmer, 1988.

Jacobs, Jane, *The Economy of Cities*, London: Jonathan Cape, 1969.

Jacoby, David, 'Jews and Christians in Venetian Crete: Segregation, Interaction, and Conflict', in *Interstizi: Culture ebraico-cristiane a Venezia e nei suoi domini tra basso medioevo a prima età moderna*, ed. Uwe Israel, Robert Jütte, and Reinhold Mueller, Rome: Edizioni di storie e letteratura, 2010, pp. 243–79.

Jahnke, Carsten, 'The City of Lübeck and the Internationality of Early Hanseatic Trade', in *The Hanse in Medieval and Early Modern Europe*, ed. Justyna Wubs-Mrozewicz and Stuart Jenks, Leiden: Brill, 2013, pp. 37–58.

Janaczek, Andrzej, 'Ethnicity, Religious Disparity and the Formation of the Multicultural Society of Red Ruthenia in the Late Middle Ages', in *On the Frontier of Latin Europe: Integration and Segregation in Red Ruthenia, 1350–1600*, ed. Andrzej Janaczek and Thomas Wünsch, Warsaw: Institute of Archaeology and Ethnology of the Polish Academy of Sciences, 2004, pp. 15–45.

Jansen, Katherine Ludwig, *Peace and Penance in Late Medieval Italy*, Princeton University Press, 2018.

Jervis, Ben, *Assemblage Thought and Archaeology*, London: Routledge: 2018.

Johanek, Peter, 'Die Frühzeit jüdischer Präsenz in Westfalen', in *Historisches Handbuch der Jüdischen Gemeinschaften in Westfalen und Lippe: Grundlagen – Erträge – Perspektiven*, Susanne Freund, Münster: Ardey, 2013, pp. 21–58.

'Merchants, Markets and Towns', in *The New Cambridge Medieval History, vol. III*, ed. Timothy Reuter, Cambridge University Press, 1999, pp. 64–94.

'Seigneurial Power and the Development of Towns in the Holy Roman Empire', in *Lords and Towns in Medieval Europe: The European Historic Towns Atlas Project*, ed. Anngret Simms and Howard B. Clarke, Farnham: Ashgate, 2015, pp. 117–54.

Johanek, Peter and Franz-Joseph Post (eds.), *Vielerlei Städte: Der Stadtbegriff*, Städteforschung A/61, Cologne: Böhlau, 2004.

Jordan, William Chester, *From England to France: Felony and Exile in the High Middle Ages*, Princeton University Press, 2015.

Men and the Center: Redemptive Governance under Louis IX, Budapest: Central European University Press, 2012.

The Apple of his Eye: Converts from Islam in the Reign of Louis IX, Princeton University Press, 2019.

The French Monarchy and the Jews: From Philip Augustus to the Last Capetians, Philadelphia: University of Pennsylvania Press, 1989.

The Great Famine: Northern Europe in the Early Fourteenth Century, Princeton University Press, 1996.

'The Jewish Cemeteries of France after the Expulsion of 1306', in *Studies in Medieval Jewish Intellectual and Social History: Festschrift in Honor of Robert Chazan*, ed. David Engel, Lawrence H. Schiffman, and Elliot R. Wolfson, Leiden: Brill, 2012, pp. 227–44.

Women and Credit in Pre-Industrial and Developing Societies, Philadelphia: University of Pennsylvania Press, 1993.

Kagan, Ricard L. and Philip D. Morgan (eds.), *Atlantic Diasporas: Jews, Conversos, and Crypto-Jews in the Age of Mercantilism, 1500–1800*, Baltimore, MD: Johns Hopkins University Press, 2009.

Kallioinen, Mika, 'Inter-communal Institutions in Medieval Trade', *Economic History Review* 70 (2017), 1131–52.

Kane, Bronach, *Popular Memory and Gender in Medieval England: Men, Women, and Testimony in the Church Courts, c. 1200–1500*, Woodbridge: Boydell, 2019.

Kantrowicz, Stephen, *More than Freedom: Fighting for Black Citizenship in a White Republic, 1829–1889*, New York: Penguin, 2012.

Karras, Ruth Mazo, *Common Women: Prostitution and Sexuality in Medieval England*, Oxford University Press, 1996.

Katz, Dana E., *The Jew in the Art of the Italian Renaissance*, Philadelphia: University of Pennsylvania Press, 2008.

The Jewish Ghetto and the Visual Imagination of Early Modern Venice, Cambridge University Press, 2017.

Katznelson, Ira and Miri Rubin (eds.), *Religious Conversion: History, Experience and Meaning*, Farnham: Ashgate, 2014.

Kaye, Joel, *A History of Balance, 1250–1375: The Emergence of a New Model of Equilibrium and Its Impact on Thought*, Cambridge University Press, 2014.

Kedar, Benjamin Z., *Merchants in Crisis: Genoese and Venetian Men of Affairs and the Fourteenth-Century Depression*, New Haven, CN: Yale University Press, 1976.

Keen, Catherine, *Dante and the City*, Stroud: Tempus, 2003.

Keene, Derek, 'Du Seuil de la Cité à la formation d'une économie morale: L'Environnement hanséatique à Londres entre XIIe et XVIIe siècle', in *Les Étrangers dans la ville: Minorités et espace urbain du bas Moyen Âge à l'époque moderne*, eds. Jacques Bottin and Donatella Calabi, Paris: Maison des sciences de l'homme, 1999, pp. 409–24.

Keil, Martha, 'Der Liber Judeorum von Wr. Neustadt (1453–1500) – Edition', in *Studien zur Geschichte der Juden in Österreich I*, ed. Martha Keil and Klaus Lohrmann, Vienna and Cologne: Böhlau, 1994, pp. 41–99.

Kempshall, M. S., *The Common Good in Late Medieval Political Thought*, Oxford University Press, 1999.

Kennedy, Hugh, 'How to Found an Islamic City', in *Cities, Texts and Social Networks, 400–1500*, ed. Caroline Goodson, Anne E. Lester, and Carol Symes, Farnham: Ashgate, 2010, pp. 45–63.

Keyser, Richard, 'The Transformation of Traditional Woodland Management: Commercial Sylviculture in Medieval Champagne', *French Historical Studies* 32 (2009), 353–84.

Kilgallon, Ella, 'Creating a Space of Penance: Women of the Franciscan Third Order in the Cities of Central Italy', unpublished doctoral thesis, Queen Mary University of London, 2018.

Kim, Keechang, *Aliens in Medieval Law: The Origins of Medieval Citizenship*, Cambridge University Press, 2000.

Kirshner, Julius, '*Civitas sibi faciat civem*: Bartolus of Sassoferrato's Doctrine on the Making of a Citizen', *Speculum* 48 (1973), 694–713.

Pursuing Honor while Avoiding Sin: The Monte dell doti of Florence, Milan: Giuffré, 1978.

'Women Married Elsewhere: Gender and Citizenship in Italy', in *Time, Space, and Women's Lives in Early Modern Europe*, ed. Anne Jacobson Schutte, Thomas Kuehn, and Silvana Seidel Menchi, Kirksville, MI: Truman State University Press, 2001, pp. 117–49.

Kis, Péter and Iván Petrik, 'Mittelalterliche Urkunden der deutschen Fleischerzunft zu Ofen (1235/70–1519)', in *Zunftbuch und Privilegien der Fleischer zum Ofen aus dem Mittelalter*, ed. István Kenyeres, Budapest Historical Museum, 2008, pp. 329–39.

Kittell, Ellen E., 'The Construction of Women's Social Identity in Medieval Douai: Evidence from Identifying Epithets', *Journal of Medieval History* 25 (1999), 215–27.

Klaniczay, Gabor, 'The "Bonfires of the Vanities" and the Mendicants', in *Emotions and Material Culture*, ed. Gerhard Jaritz, Vienna: Verlag der Österreichischer Akademie der Wissenschaften, 2003, pp. 31–59.

Klapisch-Zuber, Christiane, 'Kin, Friends, and Neighbors: The Urban Territory of a Merchant', in her *Work, Family, and Ritual in Renaissance Italy*, trans. Lydia Cochrane, University of Chicago Press, 1985, pp. 68–93.

'Les Femmes dans les espaces publics de la ville italienne (XIVe–XVe)', in *Anthropologie de la ville médiévale*, ed. Mychal Tymowski, Warsaw: Wydawnictwo Dig, 1999, pp. 83–90.

Koch, Bruno, '*Quare magnus artificus est*: Migrierende Berufsleute als Innovationsträger im späten Mittelalter', in *Neubürger im späten Mittelalter: Migration und Austausch in der Städtelandschaft des alten Reiches (1250–1550)*, ed. Rainer Christoph Schwinges, Berlin: Taschenbuch, 2002, pp. 409–43.

Kohn, Roger, *Les Juifs de la France du Nord dans la seconde moitié du XIVe siècle*, Leuven: Peeters, 1988.

Kontler, László and Mark Somos (eds.), *Trust and Happiness in the History of European Political Thought*, Leiden: Brill, 2018.

Kosche, Rosemarie, *Studien zür Geschichte der Juden zwischen Rhein und Weser in Mittelalter*, Hanover: Hahnsche, 2002.

Kowaleski, Maryanne, '"Alien" Encounters in the Maritime World of Medieval England', *Medieval Encounters* 13 (2007), 96–121.

Local Markets and Regional Trade in Medieval Exeter, Cambridge University Press, 1995.

'Medieval People in Town and Country: New Perspectives from Demography and Bioarchaeology', *Speculum* 89 (2014), 573–600.

Kozubska-Andrusiv, Olha, 'Comparable Aspects in Urban Development: Kievan Rus and the European Middle Ages', in *Medieval East Central Europe in a Comparative Perspective: From Frontier Zones to Lands in Focus*, ed. Gerhard Jaritz and Katalin Szende, Abingdon: Oxbow Books, 2016, pp. 139–56.

'"Propter disparitatem linguae et religionis pares ipsis non esse...": "Minority" Communities in Medieval and Early Modern Lviv', in *Segregation – Integration – Assimilation: Religious and Ethnic Groups in Medieval Towns of Central and Eastern Europe*, ed. Derek Keene, Balász Nagy, and Katalin Szende, Farnham: Ashgate, 2009, pp. 51–66.

Kras, Pawel and James D. Mixson (eds.), *The Grand Tour of John of Capistrano in Central and Eastern Europe (1451–1456): The Transfer of Ideas and Strategies of Communication and the Transfer of Ideas in the Late Middle Ages*, Lublin: Institute of History – Polish Academy of Sciences, 2018.

Kucher, Michael, 'The Use of Water and Its Regulation in Medieval Siena', *Journal of Urban History* 31 (2005), 504–36.

Kümmeler, Fabian, 'The World in a Village: Foreigners and Newcomers on Late Medieval Korčula', in *Towns and Cities of the Croatian Middle Ages: The City and the Newcomers*, ed. Irena Benyovski Latin and Zrinka Pešorda Vardić, Zagreb: Croatian Institute of History, 2019, forthcoming.

Laguzzi, María del Pilar, 'Ávila a comienzos del siglo XIV', *Cuadernos de Historia de España* 12 (1949), 145–80.

Lambert, Bart, and W. Mark Ormrod, 'Friendly Foreigners: International Warfare, Resident Aliens and the Early History of Denization in England, c. 1250–c. 1400', *English Historical Review* 130 (2015), 1–24.

Lambert, Bart and Milan Pajic, 'Drapery in Exile: Edward III, Colchester and the Flemings', *History: The Journal of the Historical Association*, 99 (2014), 733–53.

Langmuir, G. I., '"Tanquam servi": The Change in Jewish Status in French Law about 1200', in *Toward a Definition of Antisemitism*, Berkeley, CA: University of California Press, 1990, pp. 167–94.

Lansing, Carol, 'Concubines, Lovers, Prostitutes: Infamy and Female Identity in Medieval Bologna', in *Beyond Florence: The Contours of Medieval and Early Modern Italy*, ed. Paula Findlen, Micelle M. Fontaine, and Duane J. Osheim, Stanford University Press, 2003, pp. 85–100.

Lantschner, Patrick, 'Fragmented Cities in the Later Middle Ages: Italy and the Near East Compared', *English Historical Review* 130 (2015), 546–82.

  The Logic of Political Conflict in Medieval Cities: Italy and the Southern Low Countries, 1370–1440, Oxford University Press, 2015.

Latour, Bruno, *Reassembling the Social: An Introduction to Actor-Network-Theory*, Oxford University Press, 2005.

Laughton, Jane, 'Mapping the Migrants: Welsh, Manx and Irish Settlers in Fifteenth-Century Chester', in *Mapping the Medieval City: Space, Place and Identity in Chester c. 1200–1600*, ed. Catherine A. M. Clarke, Cardiff: University of Wales Press, 2011, pp. 169–83.

Lecuppre-Desjardin, Élodie and Anne-Laure Van Bruaene (eds.), 'Introduction', in their *De Bono Communi: The Discourse and Practice of the Common Good in the European City (13th–16th Centuries)*, Brepols: Turnhout, 2010, pp. 1–9.

Lecuppre-Desjardin, Élodie and Anne-Laure Van Bruaene (eds.), *Emotions in the Heart of the City (14th–16th Century)*, Turnhout: Brepols, 2005.

L'Engle, Susan, 'Justice in the Margins: Punishment in Medieval Toulouse', *Viator* 33 (2002), 133–65.

Le Goff, Jacques, *Money and the Middle Ages: An Essay in Historical Anthropology*, trans. Jean Birrell, Cambridge: Polity, 2012.

  The Birth of Purgatory, trans. Arthur Goldhammer, University of Chicago Press, 1984.

  Time, Work and Culture in the Middle Ages, trans. Arthur Goldhammer, University of Chicago Press, 1982.

Leroy, Nicolas, '*Carta, consuetudines, statuta…* Langue et conservation des statuts municipaux en Languedoc', *Mélanges de l'École française de Rome* 126/2 (2014), 567–80.

Lévinas, Emmanuel, *Autrement qu'être ou au-delà de l'essence*, The Hague: Martinus Nijhoff, 1974 [*Otherwise Than Being or beyond Essence*, trans. Alphonso Lingis, Dordrecht and Boston, MA: Kluwer Academic Publishers, 1978].

Lichtert, Katrien, Jan Dumolyn, and Maximiliaan P. J. Martens, 'Images, Maps, Texts: Reading the Meanings of the Later Medieval and Early Modern City', in *Portraits of the City: Representing Urban Space in Later Medieval and Early Modern Europe*, ed. Katrien Lichtert, Jan Dumolyn, and Maximiliaan P. J. Martens, Turnhout: Brepols, 2014, pp. 1–8.

Lilley, Keith D., *City and Cosmos: The Medieval World in Urban Form*, London: Reaktion Books, 2009.

'Decline or Decay? Urban Landscapes in Late-Medieval England', in *Towns in Decline: AD 100–1600*, ed. T. R. Slater, Aldershot: Ashgate, 2000, pp. 235–65.

Little, Lester K., *Religious Poverty and the Profit Economy in Medieval Europe*, London: Elek, 1978.

Lloyd, T. H., *The English Wool Trade in the Middle Ages*, Cambridge University Press, 1977.

Lombardi, Teodosio, *Presenza e culto di san Bernardino da Siena nel Ducato Estense*, Ferrara: Centro culturale città di Ferrara, 1981.

Lonza, Nella, 'The Statute of Dubrovnik of 1272: Between Legal Code and Political Symbol', in *The Statute of Dubrovnik 1271 = Liber statutorum civitatis Ragusii compositus anno MCCLXXII*, trans. Vesna Rimać and ed. Nella Lonza, Dubrovnik: Državni arhiv u Dubrovniku, 2012, pp. 7–25.

Lowe, Kate J. P., 'Introduction', in *Black Africans in Renaissance Europe*, ed. T. F. Earle and K. J. P. Lowe, Cambridge University Press, 2005, pp. 1–14.

Lug, Robert, 'Politique et littérature à Metz autour de la Guerre des Amis (1231–1234): Le témoignage du Chansonnier de Saint-Germain-des-Prés', in *Lettres, musique et société en Lorraine médiévale: Autour du Tournoi de Chauvency (Ms. Oxford Bodleian Douce 308)*, ed. Mireille Chazan and Nancy Freeman Regalado, Geneva: Droz, 2012, pp. 451–86.

Luhmann, Niklas, *Trust and Power*, revised translation by Christian Morner and Michael King, based on translation by Howard Davies, John Raffan, and Kathryn Rooney, Cambridge: Polity, 2017.

MacCaughan, Patricia, *La Justice à Manosque au XIIIe siècle: Évolution et représentation*, Paris: Champion, 2005.

Maire-Vigueur, Jean-Claude, *Cavaliers et citoyens: Guerre, conflits et société dans l'Italie communale, XIIe–XIIIe siècles*, Paris: Éditions EHESS, 2003.

Mänd, Anu, *Urban Carnival: Festive Culture in the Hanseatic Cities of the Eastern Baltic, 1350–1550*, Turnhout: Brepols, 2005.

Mari, Paolo, 'Bartolo e la condizione femminile: Brevi punti dalle *lecturae* bartoliane', in *Bartolo da Sassoferrato nella cultura europea tra Medioevo e Rinascimento*, ed. Victor Crescenzi and Giovanni Rossi, Sassoferrato: Istituto internazionale di studi piceni Bartolo da Sassoferrato, 2015, pp. 239–52.

Massey, Doreen, *Space, Place, and Gender*, Minneapolis: University of Minnesota Press, 1994.

Mathison, Erik, *The Loyal Republic: Traitors, Slaves, and the Remaking of Citizenship in Civil War America*, Chapel Hill, NC: University of North Carolina Press, 2018.

Mengel, David, 'Emperor Charles IV (1346–78) as the Architect of Local Religion in Prague', *Austrian History Yearbook* 41 (2010), 15–29.

'From Venice to Jerusalem and Beyond: Milíč of Kroměříž and the Topography of Prostitution in Fourteenth-Century Prague', *Speculum* 79 (2004), 407–42.

Menjot, Denis, 'Introduction: Les gens venus d'ailleurs dans les villes médiévales. Quelques acquis de la recherche', in *'Arriver' en ville: Les migrants en milieu urbain au Moyen Âge*, ed. Cédric Quertier, Roxane Chilà, and Nicolas Pluchot, Paris: Publications de la Sorbonne, 2013, pp. 15–29.

'La Ville et ses territoires dans l'Occident médiéval: Un système spatial. État de la question', in *La ciudad medieval y su influencia territorial*, ed. Beatriz Arízaga Bolumburu and Jesús Solórzano Telechea, Nájera: Instituto de Estudios Riojanos, 2007, pp. 451–92.

'L'Immigration à Murcie, et dans son territoire, sous les premiers Trastamares (1370–1420 environ)', *Revue d'histoire économique et sociale* 53 (1975), 216–65.

Menning, Carol Bresnahan, 'The Monte's "Monte": The Early Supporters of Florence's Monte di Pietà', *The Sixteenth Century Journal* 23 (1992), 661–76.

Meyer, Hannah, 'Female Moneylending and Wet-Nursing in Jewish–Christian Relations in Thirteenth-Century England', unpublished PhD thesis, University of Cambridge, 2009.

Milani, Giuliano, *L'esclusione dal Comune: Conflitti e bandi politici a Bologna e in altre città italiane tra XII e XIV secolo*, Rome: Istituto storico italiano per il Medioevo, 2003.

Milner, Stephen J., 'Rhetorics of Transcendence: Conflict and Intercession in Communal Italy 1300–1500', in *Charisma and Religious Authority: Jewish, Christian, and Muslim Preaching, 1200–1500*, ed. Katherine L. Jansen and Miri Rubin, Turnhout: Brepols, 2010, pp. 235–51.

Montesano, Marina, 'Aspetti e conseguenze della predicazione civica di Bernardino da Siena', in *Religion civique à l'époque médiévale et moderne: Chrétienté et islam*, ed. André Vauchez, Rome: École française de Rome, 1995, pp. 265–75.

Moor, Tine de and Jan Luiten van Zanden, 'Girl Power: The European Marriage Pattern and Labour Markets in the North Sea Region in the Late Medieval and Early Modern Period', *Economic History Review* new series, 63 (2010), 1–33.

Monnet, Pierre, 'Bien Commun et bon gouvernement: Le traité politique de Johann von Soest sur la manière de bien gouverner une ville (*Wye men wol eyn statt regyrn sol, 1495*)', in *De Bono Communi: The Discourse and Practice of the Common Good in the European City (13th–16th Centuries)*, ed. Élodie Lecuppre-Desjardin and Anne-Laure Van Bruaene, Turnhout: Brepols, 2010, pp. 89–106.

'Les Révoltes urbaines en Allemagne au XIVe siècle: Un état de la question', in *Rivolte urbane e rivolte contadine nell'Europa del Trecento*, ed. Monique Bourin, Giovanni Cherubini, and Giuliano Pinto, University of Florence Press, 2008, pp. 105–53.

'Villes et citoyenneté: En guise d'introduction', in *Religion et pouvoir: Citoyenneté, ordre social et discipline morale dans les villes de l'espace Suisse (XIVe–XVIIIe siècles)*, ed. Mathieu Caesar and Marco Schnyder, Neufchâtel: Alphil, 2014, pp. 11–33.

'Villes et territoires dans l'Empire à la fin du Moyen Âge: Pour une approche régionale entre villes, principautés et royauté en Allemagne', in *La Cité médiévale en débat*, ed. Amélia Aguiar Andrade and Adelaide Millán Da Costa, Lisbon: EM – Instituto de Estudos Medievais, 2013, pp. 71–88.

Mueller, Reinhold C. *Immigrazione e cittadinanza nella Venezia medievale*, Rome: Viella, 2010.

'Merchants and Their Merchandise: Identity and Identification in Medieval Italy', in *Gens de passage en Méditerranée de l'antiquité à l'époque moderne: Procédures de contrôle et d'identification*, ed. Claudia Moatti and Wolfgand Kaiser, Paris: Maisonneuve & Larose, 2007, pp. 313–44.

'"Veneti facti privilegio": Stranieri naturalizzati a Venezia tra XIV e XVI secolo', in *La città italiana e i luoghi degli stranieri (XIV–XVIII secolo)*, ed. Donatella Calabi and Paola Lanaro, Bari: Laterza, 1998, pp. 41–50.

Müller, Martin, 'Assemblages and Actor-Networks: Rethinking Socio-Material Power, Politics and Space', *Geography Compass* 9 (2015), 27–41.

Müller, Ulrich, 'Network of the Centres – Centres of the Networks? The Relations between "Hanseatic" Medieval Towns and Their Surroundings/Hinterlands', in *Town and Country in Medieval North Western Europe: Dynamic Interactions*, ed. Alexis Wilkin, John Naylor, Derek Keene, and Arnoud-Jan Bijsterveld, Turnhout: Brepols, 2015, pp. 145–87.

Mummey, Kevin and Kathryn Reyerson, 'Whose City is This? Hucksters, Domestic Servants, Wet-Nurses, Prostitutes, and Slaves in Late Medieval Western Mediterranean Urban Society', *History Compass* 9 (2011), 910–22.

Munby, Julian, 'Zacharias's: A 14th-Century Oxford New Inn and the Origins of the Medieval Urban Inn', *Oxoniensia* 57 (1992), 245–309.

Mundill, Robin, *England's Jewish Solution: Experiment and Expulsion, 1262–1290*, Cambridge University Press, 1998.

Murray, Jacqueline, 'On the Origins and Role of "Wise Women" in Causes of Annulment on the Grounds of Male Impotence', *Journal of Medieval History* 16 (1990), 235–49.

Murray, James M., *Bruges, Cradle of Capitalism, 1280–1390*, Cambridge University Press, 2005.

Muzzarelli, Maria Giuseppina, *Il denaro e la salvezza: L'invenzione del Monte di Pietà*, Bologna: Il Mulino, 2001.

Nicholas, David, *Urban Europe, 1100–1700*, Basingstoke: Palgrave Macmillan, 2003.

Nickson, Tom, 'The Sound of Conversion in Medieval Iberia', in *Resounding Images: Medieval Intersections of Art, Music, and Sound*, ed. Susan Boynton and Diane J. Reilly, Turnhout: Brepols, 2015, pp. 91–107.

Nirenberg, David, *Communities of Violence: Persecution of Minorities in the Middle Ages*, updated edn, Philadelphia: University of Pennsylvania Press, 2015.

'Mass Conversion and Genealogical Mentalities: Jews and Christians in Fifteenth-Century Spain, *Past and Present* 174 (2002), 3–41.

'Massacre or Miracle? Valencia, 1391', in *Neighboring Faiths: Christianity, Islam, and Judaism in the Middle Ages and Today*, University of Chicago Press, 2014, pp. 75–88.

Noiriel, Gérard, *Immigration, antisémitisme et racisme en France (XIXe–XXe): Discours publics, humiliations privées*, Paris: Fayard/Pluriel, 2007.

The French Melting Pot: Immigration, Citizenship, and National Identity, trans. Geoffroy de Laforcade, Minneapolis: University of Minnesota Press, 1996 [*Le Creuset français: Histoire de l'immigration, XIXe–XXe siècles*, Paris: Seuil, 1988].

Nolf, J., *La Réforme de la bienfaisance publique à Ypres au XVIe siècle*, Ghent: Librairie scientifique E. Van Goethem, 1915.

Nowacka, Keiko, 'Prosecution, Margnalization, or Tolerance: Prostitutes in Thirteenth-Century Parisian Society', in *Difference and Identity in Francia and Medieval France*, ed. Meredith Cohen and Justine Finnhaber-Baker, Farnham: Ashgate, 2020, pp. 175–96.

Oexle, Otto G., 'Gilde und Kommune: Über die Entstehung von "Einung" und "Gemeinde" als Grundformen des Zusammenlebens in Europa', in *Theorien kommunaler Ordnung in Europa*, ed. Peter Blickle, Munich: R. Oldenbourg, 1996, pp. 75–97.

Ormrod, W. Mark and Jonathan Mackman, 'Resident Aliens in Later Medieval England: Sources, Contexts, and Debates', in *Resident Aliens in Later Medieval England*, ed. W. Mark Ormrod, Nicola McDonald, and Craig Taylor, Turnhout: Brepols, 2017, pp. 3–31.

Ormrod, W. Mark, Bart Lambert, and Jonathan Mackman, *Immigrant England, 1300–1550*, Manchester University Press, 2018.

Ortalli, Gherardo, Oliver Jens Schmitt, and Ermanno Orlando (eds.), *Il Commonwealth Veneziano tra 1204 e la fine della repubblica: Identità e peculiarità*, Venice, Istituto Veneto di Scienze, Lettere ed Arti, 2015.

Pajic, Milan, *Flemish Textile Workers in England, 1331–1400: Immigration, Integration and Economic Development*, Cambridge University Press, 2020.

Pene Vidari, Gian Savino, 'Statuti signorili', in *Signori, regimi signorili e statuti nel tardo medioevo*, ed. Rolando Dondarini, Maria Varanini, and Maria Venticelli, Bologna: Pàtron, 2003, pp. 51–62.

Peters, Robert, 'Das mittelniederdeutsche als Sprache der Hanse', in *Sprachkontakt in der Hanse: Aspekte des Sprachausgleichs im Ostsee- und Nordseeraum*, ed. Per Sture Ureland, Tübingen: Niemeyer, 1987, pp. 65–88.

Peyer, Hans Conrad, *Von der Gastfreundschaft zum Gasthaus: Studien zur Gastlichkeit im Mittelalter*, Hanover: Hahn, 1987.

Piccini, Gabriella and Lucia Travaini, *Il Libro de Pellegrino (Siena 1382–1446): Affari, uomini, monete nell'Ospedale di Santa Maria della Scala*, Naples: Liguori, 2003.

Piekalski, Jerzy, *Prague, Wrocław and Krakow: Public and Private Space at the Time of the Medieval Transition*, trans. Anna Kinecka, University of Wrocław Institute of Archaeology, 2014.

Pini, Antonio Ivan,'Nazioni mercantili, "societates" regionali e "nationes" studentesche a Bologna nel Duecento', in *Comunità forestiere e 'nationes' nell'Europa dei secoli XIII–XVI*, ed. Giovanna Petti Balbi, Naples: Liguori, 2001, pp. 23–40.

Porfyriou, Heleni, 'Gli stranieri e la città', in *Lo spazio narrabile: Scritti di storia della città in onore de Donatella Calabi*, ed. Rosa Tamborrino and Guido Zacconi, Macerata: Quodlibet, 2014, pp. 83–92.

Postan, M. M., *The Medieval Economy and Society: An Economic History of Britain in the Middle Ages*, Harmondsworth: Penguin, 1972.

Powell, James M., *Albertanus of Brescia: The Pursuit of Happiness in the Early Thirteenth Century*, Philadelphia: University of Pennsylvania Press, 1992.

Powers, James F., 'Frontier Municipal Baths and Social Interaction in Thirteenth-Century Spain', *American Historical Review* 84 (1979), 649–67.

Prak, Maarten, *Citizens without Nations: Urban Citizenship in Europe and the World, c. 1000–1789*, Cambridge University Press, 2018.

Prestwich, Michael, *York Civic Ordinances, 1301*, Borthwick Papers 49, York: Borthwick Publications, 1976.

Prevenier, Walter, 'Henri Pirenne (1862–1935)', in *French Historians 1900–2000: New Historical Writing in Twentieth-Century France*, ed. Philip Daileader and Philip Whalen, Chichester: Wiley-Blackwell, 2010, pp. 486–500.

'*Utilitas communis* in the Low Countries (Thirteenth–Fifteenth Centuries): From Social Mobilisation to Legitimation of Power', in *De Bono Communi: The Discourse and Practice of the Common Good in the European City (13th–16th Centuries)*, ed. Élodie Lecuppre-Desjardin and Anne-Laure Van Bruaene, Turnhout: Brepols, 2010, pp. 205–16.

Previdi, Emilia Saracco, 'L'Inserimento dei forestieri nel complesso urbanistico delle città marchigiane e nel paesaggio medievale', in *Stranieri e forestieri nella Marca dei secc. XIV–XVI: Atti del 30 convegno di studi maceratesi, Macerata, 19–20 novembre 1994*, Macerata: Centro di studi storici maceratesi, 1996, pp. 1–28.

Prodi, Paolo, *Il sacramento del potere: Il giuramento politico nella storia costituzionale dell'Occidente*, Bologna: Il Mulino, 1992.

Prodi, Paolo (ed.), *La fiducia secondo i linguaggi del potere*, Bologna: Il Mulino, 2007.

Quaglioni, Diego, 'The Legal Definition of Citizenship in the Late Middle Ages', in *City States in Classical Antiquity and Medieval Italy*, ed. Anthony Molho, Kurt Raaflaub, and Julia Emlen, Stuttgart: F. Steiner, 1991, pp. 155–67.

Quertier, Cédric, 'La Stigmatisation des migrants à l'épreuve des faits: Le règlement de la faillite Aiutamicristo da Pisa devant la *Mercanzia* florentine (1390)', in *'Arriver' en ville: Les migrants en milieu urbain au Moyen Âge*, ed. Cédric Quertier, Roxane Chilà, and Nicolas Pluchot, Paris: Publications de la Sorbonne, 2013, pp. 243–59.

Quertier, Cédric, Roxane Chilà, and Nicolas Pluchot (eds.), *'Arriver' en ville: Les migrants en milieu urbain au Moyen Âge*, Paris: Publications de la Sorbonne, 2013.

Raccagni, Gianluca, *The Lombard League 1164–1225*, Oxford University Press, 2010.

Rady, Martyn, 'The Government of Medieval Buda', in *Medieval Buda in Context*, ed. Balázs Nagy, Martyn Rady, Katalin Szende, and András Vadas, Leiden: Brill, 2016, pp. 301–32.

Rawcliffe, Carole, *Urban Bodies: Communal Health in Late Medieval English Towns*, Woodbridge: Boydell, 2013.

Raymond, André, 'Islamic City, Arab City: Orientalist Myths and Recent Views', *British Journal of Middle Eastern Studies* 21 (1994), 3–18.

Rees Jones, Sarah, 'Building Domesticity in the City: English Urban Housing before the Black Death', in *Medieval Domesticity: Home, Housing and Household in Medieval England*, ed. Maryanne Kowaleski and P. J. P. Goldberg. Cambridge University Press, 2008. pp. 66–91.

'Scots in the North of England: The First Alien Subsidy, 1440–43', in *Resident Aliens in Later Medieval England*, ed. W. Mark Ormrod, Nicola McDonald, and Craig Taylor, Turnhout: Brepols, 2017, pp. 51–75.

Reiner, Avraham (Rami), 'Bible and Politics: A Correspondence between Rabbenu Tam and the Authorities of Champagne', in *Entangled Histories: Knowledge, Authority, and Jewish Culture in the Thirteenth Century*, ed. Elisaheva Baumgarten, Ruth Mazo Karras, and Katelyn Mesler, Philadelphia: University of Pennsylvania Press, 2016, pp. 59–72.

Reyerson, Kathryn L., 'Public and Private Space in Medieval Montpellier: The Bon Amic Square', *Journal of Urban History* 1 (1997), 3–27.

'Urban Sensations: The Medieval City Imagined', in *A Cultural History of the Senses in the Middle Ages*, ed. Richard G. Newhauser, London: Bloomsbury, 2016, pp. 45–65.

Reynolds, Susan, *Kingdoms and Communities in Western Europe, 900–1300*, 2nd edn, Oxford: Clarendon, 1997.

Rich, John (ed.), *The City in Late Antiquity*, London: Routledge, 1992.

Ries, Rotraud '"De joden to verwisen" – Judenvertreibungen in Nordwestdeutsch-land im 15. Und 16. Jahrhundert', in *Judenvertreibungen in Mittelalter und früher Neuzeit*, ed. Friedhelm Burgard, Alfred Haverkamp, and Gerd Ment-gen, Hanover: Hahnsche Buchhandlung, 1999, pp. 189–224.

Rigaudière, Albert, 'Donner pour le Bien Commun et contribuer pour les biens communs dans les villes du Midi français du XIIIe au XVe siècle', in *De Bono Communi: The Discourse and Practice of the Common Good in the European City (13th–16th Centuries)*, ed. Élodie Lecuppre-Desjardin and Anne-Laure Van Bruaene, Brepols: Turnhout, 2010, pp. 11–53.

'Municipal Citizenship in Jacobi's *Practica aurea libellorum*', in *Privileges and Rights of Citizenship: Law and the Juridical Construction of Civil Society*, ed. Julius Kirshner and Laurent Mayali, Berkeley, CA: University of California Press, 2002, pp. 1–25.

Rinaldi, Rossella, '"Mulieres publicae": Testimonianze e note sulla prostituzione tra pieno e tardo medioevo', in *Donna e lavoro nell'Italia medievale*, ed. Maria Giuseppina Muzzarelli, Paola Galetti, and Bruno Andreolli, Turin: Rosen-berg & Sellier, 1991, pp. 105–25.

Rollo-Koster, Joëlle, *Avignon and Its Papacy, 1309–1417: Popes, Institutions, and Society*, Lanham, MD: Rowman & Littlefield, 2015.

'*Mercator Florentinensis* and Others: Immigration in Papal Avignon', in *Urban and Rural Communities in Medieval France: Provence and Languedoc, 1000–1500*, ed. Kathryn Reyerson and John Drendel, Leiden: Brill, 1998, pp. 73–100.

Romano, Dennis, 'Gender and the Urban Geography of Renaissance Venice', *Journal of Social History* 23 (1989), 229–53.

Rosser, Gervase, *The Art of Solidarity in the Middle Ages: Guilds in England 1250–1550*, Oxford University Press, 2015.

Rouse, Barbara, 'Nuisance Neighbours and Persistent Polluters: The Urban Code of Behaviour in Late Medieval London', in *Medieval Urban Culture*, ed. Andrew Brown and Jan Dumolyn, Turnhout: Brepols, 2017, pp. 75–92.

Rubin, Miri, *Charity and Community in Medieval Cambridge*, Cambridge University Press, 1987.

Gentile Tales: The Narrative Assault on Late Medieval Jews, London and New Haven, CN: Yale University Press, 1999.

'Presentism's Useful Anachronisms', *Past and Present* 234 (2017), 236–44.

Rubinstein, Nicolai, 'Political Ideas in Sienese Art: The Frescoes by Ambrogio Lorenzetti and Taddeo di Bartolo in the Palazzo Pubblico', *Journal of the Warburg and Courtauld Institutes* 21 (1958), 179–207.

Ruiz, Theofilo F., 'Expansion et changement: La conquête de Séville et la société castillane (1248–1350)', *Annales: Histoire, Sciences Sociales* 34 (1979), 548–65.

Sabapathy, John, *Officers and Accountability in Medieval England, 1170–1300*, Oxford University Press, 2014.

Safran, Linda, *The Medieval Salento: Art and Identity in Southern Italy*, Philadelphia: University of Pennsylvania Press, 2014.

Sansy, Danièle, 'Signes de judéité dans l'image', *Micrologus* 15 (2007), 87–105.

Sbriccoli, Mario, *L'interpretazione dello statuto: Contributo allo studio della funzione dei giuristi nell'età comunale*, Milan: Giuffrè, 1969.

Scarcia, Giulia, '"Comburgenses et cohabitatores": Aspetti e problemi della presenza dei "Lombardi" tra Savoia e Svizzera', in *Comunità forestiere e 'nationes' nell'Europa dei secoli XIII–XVI* , ed. Giovanna Petti Balbi, Naples: Liguori, 2001, pp. 113–33.

Schich, Winfried, *Wirtschaft und Kulturlandschaft: Gesammelte Beiträge 1977 bis 1999 zur Geschichte der Zisterzienser und der 'Germania Slavica'*, Berlin: BWV, 2007.

Schmieder, Felicitas, 'Stadtstatuten deutscher Städte? Einige Überlegungen im europäischen Vergleich', in *Von der Ordnung zur Norm: Statuten im Mittelalter und Früher Neuzeit*, ed. Gisela Drossbach, Paderborn: Ferdinand Schöningh, 2010, pp. 217–23.

'Various Ethnic and Religious Groups in Medieval German Towns? Some Evidence and Reflections', in *Segregation – Integration – Assimilation: Religious and Ethnic Groups in Medieval Towns of Central and Eastern Europe*, ed. Derek Keene, Balázs Nagy, and Katalin Szende, Farnham: Ashgate, 2009, pp. 15–31.

Schryver, James G., 'Identities in the Crusader East', in *Mediterranean Identities in the Premodern Era: Entrepôts, Islands, Empires*, ed. John Watkins and Kathryn L. Reyerson, Farnham: Ashgate, 2014, pp. 173–89.

Schulz, Knut, *'Denn sie lieben dies freiheit so sehr...': Kommunale Aufstände und Entstehung des europäischen Bürgertums im Hochmittelalter*, Darmstadt: Wissenschaftliche Buchgesellschaft, 1992.

Scott, Joan Wallach, *Gender and the Politics of History*, New York: Columbia University Press, 1988.

Selart, Anti, 'Non-German Literacy in Medieval Livonia', in *Uses of the Written Word in Medieval Towns: Medieval Urban Literacy, vol. II*, ed. Marco Mostert and Anna Adamska, Turnhout: Brepols, 2014, pp. 37–63.

Serchuk, Camille, 'Paris and the Rhetoric of Town Praise in the *Vie de St. Denis* Manuscript (Paris Bibliothèque Nationale de France, ms 2090–2)', *Journal of the Walters Art Gallery* 57 (1999), 35–47.

Shahar, Shulamith, 'Religious Minorities, Vagabonds and Gypsies in Early Modern Europe', in *The Roma – A Minority in Europe: Historical, Political and Social Perspectives*, ed. Roni Stauber and Raphael Vago, Budapest: Central European University Press, 2007, pp. 1–18.

Shalev-Eyni, Sarit, *Jews among Christians: Hebrew Book Illumination from Lake Constance*, Turnhout: Brepols, 2010.

Shatzmiller, Joseph, *Shylock Reconsidered: Jews, Moneylending, and Medieval Society*, Berkeley, CA: University of California Press, 1990.

Sherman, Claire Richter, 'Representations of Maternal and Familial Roles in French Translations of the Pseudo-Aristotelian "Economics" Book I', in *Tributes to Lucy Freeman Sandler: Studies in Iluminated Manuscripts*, ed. Kathryn A. Smith and Carol H. Krinsky, London: Harvey Miller, 2007, pp. 287–98.

Shoham-Steiner, Ephraim, '*"And in most of their business transactions they rely on this"*: Some Reflections on Jews and Oaths in the Commercial Arena in Medieval Europe", in *On the Word of a Jew: Religion, Reliability, and the Dynamics of Trust*, ed. Nina Caputo and Mitchell B. Hart, Bloomington, IN: Indiana University Press, 2019, pp. 36–61.

'"For in every city and town the manner of behaviour of the Jews resembles that of their non-Jewish neighbours": The Intricate Network of Interfaith Connections – A Brief Introduction', in *Intricate Interfaith Networks in the Middle Ages: Quotidian Jewish–Christian Contacts*, ed. Ephraim Shoham-Steiner, Turnhout: Brepols, 2016, pp. 1–32.

Simon, Ulrich, 'Das Lübecker Niederstadtbuch: Seine Charakterisierung über das Jahr 1400 hinaus', in *Gelebte Normen im urbanen Raum?: Zur sozial- und kulturgeschichtlichen Analyse rechtlicher Quellen in Städten des Hanseraums (13. bis 16. Jahrhundert)*, ed. Hanno Brand, Sven Rabeler, and Harm von Seggern, Hilversum: Uitgeverij Verloren, 2014, pp. 63–82.

Simons, Walter, *Cities of Ladies: Beguine Communities in the Medieval Low Countries, 1200–1565*, Philadelphia: University of Pennsylvania Press, 2001.

'In Praise of Faithful Women: Count Robert of Flanders' Defense of Beguines against the Clementine Decree *Cum de quibusdam mulieribus* (c. 1318–1320)', in *Christianity and Culture in the Middle Ages: Essays in Honor of John Van Engen's 35th Anniversary of Teaching at Notre Dame*, ed. David Mengel and Lisa Wolverton, South Bend, IN: University of Notre Dame Press, 2014, pp. 331–57.

Skinner, Quentin, 'Ambrogio Lorenzetti: The Artist as Political Philosopher', *Proceedings of the British Academy* 72 (1986), 1–56.

Smail, Daniel Lord, 'Démanteler le patrimoine: Les femmes et les biens dans la Marseille médiévale', *Annales* 52 (1997), 343–68.

Imaginary Cartographies: Possession and Identity in Late Medieval Marseille, Ithaca, NY: Cornell University Press, 1999.

Legal Plunder: Households and Debt Collection in Late Medieval Europe Cambridge, MA: Harvard University Press, 2016.

The Consumption of Justice: Emotions, Publicity, and Legal Culture in Marseille, 1264–1423, Ithaca, NY: Cornell University Press, 2003.

Smelyansky, Eugene, 'Urban Order and Urban Other: Anti-Waldensian Inquisition in Augsburg, 1393', *German History* 34 (2016), 1–20.

Snijders, Tjamke, 'Near Neighbours, Distant Brothers: The Inter-Monastic Networks of Benedictine Houses in the Southern Low Countries (900–1200)', in *Medieval Liège at the Crossroads of Europe: Monastic Society and Culture, 1000–1300*, ed. Steven Vanderputten, Tjamke Snijders, and Jay Diehl, Turnhout: Brepols, 2017, pp. 69–108.

Sobecki, Sebastian, '"The writyng of this tretys": Margery Kempe's Son and the Authorship of Her Book', *Studies in the Age of Chaucer* 37 (2015), 257–83.

Spindler, Erik, 'Between Sea and City: Portable Communities in Late Medieval London and Bruges', in *London and Beyond: Essays in Honour of Derek Keene*, ed. Matthew Davies and James A. Galloway, London: Institute of Historical Research, 2012, pp. 181–99.

'Flemings in the Peasants' Revolt, 1381', in *Contact and Exchange in Later Medieval Europe: Essays in Honour of Malcolm Vale*, ed. Hannah Skoda, Patrick Lantschner, and R. L. J. Shaw, Woodbridge: Boydell, 2012, pp. 59–78.

Stejksal, Jan, 'A Catholic City in the Hussite Era, 1400–1450s', in *The Transformation of Confessional Cultures in a Central European City: Olomouc, 1400–1750*, ed. Antonin Kalous, Rome: Viella, 2015, pp. 23–39.

Stevens, Matthew Frank, *Urban Assimilation in Post-Conquest Wales: Ethnicity, Gender and Economy in Ruthin, 1282–1348*, Cardiff: University of Wales Press, 2010.

Storti Storchi, Claudia, 'Appunti in tema di "potestas condendi statuta"', in *Statuti città territori in Italia e Germania tra medioevo e età moderna*, ed. Giorgio Chittolini and Dietmar Willoweit, Bologna: Il Mulino, 1991, pp. 319–43.

Stranieri e forestieri nella Marca dei secc. XIV–XVI: Atti del Convegno di Studi Maceratesi, Macerata: Centro di studi storici maceratesi, 1996.

Strazyński, Marcin, *Das mittelalterliche Krakau: Der Stadtrat im Herrschaftsgefüge der polnischen Metropole*, trans. Christian Prüfer and Kai Witzlack-Makarevich, Vienna: Böhlau, 2015.

Strohm, Paul, *Theory and the Premodern Text*, Minneapolis: University of Minnesota Press, 2000.

Stuard, Susan Mosher, '"To Town to Serve": Urban Domestic Slavery in Medieval Ragusa', in *Women and Work in Pre-industrial Europe*, ed. Barbara Hanawalt, Bloomington: Indiana University Press, 1987, pp. 39–55.

Studer, Barbara, 'Frauen im Bürgerschaft: Überlegungen zur rechtlichen und sozialen Stellung der Frau in spätmittelalterlichen Städten', in *Neubürger im späten Mittelalter: Migration und Austausch in der Städtelandschaft des alten Reiches (1250–1550)*, ed. Rainer Christoph Schwinges, Berlin: Duncker & Humblot, 2002, pp. 169–200.

Subrahmanyam, Sanjay, *Three Ways to Be Alien: Travails and Encounters in the Early Modern World*, Waltham, MA: Brandeis University Press, 2011.

Symes, Carol, *A Common Stage: Theater and Public Life in Medieval Arras*, Ithaca, NY: Cornell University Press, 2007.

Szende, Katalin, 'Integration through Language: The Multilingual Character of Late Medieval Hungarian Towns', in *Segregation – Integration – Assimilation: Religious and Ethnic Groups in the Medieval Towns of Central and Eastern Europe*, ed. Derek Keene, Balázs Nagy, and Katalin Szende, Farnham: Ashgate, 2009, pp. 205–33.

'*Iure Theutonico?* German Settlers and Legal Frameworks for Immigrations to Hungary in an East–Central European Perspective', *Journal of Medieval History* 45 (2019), 1–20.

'Laws, Loans, Literates: Trust in Writing in the Context of Jewish–Christian Contacts in Medieval Hungary', in *Religious Cohabitation in Medieval Towns*, ed. Stephane Bosselier and John Tolan, Turnhout: Brepols, 2014, pp. 243–71.

'Power and Identity: Royal privileges to the Towns of Medieval Hungary in the Thirteenth Century', *Urban Liberties and Civic Participation from the Middle Ages to Modern Times*, ed. Michel Pauly and Alexander Lee, Trier: Porta Alba, 2015, pp. 27–67.

'Some Aspects of Urban Landownership in Western Hungary', in *Power, Profit and Urban Land: Landownership in Medieval and Early Modern Northern European Towns*, ed. Finn-Einar Eliassen and Geir Atle Ersland, Aldershot: Scolar Press, 1996, pp. 141–66.

Trust, Authority, and the Written Word in the Royal Towns of Medieval Hungary, Turnhout: Brepols, 2018.

Tadmor, Naomi, *The Social Universe of the English Bible: Scripture, Society, and Culture in Early Modern England*, Cambridge University Press, 2010.

Theuws, Frans and Arnoud-Jan Bijsterveld, 'Early Town Formation in the Northern Low Countries: Roman Heritage, Carolingian Impulses, and a New Take-Off in the Twelfth Century', in *Town and Country in Medieval North-Western Europe: Dynamic Interactions*, ed. Alexis Wilkin, John Naylor, Derek Keene, and Arnoud-Jan Bijsterveld, Turnhout: Brepols, 2015, pp. 87–118.

Toch, Michael, *Die Juden im mittelalterlichen Reich*, 2nd edn, Munich: Oldenbourg Wissenschaftsverlag, 2010.

Todeschini, Giacomo, '*Intentio e dominium* come caratteri di cittadinanza: Sulla complessità della rappresentazione dell'estraneo fra medioevo e modernità', in *Cittadinanze medievali: Dinamiche di appartenenza a un corpo communitario*, ed. Sara Menzinger, Rome: Viella, 2017, pp. 229–45.

Richezza francescana: Dalla povertà volontaria alla società del mercato, Bologna: Il Mulino, 2004 [*Franciscan Wealth: From Voluntary Poverty to Market Society*, trans. Donatella Melucci, New York: Franciscan Institute Publications, 2009].

Tognetti, Sergio, 'The Trade in Black African Slaves in Fifteenth-Century Florence', in *Black Africans in Renaissance Europe*, ed. T. F. Earle and K. J. P. Lowe, Cambridge University Press, 2005, pp. 213–24.

Tomas, Natalie, 'Did Women Have a Space?', in *Renaissance Florence: A Social History*, ed. Roger J. Crum and John T. Paoletti, Cambridge University Press, 2006, pp. 311–28.

Tomei Alessandro (ed.), *Le Bicherne di Siena: Arte e finanza all'alba dell'economia moderna*, Rome: Retablo, 2002.

Tóth, Csaba, 'Minting, Financial Administration and Coin Circulation in Hungary in the Árpádian and Angevin Periods (1000–1387),' in *The Economy of Medieval Hungary*, ed. József Laszlovszky, Balázs Nagy, Péter Szabó and András Vadas, Leiden: Brill, 2018, pp. 279–94.

Toureille, Valérie, *Vol et brigandage au Moyen Âge*, Paris: Pressses Universitaires de France, 2006.

Treggiari, Ferdinando, 'Bartolo e gli ebrei', in *Bartolo da Sassoferrato nella cultura europea tra Medioevo e Rinascimento*, ed. Victor Crescenzi and Giovanni Rossi, Sassoferrato: Istituto internazionale di studi piceni 'Bartolus da Sassoferrato', 2015, pp. 155–206.

Trivellato, Francesca, *The Promise and Peril of Credit: What a Forgotten Legend about Jews and Finance Tells Us about the Making of European Commercial Society*, Princeton University Press, 2019.

Trivellato, Francesca, Leor Halevi, and Cátia Antunes (eds.), *Religion and Trade: Cross-Cultural Exchanges in World History, 1000–1900*, Oxford University Press, 2014.

Turrini, Patrizia, *La comunità ebraica di Siena: I documenti dell'Archivio di Stato dal Medioevo alla Restaurazione*, Siena: Pascal, 2008.

Unger, Richard, 'Feeding Low Countries Towns: The Grain Trade in the Fifteenth Century', *Revue belge de philologie et d'histoire* 77 (1999), esp. 329–58.

Van Engen, John, 'A World Astir: Europe and Religion in the Early Fifteenth Century', in *Europe after Wyclif*, ed. J. Patrick Hornbeck and Michael Van Dussen, New York: Fordham University Press, 2017, pp. 11–45.

Vauchez, André, *Catherine of Siena: A Life of Passion and Purpose*, Mahwah, NJ: Paulist Press, 2018.

Francis of Assisi: The Life and Afterlife of a Medieval Saint, trans. Michael F. Casuto, New Haven, CN: Yale University Press, 2012.

Vauchez, André (ed.), *La Religion civique à l'époque médiévale et moderne (chrétienté et islam): Actes du colloque organisé par le Centre de recherche 'Histoire sociale et culturelle de l'Occident, XIIe–XVIIIe siècle' de l'Université de Paris X–Nanterre et l'Institut universitaire de France (Nanterre, 21–23 juin 1993)*, Rome: École française de Rome, 1995.

Veldhuizen, Martine, *Sins of the Tongue in the Medieval West: Sinful, Unethical, and Criminal Words in Middle Dutch (1300–1500)*, Turnhout: Brepols, 2017.

Verger, Jacques, 'Le nazioni studentesche a Parigi nel Medio Evo: Qualche osservazione', in *Comunità forestiere e 'nationes' nell'Europa dei secoli XIII–XVI*, ed. Giovanna Petti Balbi, Naples: Liguori, 2001, pp. 3–10.

Verhulst, Adriaan, *The Rise of Cities in North-West Europe*, Cambridge University Press, 1999.

Viazzo, Pier Paolo, *Upland Communities: Environment, Population and Social Structure in the Alps since the Sixteenth Century*, Cambridge University Press, 1989.

Vincent, Catherine, *Les Confréries médiévales dans le royaume de France, XIIIe–XVe siècle*, Paris: Albin Michel, 1994.

Violante, Cinzio, *La società milanese nell'età precomunale*, Bari: G. Laterza, 1953.

von Heusinger, Sabine, *Johannes Mulberg OP (+1414): Ein Leben im Spannungsfeld von Dominikanerobservanz und Beginenstreit*, Berlin: Akademie, 2000.

von Moos, Peter, '"Public" et "privé" à la fin du Moyen Âge: Le "bien commun" et la "loi de conscience"', *Studi Medievali* 3rd series, 41 (2000), 505–48.

Weber, Max, *The City*, trans. Don Martindale and Gertrud Neuwirth, New York: Free Press, 1958.

Wei, Ian P., *Intellectual Culture in Medieval Paris: Theologians and the University c. 1100–1330*, Cambridge University Press, 2012.

'Scholars and Travel in the Twelfth and Thirteenth Centuries', in *Freedom of Movement in the Middle Ages: Proceedings of the 2013 Northern Symposium*, ed. Peregrine Horden, Harlaxton Medieval Studies 15, Donnington: Shaun Tyas, 2007, pp. 73–85.

Wenninger, Markus J., *Man bedarf keiner Juden mehr: Ursachen und Hintergründe ihrer Vertreibung aus den deutschen Reichsstädten im 15. Jahrhundert*, Cologne, Vienna and Graz: Böhlau, 1981.

Wickham, Chris, *Courts and Conflict in Twelfth-Century Tuscany*, Oxford University Press, 2003.

Framing the Early Middle Ages: Europe and the Mediterranean, 400–800, Oxford University Press, 2005.

Medieval Rome: Stability and Crisis of a City, 900–1500, Oxford University Press, 2015.

Wiedl, Brigit, 'Jews and the City: Parameters of Jewish Urban Life in Late Medieval Austria', in *Urban Space in the Middle Ages and the Early Modern Age*, ed. Albrecht Classen, Berlin and New York: de Gruyter, 2009, pp. 273–308.

Wilke, Carsten, 'Jewish Erotic Encounters with Christians and Muslims in Late Medieval Iberia: Testing Ibn Verga's Hypothesis', in *Intricate Interfaith Networks in the Middle Ages: Quotidian Jewish–Christian Contacts in the Middle Ages*, ed. Ephraim Shoham-Steiner, Turnhout: Brepols; 2016, pp. 193–230.

Wubs-Mrozewicz, Justyna, 'The Hanse in Medieval and Early Modern Europe: An Introduction', in *The Hanse in Medieval and Early Modern Europe*, ed. Justyna Wubs-Mrozewicz and Stuart Jenks, Leiden: Brill, 2013, pp. 1–35.

Zelić, Danko, 'Wooden Houses in the Statutes and Urban Landscapes of Medieval Dalmatian Communes', in *Splitski statut iz 1312. godine – povijest i pravo [The Statute of Split – the History and the Law]*, ed. Željko Radić, Marko Trogrlić, Massimo Meccarelli, and Ludwig Steindorff, Split: Književni krug Split – Odsjek za povijest Filozofskoga fakulteta Sveučilišta u Splitu – Pravni fakultet Sveučilišta u Splitu, 2015, pp. 489–507.

Zientara, Benedykt, 'Foreigners in Poland in the 10th–15th Centuries: Their Role in the Opinion of the Polish Medieval Community', *Acta Poloniae Historica* 29 (1974), 5–27.

Ziwes, Franz-Josef, 'Territoriale Judenvertreibungen in Südwesten und Süden Deutschlands im 14. und 15. Jahrhundert', in *Judenvertreibungen in Mittelalter und früher Neuzeit*, ed. Friedhelm Burgard, Alfred Haverkamp, and Gerd Mentgen, Hanover: Hahnsche Buchhandlung, 1999, pp. 165–87.

Zorzi, Andrea, 'Bien Commun et conflits politiques dans l'Italie communale', in *De Bono Communi: The Discourse and Practice of the Common Good in the European City (13th–16th Centuries)*, ed. Élodie Lecuppre-Desjardin and Anne-Laure Van Bruaene, Brepols: Turnhout, 2010, pp. 267–90.

Index

Aachen, 3
adultery, 76, 80, 87
Agen, 38, 80
Agnes (wife of Michael Norton), 80
Agostino Novello, 74–5
Albanians, 69
Albertanus, 10
Alberto di Francesco, 79
Alfonso V of Aragon, 48
Ancona, 35
Andrew III of Hungary, 54
Angela da Foligno, 83
Antonino of Florence, 67
Arles, 4
Arras, 4, 10
artisan and craft groups, 40, 48, 75–9
Art of Speaking and Keeping Silent
    (Albertanus), 10
Ascheri, Mario, 33
Ascoli Piceno, 44, 56
Augustine of Hippo, 52
Auragne, 84
Auxonne, 48
Avignon, 4, 7, 17, 30, 46, 49, 93
Àvila, 58

Baldus de Ubaldis, 17
bankers. *See* moneylenders and bankers
Barcelona, 55, 73
Barnim, Duke of Pomerania, 5
Bartholomew 'the English', 6
Bartolus of Sassoferrato, 10, 16, 56
baths and bathing, 68
Beatrice (daughter of Pieter de Wilde), 78
beguines, 49, 83–4
Bela IV of Hungary, 28, 54, 126
Benjamin of Tudela, 52, 99
Bergamo, 34, 81, 89
Bernardino da Feltre, 67
Bernardino of Siena, 62–6
Berne, 45

bigamy, 76
Birger Jarl, 28
bishops, authority of, 2, 63
Black African slaves, 88
Black Death, 24, 47, 55, 60
Bodel, Jean, 10
Boileau, Etienne, 78
Bolesław V of Poland, 13
Bologna, 7, 33, 36, 43
Bona, 85
The Book of Sir Thomas More (Shakespeare),
    97
The Book of the City of Women (Christine de
    Pizan), 72
Boone, Marc, 48
Brescia, 63
Brno, 68
brothels, 87, 89–90
Bruges, 5, 7, 48, 77, 83
Brunetto Latini, 9–10, 26
Buda, 12–13, 28, 37, 77, 81, 88
burgage plots, 5
burial rituals, 77, 80

Cairo Montenotte, 40, 106
Camerino, 35, 43, 90, 121
Campbell, Bruce, 47
Carcassone, 60, 119
Catherine of Siena, 83
Cavallar, Oswaldo, 57
Cecina, 37, 43
Cellarius, Christianus, 96–7
Cerutti, Simona, 1
Charles IV, Holy Roman Emperor, 54, 89
Charles V, Holy Roman Emperor, 96
Chaucer, Geoffrey, 9
Chester, 78
Chioggia, 43
Christians and Christianity
    clerics as civic office-holders, 44
    episcopal authority, 2, 63

Christians and Christianity (cont.)
  and ideology of Jewish service, 52–3
  preaching campaigns, 45, 49, 62–4, 66–8
  relationship with Jews, coexistence, 56–9
  relationship with Jews, intolerance, 59–68
  urban religious orders, 7
  women's religious participation, 82–4
Christine de Pizan, 72
Christoph van der Hove, 78
cities
  as assemblages, 22–3
  cohesion and diversity, overview, 8–13
  development and growth, overview, 2–8
  historiography, 18
  walls and fortifications, 15–16
citizenship
  of Jews, 45, 57
  and marriage, 37, 120
  requirements for, 16–18, 27, 37–43, 48, 92
  of women, 77, 92
Clare of Assisi, 83
Clarke, Paula, 79
Clement V, Pope, 84
Clement VI, Pope, 61
clothing
  distinguishing Jews, 62, 64–5, 69, 85
  distinguishing prostitutes, 65, 88
Cologne, 5, 61
colonial extension, 30
commerce. See merchants and
    mercantilism; moneylenders and
    bankers
common good, 9–12, 47, 49, 64
Commonwealth Veneziano, 30
communal movement, 4
Compagni, Dino, 44
concubines, 72
Constable, Olivia Remie, 6, 68
Constance, Council of (1414–1418), 62
controlled anachronism, 19
cosmopolitanism, 6–7
Council of Constance (1414–18), 62
Council of Lyons (1274), 62
Courtemanche, Andrée, 42
courts, women's access to, 80–2
craft and artisan groups, 40, 48, 75–9
credit and loans, 13, 45, 49, 54, 62–3, 65–7,
    81–2

Danes, 48, 51
Dante Alighieri, 9, 34, 44
Datini, Francesco and Margherita, 76
Davies, Rees, 12
death and burial rituals, 77, 80
denization (naturalisation), 17, 27
The Description of the World (Polo), 8
diaspora, as concept, 7–8

disfigurement, 80
Le Dit des rues de Paris (Guillot), 79, 84, 89
Domenico da Leonessa, 66
Dorin, Rowan, 62
Dorpat/Tartu, 12
dowries, 41–2, 75
Drossbach, Gisela, 114
Dublin, 4, 36
Dubrovnik/Ragusa, 73

economy. See also merchants and
    mercantilism; moneylenders and
    bankers
  affected by migration, 14
  challenges of fourteenth century, 23–4,
    47, 60
Edward I of England, 26–7, 75, 88–9
Edward II of England, 27
Elena Somerset, 80
Elisabeth of Ghent, 83
Ennen, Edith, 104
episcopal authority, 2, 63
Exeter, 78

Fancy, Hussein, 53
Farmer, Sharon, 7, 82
Federico da Montefeltro, 66
Ferrara, 34
financiers. See moneylenders and bankers
Fitz Robert, Geoffrey, 29
Flemings, 46, 51, 69
Flora (widow), 81
Florence, 5, 40, 43–4, 88, 135
Fonte Avellana, 43
Forlì, 36, 39
fortifications and walls, 15–16
Franceschina (public merchant), 79
Franciscans, Third Order, 83
Francis of Assisi, 83
Frederick I, Holy Roman Emperor, 54
Frederick II, Holy Roman Emperor, 34
Frederick II, Duke of Austria, 53
Fribourg, 42, 123
Friuli, 45
fueros (royal statutes), 52, 68
Fuero de Teruel (1177), 53
Fuero of Cuenca (1177), 120
Fuero of Úbeda, 118

Galbert of Bruges, 9–12
gender, as category of analysis, 72. See also
    women
Genoa, 4–5, 7, 33, 73, 88
Gerino di ser Tano of Casole, 42
Ghent, 5, 48, 79, 83
ghettos, 69
Gian Galeazzo Visconti, Duke of Milan, 47

Giovanni da Capistrano, 67–8
Gourdon, 56, 80, 85–6
governance. *See also* citizenship; statutes and
   legislation
  communal movement, 4
  political theory, 9–12
  taxes, 40–1, 45, 120, 123
  varieties of, 13, 26, 28–9
Great Yarmouth, 87
Guglielma Nadala, 86
guilds, 11, 40, 48, 77–8
Guillot of Paris, 79, 84, 89

Handlin, Oscar, 21
Hanseatic network, 6, 30–1
Haverkamp, Alfred, 57
Henry III of England, 54, 56
Henry IV, Holy Roman Emperor, 4
hospitality networks, 6–7
hospitals, 31
house-building, 42–3, 121
Hus, Jan, 68
Hussites, 67–8

inheritance customs, 41–2, 75
inns and taverns, 36, 118
The Institution of the Eucharist (Justus van
   Ghent), 66
interest (financial), 45, 49, 62–3, 65–7, 81–2
Isidore of Seville, 9
Izaac of Bordeaux, 56

Jeu de St Nicholas (Bodel), 10
Jews, 50–70, 95
  civic status, 45, 57
  coexistence in mixed communities, 14,
   56–9
  distinguishing clothing for, 62, 64–5, 69,
   85
  early settlement of, 51
  expulsion of, 50–1, 66–7
  as financial servants, 51–6, 62, 82
  guilds, excluded from, 48
  intolerance towards, 55, 59–68
  violence against, 55, 60, 67, 85–6, 93
  women's access to courts, 81
Joan Blakhay, 78
John the Armourer, 78
Jordan, William Chester, 53, 82
Judah the Pious, 14
Justus van Ghent, 66

Kaye, Joel, 45
Kempe, John, 31
Kempe, Margery, 87
Kent, 46
Kilkenny, 29, 77

Kirshner, Julius, 57
Krakow, 13

landownership, 61
language, 6, 8–9, 34
Lantschner, Patrick, 23, 110
Laureta Bonafazzy, 76
legislation. *See* statutes and legislation
Le Goff, Jacques, 18, 109
Leiden, 77
Le Mans, 4
Léon, 37
lepers, 60
Levinas, Emmanuel, 96
The Life of St Denis, 15
Le Livre dou Tresor (Brunetto Latini), 9
loans and credit, 13, 26, 45, 49, 54, 62–3,
   65–7, 81–2
Lombards, 6–7, 43, 54, 63, 82
London, 5, 7, 88, 118
Loraux, Nicole, 19
Lorenzetti, Ambrogio, 11–12, 74
Louis VIII of France, 13
Louis IX of France, 53
Louvain, 83
Low German, 6, 9–12
Lübeck, 13, 34
Lucca, 7
Lucia (public merchant), 79
Lüneburg, 48
Lviv/Lemberg, 12, 28
Lyons, Council of (1274), 62

Mabina Taverner, 77
Maddalena (midwife), 82
Magdeburg, 13, 51
Mainz, 51, 63
Maitland, Frederic William, 33
Majorca Disputation, 55
Manosque, 87
Mantua, 32, 80
Margaret of Constantinople, Countess of
   Flanders, 31, 54
mariners, 32
marriage
  adultery, 76, 80, 87
  and citizenship, 37, 120
  exemption from military service through,
   119
  and inheritance, 41–2, 75
Marseilles, 4, 58, 81
Marshall, William, 29
Martínez, Ferrant, 68
Martini, Simone, 74
Martin V, Pope, 62
Massa Maritima, 63
Meinhardi, Andreas, 50

Le Menagier de Paris, 73, 84
Mengel, David, 90
merchants and mercantilism
    Hanseatic network, 6, 30–1
    hospitality networks for, 6–7
    privileges for, 12, 54–5
    statutes on settlement of, 13, 26–8, 35–6, 40
    women's involvement, 75–6, 78–80
Meresburg, 51
Meyer, Hannah, 82
midwives, 82
migrants and migration
    economic impact, 14
    historiography, 21–2
Milan, 5, 13, 47
Milič, Jan, 90
The Million (Marco Polo), 8
Modena, 63
moneylenders and bankers
    credit and interest practices, 13, 45, 49, 54, 62–3, 65–7, 81–2
    Jews as financial servants, 51–6, 62, 82
    privileges for, 44–5, 54–5
Montebuono, 37, 81
monte di pietà (charitable banks), 66–7
Monte Milone, 43
Montpellier, 4, 85
morality, 9–12, 49, 53, 62–8, 88–90
More, Thomas, 97
Mühlhausen, 36, 120
Mulberg, Johannes, 49
Murcia, 37
Muslims, 27, 48, 53, 57–9, 68

Narbonne, 4
naturalisation (denization), 17, 27
The Nine (Siena), 11
Nirenberg, David, 58
Noiriel, Gérard, 21
Norwegians, 48
Norwich, 55
notaries, 44, 122
Novgorod, 7
Nuremberg Chronicles, 24

Oak Book of Southampton, 32
oath-taking, 17, 26, 49, 57
Observant movement, 63, 66–7
Olomouc, 68
Oxford, 4

Padua, 33
Paris, 5, 7, 13, 55, 78, 82, 89–90
Parma, 17
Pasqua Zantani, 79
Pere II of Aragon, 53
Péronete (wife of Jacquot le Pitoul), 86

Perugia, 38, 62–3
Peyre de Farganel, 85
Philip the Good, Duke, 48
Piacenza, 34, 122
pilgrims, 31
Pirenne, Henri, 3, 18
Pisa, 4, 33
Pisactor, Siffridus, 63
Pistoia, 33, 36, 44
Plato, 5
political theory, 9–12. *See also* governance
Polo, Marco, 8
Pons of Gourdon, 56
population
    decline, 47, 64
    growth, 3
    male *vs* female, 73
Porfyriou, Heleni, 96
Porlezza, 35, 42
Pozsony/Pressburg, 54
Prague, 6, 12, 89
preaching campaigns, 45, 49, 62–4, 66–8
Prenzlau, 5
property ownership, 61
prostitutes, 53, 65, 87–90, 142
Proulx, E. Annie, 21
public merchants, 78–9
purity, discourse on, 61, 67–8

Ragusa/Dubrovnik, 35, 40
Ravenna, 3
Recanati, 40, 43
redemptive governance, 53
reform, preaching campaigns, 45, 49, 62–4, 66–8
Regensburg, 51
regulations. *See* statutes and legislation
religion. *See* Christians and Christianity;
    Jews; Muslims
Reval/Tallinn, 12
Riga, 12
Rintfleisch massacres (1298–1300), 55
Rivarolo, 48
Roger II of Sicily, 12
Roll of Oléron, 32
Roman law, 33–4, 45
Rome, 30
Roncinelli, Giacomo, 82
Rustichello da Pisa, 8
Ruthin, 29, 79, 81, 87

Salisbury, 78
San Gimignano, 36, 80
San Salvatore (religious house), 88
Sassari, 81, 86
Sassoferrato, 41
Sefer Hasidim (Judah the Pious), 14, 87

Seville, 27, 67
sexual contacts, 59, 68
Shakespeare, William, 97
Shepherds Crusade, 60
Siena, 11, 13, 16, 31, 34, 42, 47, 64–6, 75, 88
Sigismund, King of the Germans, 62
Simons, Walter, 83
slaves, 88
Slavs, 43, 48, 69
Smail, Daniel, 58, 76, 81
Sopron, 61
Spoleto, 44
statutes and legislation
    on adultery, 76, 80, 87
    on citizenship, for Jews, 45, 57
    on citizenship, for women, 77, 92
    on citizenship, requirements for, 16–18,
        27, 37–43, 48
    on clothing, 62, 64–5, 69, 85, 88
    on death and burial rituals, 77, 80
    on inheritance, 41–2, 75
    on Jewish financial service, 51–6
    making of, 33–5
    on prostitution, 65, 88–90
    on settlement of strangers, overview, 13,
        26–8
    on short-term settlement, 35–7, 117
    on violence against women, 84, 86
    and women's access to courts, 80–2
Stevens, Matthew, 29
strangers. See also Jews; statutes and
        legislation; women
    desire for, 27–8, 43–5, 92–3
    fourteenth- and fifteenth-century
        challenges for, 46–9
    historiography, 21–3
    as term, 1–2, 16
    varieties of, 30–3
students, 31–2, 121
Subrahmanyam, Sanjay, 23
Summa of Vices (William Perault), 10
sumptuary laws, 62, 64–5, 69, 85, 88
Swedes, 48, 69
Symes, Carol, 10

Tàrrega, 60
taverns and inns, 36, 118
taxes, 40–1, 45, 120, 123
Tefilah li-Shlom Malchut, 55
Thibaut, Count of Champagne, 53
Third Order (Franciscans), 83
Thomas Aquinas, 54
Todeschini, Giacomo, 64

Tortosa, 67
Toulouse, 38, 80
Treaty of Stralsund (1370), 30
Tresor (Brunetto Latini), 26
Treviso, 31, 41
Troyes, 53
Tuscans, 8, 46, 51, 93

universities, 7, 31–2, 57, 121
Urbino, 66
Usurarum voraginem, 62
usury, 45, 49, 62–3, 65–7, 81–2

vagrancy, 87
Valencia, 82, 88
Valréas, 117
Valsolda, 36
Van Engen, John, 68
Venice, 5–6, 30, 33, 35, 40, 69, 73, 77–9, 82,
    90
vernacular language, 6, 8–9, 34
Verona, 44, 63, 76
Villani, Giovanni, 67
Vincent Ferrer, 62
violence
    against Jews, 55, 60, 67, 85–6, 93
    against and between women, 84–5

walls and fortifications, 15–16
Weber, Max, 18, 108
wet-nurses, 82
William Perault, 10
William the Conqueror, 52
William Wymark, 78
Wittenberg, 50
women, 71–90, 95
    access to courts, 80–2
    appearance in public, 84–5
    civic status, 77, 92
    diversity of roles for, 72–5
    in female households, 73, 134
    as prostitutes, 53, 65, 87–90, 142
    religious participation, 82–4
    urban labour roles, 73, 75–80
    violence against and between, 84–7
Worms, 51
Wroclaw, 68
Wurm, Nikolaus, 10

York, 4, 75, 88–9, 121
Ypres, 16

Znojmo, 68